Tomboy Ballerina

Tomboy Ballerina
My Life from Baseball to American Ballet Theatre and Beyond

RONI MAHLER *with*
CAROLINE O'CONNOR

Foreword by Cynthia Gregory

McFarland & Company, Inc., Publishers
Jefferson, North Carolina

This memoir reflects Roni Mahler's present recollections of experiences over time. Some dialogue has been recreated to the best of the author's ability. The authors have made efforts to contact photographers and other sources for permission to use their work/image.

Library of Congress Cataloging-in-Publication Data

Names: Mahler, Roni, author. | O'Connor, Caroline, 1991– author.
Title: Tomboy ballerina : my life from baseball to American ballet theatre and beyond / Roni Mahler with Caroline O'Connor ; Foreword by Cynthia Gregory.
Description: Jefferson, North Carolina : McFarland & Company, Inc., Publishers, 2025 | Includes bibliographical references and index.
Identifiers: LCCN 2025005393 | ISBN 9781476695891 (paperback : acid free paper) ∞ ISBN 9781476654539 (ebook)
Subjects: LCSH: Mahler, Roni. | Ballerinas—United States—Biography. | Dance teachers—United States—Biography. | Ballet Russe de Monte Carlo. | National Ballet (Washington, D.C.) | American Ballet Theatre.
Classification: LCC GV1785.M2447 A3 2025 | DDC 792.802/8092 [B]—dc23/eng/20250212
LC record available at https://lccn.loc.gov/2025005393

ISBN (print) 978-1-4766-9589-1
ISBN (ebook) 978-1-4766-5453-9

© 2025 Roni Mahler and Caroline O'Connor. All rights reserved

No part of this book may be reproduced or transmitted in any form or by any means, electronic or mechanical, including photocopying or recording, or by any information storage and retrieval system, without permission in writing from the publisher.

Front cover images: Roni Mahler as "Dawn" in *Coppélia* with American Ballet Theatre in Winter 1970. (Photograph by Martha Swope. ©Billy Rose Theatre Division, The New York Public Library for the Performing Arts. Courtesy of American Ballet Theatre.) *Background* Mahler, age 12, at Camp Wicosuta in New Hampshire (author image).

Printed in the United States of America

McFarland & Company, Inc., Publishers
Box 611, Jefferson, North Carolina 28640
www.mcfarlandpub.com

For my Son, Erik, ... who will always hate the Yankees.

For my Godson, Lloyd Gregory Miller, ... whom I came *this* close to turning into a diehard fan.

—Roni Mahler

Table of Contents

Foreword by Cynthia Gregory   1
Overture   3
Prologue: My Early Years   5

First Intermission: Life Lessons   53
Act One: Ballet Russe and National Ballet   59
Second Intermission: The Kennedys   122
Act Two: American Ballet Theatre   126
Third Intermission: Looking Back   154
Act Three: Onward and Upward   158
Finale: Curtain Calls   207

Team Gratitude   215
Chapter Notes   219
Bibliography   223
Index   227

Foreword

by Cynthia Gregory

How does one describe my dear friend, Roni Mahler? One of a kind, I'm sure. But also, a unique woman for "all seasons"!

Ballet seasons: As a soloist with American Ballet Theatre at New York's Lincoln Center.

Baseball seasons: As an avid, devoted fan of the New York Yankees.

Summer seasons: As a beloved teacher for dance conventions and schools around the world.

Football seasons: As a teacher for college and professional teams.

So many seasons!! So many stories!!

Our story began way back in 1965 when we were introduced to each other by a writer for *Dance Magazine*. It was backstage at the New York State Theater at Lincoln Center. A few years later we were both dancing there, with American Ballet Theatre.

Readers … I believe you will find this to be a cozy, confidential and conversational memoir … personal, intimate, humorous, and fascinating.

First of all, Roni was a marvelous dancer who worked with some of the best ballet companies in the U.S. She could fly across the stage in great bounding leaps. She was a fine dramatic dancer, as well. Early on, dance became her life.

Also, early on, she fell in love with baseball and the New York Yankees. She was a die-hard fan, with Mickey Mantle a personal favorite. Baseball became part of her life as well.

When Roni began teaching, even while she was still performing, she knew that she had much to offer. Her classes were unique, and they spoke to her students in many different ways. Each class, an adventure in itself.

Then, later on, she began working with college and pro-football teams in Kansas and Ohio, at the same time as she worked with the ballet in those places. Picture this… Roni teaching ballet classes to the Cleveland Browns!! The slim, 5'4" Roni working on balance and stretching with a 6'4", 310 lb. offensive tackler, and jumping across the studio with all those guys. It was quite an experience for her! And also for them, I'm certain!!

On top of it all, Roni was a devoted, loving mom, who shared her passion for sports with her son, Erik. As he grew up, she watched him become an amazing, walking sports encyclopedia. And … a really wonderful guy!

I want to say here and now, that I am so blessed to have been Roni's close friend for over fifty years! We've shared so much together. She is a passionate human being and a caring, loyal friend.

So, dear readers…. I really hope you will enjoy Roni's pages of memories and stories. At the risk of sounding trite and clichéd, I believe my friend, Roni, has hit a home run with this very special book!

Cynthia Gregory is celebrated as one of the foremost ballerinas of her time. Beginning her career at San Francisco Ballet, she became a principal dancer at American Ballet Theatre, where she danced for 26 years. Cynthia was dubbed "America's prima ballerina assoluta" by the great Rudolf Nureyev.

Overture

When I was only 21, I was coached by George Balanchine. Unmolded clay in the master sculptor's hands. At 83, so many names now drift through my mind. Impossible to name them all in any one conversation. Balanchine and Frederic Franklin, Rudolf Nuryev, José Limón, Cynthia Gregory, Erik Bruhn, Natalia Makarova, Carla Fracci, Jerome Robbins, Agnes de Mille, Antony Tudor, Nora Kaye, Herbert Ross. Even Mickey Mantle's voice on the telephone, and JFK grinning at me through a limousine window.

And with each name there is an image stuck in my mind; a smile, a leap, a glance from the wings, a memory to hold close to my heart.

Back when I was four, my Mother took me to my first ballet performance. I came home and announced that I wanted to be a ballerina.

When I was nine, my parents took me to my first baseball game at Yankee Stadium. I came home and announced that I wanted to be Mickey Mantle.

I agonized when I missed a double pirouette. I was inconsolable when Mickey struck out. I asked myself, "How can a ballerina feel so connected to a baseball player?" Well, they say he's got talent. They say I've got talent. He's got a bad temper. I've got a bad temper. He plays hurt. I dance hurt.

I wondered if it was possible to love ballet and also become fixated on something so utterly different. Perhaps it was destiny. Was I meant to be a tomboy because Roni is a boy's name, my voice is low, and my hair is short?

But ballet is definitely my oxygen. In class and onstage I could challenge myself, pushing my body to extremes, very much like an elite athlete. And I relied on my "coaches." Maria Yurieva Swoboda as my first and forever ballet teacher. Frederic Franklin as a mentor for life. George Balanchine, molding me in surprising ways.

Looking back, it's clear that fate has smiled upon me. I've been taught, mentored and sculpted by the best. I've found a home first under the stage lights, and later, in the studio as a teacher. I even embraced the opportunity to connect my two passions, by teaching ballet to NFL players.

Thanks, Fate. You've been a great companion. You've given me a life that reads like a full-length ballet. Complete with Three Acts, and Curtain Calls.

Okay. This Overture is over. Curtain going up…

Prologue
My Early Years

In the Beginning

It is March 5, 1942. A Thursday afternoon in the Fort Tryon section of Upper Manhattan, near The Cloisters. While my very, very pregnant mother is shopping in a local drugstore, she notices a brand of false eyelashes named "Roni." "Hmmm…" she thinks. "Nice name; not wild about the spelling." It makes her want to pronounce it like "macaroni."

When I am born the following morning around 6:30, my father is in a definite state of denial. Their firstborn, Stephanie, is now an adorable two-year-old girl. According to my dad's logic, the next child will be the boy.

My Dad: "Soon I'll have someone to take to the Turkish baths."
His Dad: "But, you don't even go to the Turkish baths."

The story has it that, upon my arrival, my dad even growls to the doctor, "Go back and check. Are you sure you didn't knock something off?" My mother is obviously the only one capable of clear-headed thinking. She remembers those drugstore eyelashes, changes the "spaghetti spelling," and names me "Ronnie." She adds a middle name of "Joan," so people will know I'm a girl. One would think.

* * *

It is a Sunday afternoon. I am four. Mommy tells us that Daddy's playing golf, but she's taking my six-year-old sister, Stephanie, and me to a special Children's Matinee. We pronounce the name on the program together: A-m-e-r-i-c-a-n B-a-l-l-e-t T-h-e-a-t-r-e. Mommy says we will see "*Les Sylphides, Peter and the Wolf,* and *Aurora's Wedding.*" I can't understand the first one, or the last one. *Peter and the Wolf* sounds like fun. I'm only four. Please don't ask me anything else.

The show begins. I'm looking at beautiful Fairies coming to life. Silly Hunters walking backwards, looking for a Wolf. And, Little Red Riding Hood and a flying Bluebird dancing for a Princess. I'm thinking, "This is a magic land. I want to live here forever." I know this is what I want to do.

Back at home, Stephanie and I both have 102-degree fevers. And the beginnings of the measles. Maybe I just saw everything through a feverish haze? I'll never know.[1]

After watching me dance around the house for another year, my mother decides

My sister Lyn and me in our Upper West Side apartment in 1948.

it is time to sign me up for something. She has loved to dance ever since she can remember. Her arms and hands and head move together like a beautiful song. When Mom was a teenager at summer camp, she remembers a wonderful Isadora Duncan Technique dance instructor named Lillian Rosenberg. Lillian was trained by Irma Duncan, one of the six "Isadorables" from Isadora Duncan's famous dance company.[2] Right now, Lillian happens to be teaching at Irma's dance studio in New York City. Lillian also happens to have a Saturday morning class of five- and six-year-olds. I am five.

I remember bare feet. I remember a red chiffon scarf. It goes under my right armpit and is safety-pinned on top of my left shoulder. A woman in the corner is tapping softly on a small drum. I am standing in a circle and told to fly like a butterfly to the beat of that drum. I can still duplicate exactly what I did that first Saturday morning: lifting my chin, running a few steps, softly leaping around in the circle, waving my arms up and down, smiling and murmuring, "But-ter-fly … but-ter-fly … but-ter-fly." I'm so lucky. Thank you, Mommy.

* * *

One year later, Mommy sets out to find me a ballet teacher. The process never changes. She signs me up for a single Saturday class at a ballet school in the city, and observes. She is not pleased. Apparently, I am very good at imitating movement. If the teacher has ugly ballet hands when she demonstrates, then I have ugly ballet hands. We never go back to that class again. Good thing Mommy is so picky. Bad habits are hard to forget.

People say that the very best children's school is called School of American Ballet.

But when Mommy tries to sign me up, they tell her that I am too young. I haven't turned seven yet. The search continues.

I think I end up going to three or four different Saturday classes in a row, before Mommy decides it is time to seek some first-rate advice. Early in the fall of 1948, she writes to someone whose name I can't pronounce—Anatole Chujoy. He is the Founder, Publisher, and Editor of *Dance News*, a monthly publication based in New York City.[3] But, right now, he's reading my mother's letter requesting a meeting. She wishes to be pointed in the direction of the best ballet teacher for her six-year-old daughter. They say she has talent.

Explaining to her that his position doesn't allow him to recommend a teacher, Anatole Chujoy states a well-known "fact." Madame Maria Yurieva Swoboda is considered the best teacher of children "this side of the Mississippi."

As a child in her native St. Petersburg, 11-year-old Maria Yurieva's mother enrolls her daughter in ballet classes taught by good friend, Lydia Nelidova. At 15, talented Maria successfully auditions for the famed Bolshoi Ballet. (*"They have to take me. I do 64 fouettés, right, left, on toe."*) She's the first dancer ever accepted into the Bolshoi Ballet, not trained in the Bolshoi's famous School.[4]

Mikhail Mordkin is among the famous Bolshoi Ballet stars judging Maria's successful audition that day. One year later, he requests that she perform the title role in *Giselle ... with him*. But the fairy tale is short-lived when the clouds of revolution begin to swirl. Maria and her mother flee to the Balkans, where Maria performs with her own small ballet company.

They eventually make their way to Paris in the early '20s. Maria and her mother are attending one of those elegant "salons" of the day, when Maria encounters the handsome Bolshoi Ballet principal dancer, Vescheslav Swoboda. He knows her because he was also a judge at her audition. The fairy tale picks right up again when they marry. And, together, listen to the likes of Sergei Rachmaninoff and Léon Bakst converse about the arts.[5]

The newlyweds eventually sail to America and become principal dancers with the Chicago Civic Opera. Maria Swoboda performs under her maiden name of Yurieva. After several successful seasons, she suffers a career-ending knee injury. The couple moves to New York City and opens the Swoboda-Yurieva School of Ballet. Mr. Swoboda teaches the Professional Class, the Men's Class, and *Pas de Deux*. Maria Yurieva teaches the Children's Professional Class, Pointe Class, and Variations.

When Mr. Swoboda passes away from cancer in August of 1948, his widow assumes his last name and drops the "Yurieva" from the School's name. And that's how come, on an otherwise-ordinary Saturday afternoon, it's "Madame Swoboda" whom my mother comes to observe teaching a children's ballet class.

It's an early October Saturday, in 1948. My sisters Stephanie and Lyn and I are running around trying to get dressed in something nice. Mommy and Nana are taking us downtown. While Mommy meets the new ballet teacher, Nana will be taking her three granddaughters to eat lunch at Schrafft's. Stephanie is eight, I'm six, and Lyn is four. Schrafft's is a very special treat for us. I love the waitresses' starched white aprons and those little pleated cloth tiaras on their heads.

The Swoboda School of Ballet is at 50 W. 57th Street. On the second floor, David

Furs, fur-coated mannequins are visible through tall glass windows. Two floors above that, more tall glass windows of a ballet studio. After getting off the elevator, you open the frosted-glass door with neat black lettering and enter a small and cozy waiting room. A few upholstered chairs and a quaint wooden end table with a decorative lamp on top.

To the left, the small office of School Administrator Violet. My mother is invited to take a seat. The wall behind Violet's desk is home to two beautiful photographs of a ballerina in a white tutu. In both of them, the pose is an extraordinary *arabesque allongé* (*en pointe*). My mother mentions that the photos appear to be identical mirror images of one another. Violet is quick to intervene. Although many people assume the one to be a flipped negative of the other, Madame Swoboda most assuredly posed separately for each.

My mother explains to Violet that she is thinking of enrolling her young daughters. However, before she decides, she would first like to watch Mme. Swoboda teach a children's class. Violet invites her to take a seat in the waiting room.

After a while, a woman walks into Violet's office. Mid-to-late forties. All in black. A mid-calf black wool skirt. A black wool sweater, whose long sleeves are pushed up to mid-forearm. Black open-toed, canvas comfort shoes. Flaming red hair, neatly ending in a horizontal oblong braided bun, at the nape of a long neck. A short, grayish necklace of "black pearls" and matching stud earrings complete the picture.

Can this be Madame Swoboda? My mother can't make out what Violet is muttering to Madame. (Years later, when Mom and Violet have become friends, Violet 'fesses up. Right before bringing Mom in to watch that class, she had whispered to Madame, "We have a live one here.")

The woman in black enters the studio. It *is* Madame Swoboda. Violet leads my mom just inside the door and points to the three "viewing" chairs already in place.

Then class begins, and it's obvious the search is over. My mother is completely entranced. Watching Madame move is mesmerizing. The presence; the carriage; the long, regal neck; the majestic arms; the graceful hands. Everything cries *prima ballerina*. Mom can't wait to see me mimic *that*.

When we come home, Mommy tells us everything. She's found a wonderful teacher who owns a wonderful school. Stephanie and I will begin classes next Saturday. (Lyn is only four. Too young.) Mommy describes how beautiful Madame Swoboda is when she moves around the room. She says her voice can sound like she's screaming, but she's not. That's just the way she talks. We'll get used to her Russian accent.

She tells us that *her* Daddy came from a place called Minsk, in a place called Russia. When he was just a little boy, they had to run away from Russia because it wasn't safe. They landed on the Lower East Side, right here in New York City. I ask Mommy why it wasn't safe. She just says one word. "Pogroms." She doesn't tell me what it means. Instead, she tells me that my daddy's daddy came from Vienna, Austria. Russia and Austria. Hard to remember. Then Mommy says something that I don't understand, but it sounds really funny: "You are half Russian cheekbones and half Austrian ribcage." I can remember *that*.

Prologue

It's finally Saturday again. Mommy takes me to my very first ballet class. She grew up listening to her Daddy's Russian accent, so she can understand everything Madame Swoboda is saying. I can't understand *anything* Madame is saying. But it doesn't matter. I'm under a spell. In the middle of a wonderful dream. I understand one thing. I love my ballet class.

Every Saturday, my wonderful dream takes place in this very large studio with very high ceilings. The sun pours in through those four very large windows that look down on 57th Street. Under the barres, along the very long wall, are two big picture frames. Somebody has drawn just the head and neck of a person in each frame. Mommy says they're called portraits. Violet tells me one is Madame and the other, Mr. Swoboda. I am six. So, I'm sure those two faces are always staring at me, to see if I'm making mistakes.

The ballet class music is a happy surprise. It's so pretty. A lady is playing it on a very big piano. No more little drum. The dancers taking the next class have to walk into the studio and past the piano, to get to the dressing room. I get in big trouble if my attention wanders, and I start looking at those older students instead of Madame.

Things are very different this year. Gone is my red chiffon scarf. Now I'm wearing Aunt Kitty's little white beach dress. My great-aunt Kitty owns a beachwear store in Daytona Beach. Why did she send me a present for starting ballet class, from a store that sells things you wear to the beach? No one else is wearing a little white beach dress.

Also gone is my enchanted butterfly circle. Now, all of us stand in a very straight line, holding on to what looks like a banister. Only without the stairs. But I like all the

Me at age six taking one of my first ballet classes with Madame Swoboda in Aunt Kitty's white dress (Roberta [Berson] Hauser, second from left; Virginia Klein, third from left; other individuals unknown).

new things, too. Everything in ballet is French. I soon learn to call my banister a *barre*. I quickly learn how to spell this French *barre*. I love trying to learn all the steps in this brand new language, and how to spell them. I also learn that, in French, instead of pronouncing an "r," I get to gargle. It takes a while for me to learn that those half-circles on the floor are called *ronds de jambes*. I've been calling them *Ronnie Joans*.

I also like pointing my toe in front of my belly button. When Madame does it, she doesn't look straight in front. She turns her head a little bit to the side. It looks so pretty. I try it. I feel pretty, too.

When class is over, we get in line and hold Madame's right hand while doing a little curtsy. We say, "Thank you, Madame," at the same time. She looks right into my eyes, like I'm a good girl. When my mother's friends now ask me where I take ballet, I've practiced saying, "The Swoboda School."

Saturdays at the ballet school are really a magic time. So much to see. So much to hear. When I'm early, I get to watch the Professional Class before mine. The teacher's name is Boris Romanov. He comes from Russia. Just like Madame Swoboda. And my mommy's daddy.

They say Mr. Romanov was a famous choreographer. I don't know what that means, but he counts like this: "*A-vun…. Two…. Ta-ree…. Four…. A-vun…. Two…. Ta-ree…. Four!*" How come he can only count up to four?

Two of the professional dancers I watch in class are so beautiful. Violet tells me their names. Meredith Baylis and Gertrude Tyven. I ask about another dancer I really like. She looks younger. Violet says her name is Christine Hennessy, and she will be a professional one day, too. Violet then tells me that Norma Vance is another professional dancer who always takes class here when she's not performing. (Who would ever guess, back then, that *I* would one day become the first student from the Swoboda School to ever go on to a professional career, after being trained *exclusively* by Madame. Without her husband.)

These beautiful dancers are now moving sideways and spinning around on one foot. Mr. Romanov is saying, "*Tawm-bay…. Pah duh Boo-ray…. Eee Pee-roo-wet…. Eee Four…. Tawm-bay…. Pah duh Boo-ray…. Eee Pee-roo-wet…. Eee Four.*"

I really, really like the way Mr. Romanov talks. Listening to him every Saturday before my class, I begin to practice mimicking him. When I get pretty good, I entertain my mother's friends with my imitation.

Finally, Mr. Romanov's professional class is over. I run to the barre and await those magic words: "First position. One. Two." Every Saturday, it's like those words open a door. Now, an hour of moving to music I love. When I'm in first position and Madame says, "One, two," everything is going to be okay.

But, when we get home, Mommy tells me to hold onto the top of her low chest of drawers. My hands are almost as high as the top of my head. I guess I'm pretty short. She's going to teach me *pas de bourrée*, the step I couldn't do in class. "Step behind, step side, cross in front, lift my back foot; step behind, step side, cross in front, lift my back foot." I now know *pas de bourrée*.

I'm so happy. My Saturdays are now filled with new ballet steps all the time, and pretty arms. Lots and lots of pretty arms. I sometimes think they're my favorite. Because pretty arms make me feel pretty.

Posing with my children's professional class at the Swoboda School of Ballet in 1949 in my first black leotard (Roberta [Berson] Hauser, far left; Virginia Klein, far right; other individuals unknown).

No classes in the summer, but classes again in the fall. For the first time, I hear us called the Children's Professional Class. I like it. It sounds really important. I guess I'm right, because now our class has to take pictures. It's for something called a "brochure"? Only, we all have to be dressed alike.

Goodbye to Aunt Kitty's Magic White Dress. I'm in the Children's Professional Class now. Everyone has to wear the same black, short-sleeved cotton leotard. It zips up the back. That's hard to do by myself, but I'll learn.

On the day we take pictures, I'm so happy that I'm not the only one in white anymore. I am also happy because, in one of the pictures, I'm going to kneel in the center, with the other girls around me. I am *not* happy that Madame wants me to kneel on my left knee.

The other day, I fell in Susie Goldstone's front yard. On her stone path. And I bloodied my left knee. The band-aid is gone now, but the scab is as big as a quarter. It is also all puffed up. I show it to Madame and ask if I can kneel on my right knee instead. "No."

Ouch. But I kneel on my left knee without a peep. When the brochure comes out, just looking at the picture makes me hurt.

...When I Am Nine

I'm thinking of a word that has eight letters ... beginning with "b" and ending with "l" that means our national pastime?

This tomboy shrimp is about to fall in love with the New York Yankees (left to right: Lyn, me, and Stephanie).

The hot, July day that I watched my first baseball game.

The first time I hear the word "baseball," I am five. It is April 27, 1947. Mommy and Daddy have us huddled around a radio. I can barely hear a man talking in a very scratchy voice. Daddy says, "That's The Babe. Babe Ruth. He was the most famous player in baseball. He's saying goodbye." I can't understand what Babe Ruth is saying, but it must be important. (Suffering from terminal throat cancer, The Babe passes away 16 months later.)[6]

The second time I hear the word "baseball," I am eight. Mommy is telling us how she and Daddy were once waiting for a train at Penn Station. A lot of Yankees baseball players were waiting there, too. Mommy says, "There's Gehrig." Daddy says, "I'll bet you five bucks it's not."

MOMMY: "My husband just bet me five dollars you're *not* Lou Gehrig."
GEHRIG (smiling): "You win."

His dimples were all she needed, to know Daddy was wrong.

The third time I hear the word "baseball," I'm nine. It's 1951. A hot July afternoon. Mommy has just finished showing Stephanie, Lyn, and I how to fold colored construction paper into fans to cool ourselves.

All this time, something's been playing on our 14-inch Sylvania television set. This is our second television. Daddy put it together from a kit. He said our first one was a "7-inch RCA." Now, I'm pointing to the picture on this much bigger screen.

ME: "What's that?"
MOMMY: "Baseball."
ME: "What's baseball?"

And so it begins. Mommy starts explaining what is happening on the television. By the end of the game, my nine-year-old brain is dizzy with new words like "inning," "outfield," "infield," and "shortstop." Words I think I know, like "diamond" and "batter" and "pitcher" and "balls" and "strikes" and "walks," now mean something else. Sometime in early July, the whole family is off to Yankee Stadium. I'm going to my first baseball game. I can't wait.

To go into the Stadium, you have to really lean in and push a turnstile. We walk up a lot of long ramps to get to something called the Third Deck. Daddy finally looks up at one of the Section numbers. "This must be us," he says, and leads us up a short little ramp.

I see a slit of green. Then, it's a narrow stripe. Then, a thicker stripe. Then suddenly I'm looking at this huge ocean of the greenest grass I've ever seen. Yankee Stadium isn't "black-and-white?" A lot different from that television screen. Are those my arms tingling? Is that my heart pounding? I can't believe my eyes. I am short for my age, so maybe everything just seems bigger?

When the Yankees run out from the dugout, Daddy says it is now "the top of the first." The nine Yankees are wearing white uniforms with pinstripes and take their "positions" on the "field."

Daddy is pointing to the player, wearing No. 6, who has run out to right field. Miraculously, he is standing right in front of our seats.

"That's Mickey Mantle. He's a rookie and only nineteen. Next year, he'll replace the guy wearing No. 5 in centerfield. *His* name is Joe DiMaggio. He's the Yankees' star player. They say Mickey Mantle will be the next Yankees star player." Boy, Daddy sure knows a lot about the Yankees. He says that's because he and Mommy are "die-hard fans." They "live and die" with the Yankees. I want to be a die-hard fan, too.

That man in black behind the catcher is the umpire. The pitcher throws the ball to the hitter, the guy with the bat. If the umpire thinks the ball is "over the plate," he calls it a strike. If he thinks it missed, he calls it a ball. Three strikes and you're out. Four balls, and you get to "take first." The best part is, it's okay to scream at the top of my lungs at a baseball game. "You're blind, Ump!"

My head feels like it's spinning. The hotdogs sure smell good. I eat two. My stomach starts to hurt, so I stop. The game is hard to follow, so I don't really remember it. Or the other team. Or the score. But I remember Mickey Mantle.

I soon learn that Mickey's called a switch hitter. A player who bats from both sides of the plate. The sportswriters say he has "prodigious" power. In addition to hitting "tape-measure" home runs (my baseball vocabulary keeps getting bigger), he can run extremely fast. He also strikes out much too often, and takes out his frustrations on the dugout water cooler.

Me, too. I throw toe shoes at the wall in my bedroom, when I think I've had a bad ballet class. So, after hearing all that talk about the next Yankees star, I start wondering how Mickey is going to handle the pressure. I'm not handling mine when I'm at ballet. That's for sure.

The day after my first game, I begin reading everything I can get my hands on about the New York Yankees. The Yanks, as I quickly learn to call them, are having a pretty good season and winning a lot. In the blink of an eye, I become a die-hard Yankees fan. Just like Mommy and Daddy.

But, Mickey is still striking out. A lot. And kicking water coolers. A lot. The writers are wondering whether "the kid" will ever live up to all those expectations. They're right to be worried. More strikeouts. More tantrums.

It's all I can think about. I feel like I'm suffering twice: hero worship and hero worry. I'm elated when he goes 3 for 4, and miserable when he strikes out more than once. My highs and lows are tied up with Mickey's. It feels like we're the same.

I remember hearing Mommy say, when she was trying to find me a *good* ballet teacher, that it was because I've got talent. What if I don't live up to that in ballet class? I feel just like Mickey. Trying to live up to what other people expect. It scares me.

* * *

A few weeks after that first game, it's the end of July 1951. By now, we're living in New Rochelle. But, don't worry. I'm still taking all my ballet classes with Mme. Swoboda. Mommy and Daddy have joined the Westchester Country Club, to play golf. There's a huge swimming pool with two diving boards. One springs up and down when you jump on it. The other is very tall and does not.

Then there's Tom-The-Lifeguard. Tom McDermott is very handsome. He has a lot of muscles. He's very tan, and wears the tiniest red bathing suit. My 11-year-old sister, Stephanie, says it's called a Speedo. She says Tom is very sexy. I'm not sure what that means, but I am definitely in love. They say Tom is a New York State diving champ. I am taking diving lessons from the New York State champ. But only off the lower, springy board.

Tom says the "key to success" is practice. I do anything Tom tells me to. Like, work on my "approach." Stand toes straight forward, feet together. Walk right, left. Jump off left foot, right knee high. Land both feet really close to the board's edge. Push off both feet. "Execute" dive with straight knees and pointed toes, entering water straight up-and-down. Not "slanty." Swim to edge. Get out of pool. Wait turn at diving board steps. "Mount" diving board. Do it all over again.

Guessing how much space your approach will take is hard. Walk right. Walk left. Jump off left foot… Oops. Not close enough to the end of the board. Try again. You get the picture. Over and over again. That's all I do all day long. Except wave to Mommy or Daddy, as they walk by on their way to the 11th hole.

Did I mention that I always do everything Tom asks me to? One day, poolside, he introduces me to his friend. Tom is very impressed that I'm studying ballet. He says it's helping my diving "form." He asks me to show his friend one of my ballet steps. Aye aye, sir. I show a jumping step called *grand jeté en tournant*. (The shortcut name is *tour jeté*. Madame won't let us use it.) I dutifully jump off one leg, do an about-face in the air, and land on the other leg. Oops. I forget that concrete near a pool has a lot of wet spots. My landing leg slips out from underneath me. I crash on my chin. Hurting. Hurting.

Tom holds a towel under my chin to catch all the blood. My Nana and younger sister, Lyn, have seen the whole thing. Nana tells Lyn to go get our mother.

That day, only my daddy is playing golf. Mommy is playing Canasta with her friends, in back of all the people lying on their *chaise longues* (French for long sun-tanning chairs).

Lynie is seven years old and afraid. We girls are never supposed to interrupt Mommy when she's in the middle of a Canasta "hand." Lynie stands by the card table and waits patiently until the hand is over. "Mommy. Nana wants you."

After what seems like forever, I'm curled up on my mother's lap in the passenger seat of Tom's car, a Beetle. I've never seen a car this small. I'm so glad Tom is driving. Otherwise, I would be curling up in *his* lap.

Three stitches (and a lot of gentian violet) later, I am finally cuddling under my very own sheets in my very own bed. But, be careful. The pillow can't disturb that huge white "beard" of gauze and adhesive tape now attached to my chin. I guess I also banged my knee when I fell. Same knee as two years ago. It's turning blacker and bluer by the minute. But I hardly think of my knee, because my chin hurts so much. I guess you can't pay attention to two hurts at once.

But it's not only my chin and my knee that are hurting. My heart is hurting, too. Because now I know for sure that my life and Mickey's life are hopelessly connected. You see, I've started reading the daily sports pages of the *New York Times* and the *New York Herald-Tribune*. That's how I find out that, at almost the same time I'm taking my "chin dive" at the pool, Mickey is taking a "dive" of his own. Straight out of the Majors and back to AA ball in the Minor Leagues. Hard to tell which hurts more.

The worst part about my chin is having to answer everyone's questions. One person at a time. If only I could hang a sign around my neck, explaining everything. Turns out, that's actually *not* the worst part. The worst part is that, in 10 days, I have to dance onstage at a dance convention in front of 200 teachers.

Every August, C.L. Lewis, President of NADAA (National Association of Dance and Affiliated Arts), presents a huge national convention for dance teachers at the Roosevelt Hotel in Manhattan (NYC). Because the Swoboda School of Ballet is considered the best, he asks Mme. Swoboda to put on an hour-long presentation in the Grand Ballroom.

The students Madame is using are all from her Professional Class. Except one. I have been chosen to demonstrate the Children's Work. Me. The one with the huge, white gauze-and-adhesive-tape beard. The questions. The questions. How will I ever answer all the questions?

Luckily, by the time the convention rolls around, I have permission to replace the beard with one gauze pad and two ½" strips of tape. But, it's almost worse,

Stephanie (right) and me (plus equine friend) in 1947 outside our Upper West Side apartment.

because the smaller gauze pad can't cover all the gentian violet. A white beard is now purple-and-white. I tell everyone I fell practicing ballet.

I can't say how long I'm up on that stage in front of those teachers. I guess as long as it takes to show two combinations. The first is *battement tendu* with *port de bras*. Translation: pointing my toe in many directions, while changing my arms. The second is *petit allegro*. Translation: small jumps. This combines *glissade, assemblé, petit jeté coupé*, and *pas de bourrée*. Yes, that *pas de bourrée*. The first step I ever had trouble learning. Now, I can do it in my sleep. I'm happy because Madame is letting me keep both arms down in "low fifth" during all these small jumps.

To my surprise, the teachers do not just watch me dance. They are trying the steps right along with me. A pianist I know from class is playing the music. Then something happens. I have been facing the teachers the whole time. They are supposed to be "mirroring" me. They are doing okay during the first combination. When it comes to those small jumps with all those *glissades* and *jetés* and *assemblés* and *pas de bourrées*, it's a little harder. The teachers aren't getting it.

Suddenly, I hear myself blurt out, "Should I turn around?" Yes. Yes. When my back is to the teachers, everything is fine. Remember this, Ronnie.

When I'm done, I get to watch the beautiful Professional Class put on its show. Heaven. When that's over, I get to watch Madame take a bow with all of us. I imagine her in a costume, when she was a young and famous ballerina. Am I going to cry? The magic is not over yet.

I remember Madame introducing me to a man and a woman she says are stars of a very important ballet company called the Ballet Russe de Monte Carlo. Mr. Leon Danielian and Mme. Alexandra Danilova. I am excited to meet them. They tell me I did very well. They ask about my chin. Then I ask them to say the name of their famous ballet company again, slowly, so I can repeat it after them and learn it.

Highs and Lows of Junior High

The years feel like they're flying by at the Swoboda School of Ballet. I am still very much under ballet's "spell." But not my older sister, Stephanie. She prefers stables to studios. So it's horseback riding lessons for her instead of ballet.

I am finally getting used to Madame's accent. Good thing, because Mom can't really be around to "translate" for me, like she did after that first class long, long ago. My mother works full-time, as accountant and office manager, in the wholesale potato business my father owns. But, once in a while, she manages to duck out early and come see class. This one time, when I'm about twelve, Madame has a few of the mothers sitting in one corner. That day, Mom, whose first name is Ethel, is really treading on thin ice. Every time she catches my eye, she sits up a little taller and lengthens her neck. I think she's hoping I'll improve my posture.

> **MADAME (piercing the air):** *"Etel, I trow-ink you out."*
> **MY MOM:** (Speechless, slinks down low in her chair.)

Even I understand *that*.

* * *

I am 4'8" when I enter Albert Leonard Junior High School as a 7th Grader, and the whole world is taller than I. Am I the shortest 7th-grader in all of New Rochelle? Even my best friend, Sheena Macpherson, is taller. Though not by much.

Worst of all, I'm at the mercy of the 9th-Grade hall monitors. They control traffic flow when we have to change classes. Strategically stationed at points of maximum congestion, they wield an awful power. Their adamant arm signal can callously reroute you, without a word. For this neophyte munchkin, that rerouting often makes me late for class. I've nicknamed them The Quislings, because they feel like traitors to my cause.

It's not until the spring that I finally turn 12. Now, thank goodness, I'm as old as the other seventh graders. Just not as tall. But I have more important things to think about. All anyone can talk about is the Talent Show. Auditions are coming up soon.

It's 1954. *Mr. Sandman* by The Chordettes is #1 on the charts.[7] Eleanor Landres, Avery Fisher, and I decide we're going to try out. We're going to sing that very song. Never mind that there are four Chordettes, and we are only three. We make up our own harmony and rehearse like crazy. I mention all this at the dinner table one night.

> **Mom:** "Why are you auditioning as a singer, not a dancer?"
> **Me:** "Oh, no. I'm not good enough yet, as a dancer."
> **Mom:** "Maybe you can audition as both?"
> **Me:** "These kids won't like ballet."
> **Mom:** "Maybe you can ask Mme. Swoboda what she thinks?"

What happens next really takes me by surprise. In this 12-year-old's mind, Mme. Swoboda is way over here, in the world of classical ballet. Everybody else is way over there, in the real world. Wrong.

Madame knows exactly what to do. She choreographs an amazing Can-Can solo for me. Léonide Massine could put it right into his fun-filled ballet, *Gaîté Parisienne*. Before teaching me a single step, Madame has taught me a valuable lesson. Ballet choreography does not always have to be performed in a *tutu*. What do I know? I'm too busy being afraid the kids will think I'm "square" and boo me off the stage. I've got a lot to learn, besides new choreography.

Madame takes me into the small studio to start teaching me this new solo. It feels like we have a secret. First, I run on from upstage left, and pose. I take a few counts to rustle my skirt, with a little "shoulder action." Almost like flirting with the audience. Now, I'm running to pose downstage right. I repeat the skirt rustling and those shoulders. Then I run to upstage center. This time, Madame has me posing with my back to the audience. Now, the skirt-rustling happens while I'm looking over my right shoulder to flirt.

I can't believe my eyes, as I watch Madame demonstrate all this for me. Here she is, slightly heavyset and in her mid–40s. Her shoulders are shaking. Her eyes are flashing. She's transforming herself into a young Can-Can dancer right in front of me. Too bad I'm the only one seeing this.

Suddenly, the music breaks out into those often-played Can-Can melodies we all know. The steps are gradually becoming more and more athletic. This solo is going to be fun.

Fast forward to Audition Day. I sing. I dance. At the dinner table that night, the inevitable question:

Mom: "How did it go?"
Me: "Fine."
Mom: "Did you make the show?"

Performing at the Albert Leonard Junior High School talent show in a Can-Can solo choreographed by Madame Swoboda, wearing the first costume ever made just for me.

ME: "Yes."
MOM: "As a singer, or a dancer?"
ME: "Dancer."

No one speaks for what seems like a very long time. Fitting silence for the death of a singing career.

Lucky for me, Mom has a seamstress friend who can design and make my costume. It's the first time anyone has ever made a costume especially for me. Wow. A cobalt blue satin dress. Just below the knee. With cobalt blue spaghetti straps. Underneath the full-circle skirt, there are rows and rows and rows of cerise tulle ruffles. There are also rows and rows of cerise tulle ruffles sewn onto my trunks. My black velvet choker is adorned with a cerise tulle "poof," and there's another poof for my hair. Add black fishnet tights, black ballet shoes with black ribbons, and long black gloves from the middle of my upper arm to my knuckles. The picture is complete.

The night of the show, my Can-Can solo and I are a hit. Toward the end of the dance, when the audience recognizes the most famous Can-Can music of all, they begin clapping along. And Madame has saved the best for last. During the final sixteen counts of music, I am hopping around and around and around in place on my left leg. This, while my straight right leg is being held, head-high, *in my right hand*. Which is hanging on for dear life to the arch of my right foot.

The Big Finish? What else? Crashing to the floor in a split with my head face-down on my front leg, before I right myself with both arms stretched triumphantly upward. After pretty much "bringing down the house," I am declared the winner of the Talent Show. I never sing in public again. (Well, almost never.)

* * *

That summer, it's my first year of sleepaway camp. Eight weeks at Camp Wicosuta in Bristol, New Hampshire. My best friend at camp is Phyllis Rosenberg. Even though Phyllis lives in Brooklyn, she and I are already friends from Mme. Swoboda's ballet class. Phyllis is a repeat camper. The seasoned veteran. I'm the rookie. Green as can be. But I have Phyl to show me the ropes.

At mealtime in the Dining Room, Phyllis and I begin hearing murmurings about the best field trip ever. Climbing Mount Washington. Yes, that Mount Washington. The most prominent mountain east of the Mississippi River.

First, we'd have to "qualify" by climbing the beginner-level Mount Sugarloaf. Up and down in one day. Easy-peasy. Next, the intermediate-level Mount Moosilauke. More challenging, and we stay overnight on top. But, Mount Washington. Now that's a whole different ball game.

Phyllis and I decide to go for it. Mount Sugarloaf, check. Mount Moosilauke, check. Basking in the glow of our previous conquests, we send off our parental permission slips. We're in. Now we're privy to that purple-inked, mimeographed handout. The one with all the juicy details.

Our adventure will begin with the obligatory bus ride to the trail. Then, the climb. Then, an overnight stay at a lodge on top. The next day, we will ride down the mountain on the historic Mount Washington Cog Railway. Then, another bus ride back to camp. Dress requirements are: shorts, a t-shirt, a windbreaker, and sneakers.

Stop the presses. My parents don't believe that "young ladies" should ever wear sneakers, so my sisters and I don't own any. The camp okays my wearing the only lace-up shoes I have with me. My favorite magenta-colored, leather-soled oxfords. Seems okay to me.

Campers and counselors begin the trek. No memory of the early part of our climb. Maybe because it's so ordinary? Let's cut right to the part I remember crystal-clearly. The part where we're nearing the top of the mountain.

The temperature has dropped to 29°F. Hail the size of nickels is pelting us. Even if my feet and hands had not started freezing up, the terrain of tall, pointy rocks would challenge even a sneaker-wearer. How about a leather-soled-oxfords wearer? Oh, dear. Maybe the high winds and hail are a factor? (Remember shorts and a t-shirt and a windbreaker?) Anyway, we are definitely lost.

By this time, I can't feel my frozen feet. I must be falling down a lot on those tall, pointy rocks, because I am looking at blood dripping down my shins. Then out of nowhere, an "angel" scoops me up into her strong and very warm arms. This angel mercifully carries me the rest of the way to the top.

Turns out, our miracle is the Red Wing Camp for Girls. Having already completed their climb, they are nestled around the Lodge fireplace when news circulates that we are seriously overdue. They rush right out to find us. Just like the Cavalry in those Westerns on TV. Only, no bugles.

I'm not sure what exactly happens next. But one thing I *do* know. The Tall-And-Excruciatingly-Handsome Director of our "brother camp," Tomahawk, is unlacing my leather-soled oxfords. Peeling off my socks. I didn't know "Bogie" (his nickname) was climbing with us. My eyes never leave his gorgeous face, as he begins soaking my feet in warm water. (Years later I learn that rubbing frozen feet with snow is the better choice.)

Just as I'm starting to calm down, everything suddenly goes terribly wrong. Somebody has the nerve to take off my wet t-shirt. Now Bogie knows I still wear an undershirt. Can you die from embarrassment?

The railway ride down the mountain the next day is a hit, and not just because there's no hiking involved. Back at Camp that night, they're serving my favorite. Steak. But I can't eat it. The pain. Oh, the pain. All I can do is bite my fingers and dig the heel of one foot into the toes of the other. And I can only stare at that juicy steak on my plate. No one knows what to do with me. I hear the word "frostbite," and they put me in the infirmary overnight for "observation." Luckily, I wake up feeling okay. I'm a regular "Wico girl" again.

The following summer of 1955, I have a chance to vindicate myself. I sign up to climb Mount Washington again. This time, in sneakers and warmer clothing. At the halfway mark, the counselors say we are on pace to break the camp record. They ask for volunteers. We're going to have to "really haul it," if we want to try. I naturally raise my hand. And, yes. We break the record, and that "we" includes this tomboy. (When Malia and Sasha Obama go to "Wico" in 2012, I wonder if they climb Mt. Washington as well.[8])

***

That Fall, I'm finally a 9th grader. Finally on top. What a feeling. With *my* inherent power, I've bestowed an alternate nickname on The Quislings. They now double as The Brown-Nose Brigade, in service of Her Majesty, our dreaded Assistant Principal, Miss Sarah Mathison.

Fear The Brown-Nose Brigade. It is *they* who deliver those ominous pink slips to *us* at any time. In the middle of any class, no less. Cries of, "Oooooh" accompany their walking through the door. Some cat-calling may ensue, as they approach the intended recipient. That pink, Come-To slip can only mean one thing: having to leave class immediately and "come to" the Office of She-Who-Shall-Be-Feared.

So it is, on the morning of October 4, 1955, that this 13-year-old Miss Goody Two Shoes is toiling away in Study Hall. I've made it to the 9th grade without *ever* receiving a Come-To slip, so I ignore the "oooooh" until the Quisling is standing at my desk. Is it possible that this pink paper is being thrust in *my* direction? I slink out of Study Hall with my chin glued to my chest, all the way to the Assistant Principal's office.

The minute her Office Assistant glimpses *pink* in my hand, I hear, "Miss Mathison will see you now." How best to describe the sight that greets me when entering her office? Standing behind the desk, with that obligatory one hand behind her back, is a heavyset woman who seems as wide as she is tall. I have never seen such a square jaw. Her black hair is parted in the middle and slicked into a tiny low knot somewhere behind her head. She is wearing a beige dress with a white lace collar, immediately conjuring up photographs I've seen of Lizzie Borden. Then I hear the unimaginable.

"Your father just telephoned, asking my permission for you to leave school early, so you can attend today's final game of the World Series. I told him it was absolutely out of the question (long pause) … unless you root for the New York Yankees." You mean to tell me Miss Mathison is a Yankee fan *and* has a sense of humor?

Once my dad and I are in the car, he explains that his dear friend, Max Caplan, happens to be a dear friend of Isaac "Ike" Gellis. Mr. Gellis happens to be the Sports Editor of the *New York Post*.[9] Mr. Gellis called my Uncle Max with four seats to the game, and Uncle Max called Daddy.

Holy mackerel. There they are. Those huge block letters. Y-A-N-K-E-E S-T-A-D-I-U-M. Looming so large before my eyes. The front of Yankee Stadium is a sight to behold. This is only my second time seeing a game here. Everything is so different today. Okay, October is a lot cooler than July. But, this doesn't only *feel* different. It *sounds* different. Everything is buzzing. Like the Stadium, and everything in it, has been plugged into an electric outlet. The excitement is everywhere. The fans are definitely moving around faster, like they're in a rush to get somewhere. Like their seats?

Speaking of seats, ours are amazing. Mr. Gellis is, after all, the Sports Editor of the *New York Post*. We are in the third deck, maybe a third of the way up, on the third-base side of the pitcher and catcher. Uncle Max and Mr. Gellis are seven rows in front of Daddy and me, and a couple of seats more toward left field.

These '55 Dodgers are actually a great team. Filled with lots of stars of their own. Will Jackie Robinson run the bases like lightning? Will Roy Campanella throw out a base stealer? Gil Hodges, Pee Wee Reese, Duke Snider, Johnny Podres. They're all there. But I only have eyes for my Yankees. If you're not in pinstripes, you don't count.

My only disappointment is that Mickey's not starting. His legs have really been hurting. No roaming the outfield for The Mick today.

Play ball! At the end of 5½, it's a real pitcher's duel. The Dodgers' Johnny Podres against the Yankees Tommy Byrne. 2-0, Dodgers. Now, before the bottom of the sixth, the announcer says the crowd is 60,000+. My Uncle Max switches seats with me, so I can see the action closer. Seven rows forward and *much* closer to the left field foul pole.

Fatefully, in the top of the sixth, Dodger Don Zimmer had been pinch hit for, and is out of the game. Also fatefully, Manager Walter Alston moves *right-handed* Jim Gilliam in from left field, to replace Zimmer at second. And taps faster outfielder, left-handed Sandy Amorós, off the bench to replace Gilliam in left. Most fatefully of all, a southpaw wears his *glove on his right hand*.

Okay. Bottom of the sixth. No outs … two men on … with Yogi Berra coming to the plate. Yogi smacks a sharp line drive to left. A "rope" (screaming line drive), that gets out there in a nanosecond. I spring out of my seat, along with 60,000+ others. Southpaw Amorós is making a beeline toward the ball. Darn his speed. *Darn that glove on his right hand.* He catches up with Yogi's "rope" just inside the foul pole, near the 301-foot mark. You guessed it. Because Amorós is a lefty, his gloved right hand is able to reach out in front of his fully-stretched arm and body. He catches Yogi's line drive. I crash back down in my seat. My changed seat has just let me see that stab-my-heart catch seven rows closer.

Amorós quickly throws back in to shortstop Pee Wee Reese, who nabs Gil McDougald off first. Double-play. Hank Bauer grounds out, stranding Billy Martin at second. Inning over.

From delirious optimism to dashed hopes. It never dawned on me that the Yankees might lose today. I go back up the seven rows, to sit with my dad again. With two outs in the bottom of the seventh, Yankees Manager, Casy Stengel, has Mickey pinch hit for reliever, Bob Grim. He pops out to the shortstop. Inning over. Thank goodness I'm not still seven rows closer to see *that*. Two Yankee singles in the eighth amount to nothing.[10]

Nothing for the Yanks in the ninth. Game over. Series over. The Yankees become the first team in World Series history to win the first two games *at home* and fail to win the Championship. I am convinced that this devastating loss is completely my fault. The Baseball Gods have thought me greedy. I should've been grateful for my original seat. I should never have switched closer to the action. So "the action" is my punishment.

Daddy and I slowly make our way out of the Stadium. My eyes are tearing up. I can't even answer when he says, "I'm sorry you had to see this, baby." I know for certain that I'm ungrateful. *And* inconsolable.

Wait. How can I ever face all those gloating Dodger fans tomorrow in school?

I know. I'll be an ostrich. Head in the sand. Only way. And what about the screaming headlines in my beloved sports sections? Okay. A self-imposed "blackout." Three weeks of no newspaper. Or radio. Or television. Does an ostrich know how to say, "Wait till next year."

Madame and Me

While Mickey's career has been rolling along, so has my ballet life. Ever since Mr. Swoboda's passing in August of 1948, Madame has been trying to replace him. A succession of male teachers help out in the short run, but nothing permanent works out. Not until 1954.

Before you meet Sergei J. Denham, a little history. In 1909, Serge Diaghilev premieres the Ballets Russes de Serge Diaghilev, at the historic Théâtre du Châtelet in Paris.[11] This Ballets Russes (notice the plural) boasts a star-studded cast. Some of Russia's best young dancers. Do Anna Pavlova and Vaslav Nijinsky ring a bell?

After a twenty-year run, Diaghilev's death in 1929 leaves the company on the brink of demise. Instead, it is reincarnated as the Ballet Russe de Monte Carlo in 1938 by Léonide Massine and former Monte Carlo Opera director, René Blum. Banker Sergei J. Denham, whose love of ballet dates back to his Moscow childhood, is the new Director.[12] Following the outbreak of World War II, Denham turns Ballet Russe de Monte Carlo into an American company. He's been dreaming of a Ballet School in New York City ever since.

Early in 1954, Mme. Swoboda, accepting the inevitable, hands over all rights and leases to Mr. Denham.[13] The Ballet Russe de Monte Carlo School of Ballet is born. Madame is retained as Head of Faculty and, of course, continues to teach.

The new location is 157 West 54th Street, just east of Seventh Avenue. There are now two studios, one larger and one smaller. The School's entrance is sandwiched between Al & Dick's Steakhouse and a public parking garage with an attendant. After classes, I love saying goodnight to that nice man, as I dash past the garage and rush to Grand Central station for my train back to New Rochelle.

How does that saying go? Out with the old, and in with the new? Gone is the elevator to the fourth floor. I now walk a staircase of 24 uninterrupted steps to get to my second-floor ballet classes. Instant warm-up. Remember when I was six, and "Swoboda School of Ballet" was a mouthful? Try "Ballet Russe de Monte Carlo School of Ballet." Good thing I've been practicing for three years, since the Roosevelt Hotel.

At the top of those stairs is a waiting room with chairs and magazines. There's also a picture book about the Company. Wow. Mme. Danilova and Mr. Danielian really are the big stars Madame said they were. The centerpiece of this waiting room is a very large desk. Madame Irene Kotchoubey, the School Administrator, sits at it.

Mme. Kotchoubey is a tall, dignified woman with a gentle voice, which she never raises. And she has extraordinary posture. Almost regal. Her soft gray hair is always neatly coiffed. You happily do everything she asks you to do, without feeling ordered about or imposed upon.

It is whispered that Madame Kotchoubey is of royal blood. An actual princess in the time of the Tsar. "Princess Irene Kotchoubey." I like the sound of that. I never doubt it for a moment.

Even though the name of the school has changed from Swoboda School to Ballet Russe School, Mme. Swoboda continues to be my main teacher. There are two "general" gifts Madame brings to her teaching. First, she always carries herself with the most amazing "presence." You might even say that she exudes it. If I had to distill her presence down to its most basic component, I would have to say, "Consciousness of Sternum." When I just imagine "leading" with my sternum, I feel like I begin to emulate that "thing" she exudes. Picture this: Your teacher slouches ever-so-slightly (or just doesn't pay attention to how she holds herself). How long before you pick up the habit yourself?

Second, simply put: Mme. Swoboda trains "the back." She trains the student how to use his or her back, as an instrument of strength and control. She may never put into words exactly how to do that. Yet, over the years, I come to realize that the exercises themselves embody the concept.

All ballet classes are divided into two sections: a shorter segment holding onto the *barre*, and a longer segment dancing in the middle of the room (the center). I've heard Madame's *barre* work described as "always the same." Not true. Yes, the *order* of the exercises never changes, but the exercises themselves certainly do. In fact, there are three or four "variables" for each "slot." The regulars in class rotate as "leader for today." They get to choose the variables, trying to create a well-rounded result. Excellent training for future teachers.

In the "center" portion of class, Madame does away with the conventional dividing into groups. "Groups" means that most of the class stands idly by, while each group takes its turn at the exercise. Madame also turns the class away from the mirror and uses the studio space the long way. All of her combinations have steps that make you travel forward. You set yourselves up in horizontal lines, feeding in one behind the other.

You have to stay in a straight horizontal line, as you're moving forward while doing the combination. Which is more important? Doing the steps correctly, or staying in your straight line? Staying in your straight line, of course. Sooner or later, everybody gets the steps. But staying in a straight line while dancing these steps that travel forward? *That's* a skill in itself.

If you're leading off in the first three or four lines, you'd better not make any mistakes. The dancers who need to follow someone start at the back. But here's the brilliant part. When the "leaders" run out of room, they peel off, split, and go to the back, and start all over again. So, sooner or later, each line gets to the point where there's nobody in front. That's the genius of this whole setup. It builds independence in your students, which is the most important thing. Believe me when I tell you that I've only scratched the surface. There is *so* much that makes Madame's class "like no other."

Madame is not only unique. She is tough. Especially on a new pianist who is playing for her class for the first time. To be fair, playing for ballet class is an art form all its own. First, the musical measures have to be in "even 8's." That's because the barre exercises and center combinations are in "even 8's." Then, unless the dancers are pretty advanced or professional, it has to be easy to hear "the beat." Otherwise, the students cannot count those "8's."

Most important and most difficult of all, the "feeling" of the music should match the "feeling" of the exercise or combination. If the steps are slow and flowing, it helps if the music isn't too choppy (*staccato*). If the steps are quick and sharp, it helps if the music isn't too smooth (*legato*). When it comes to playing for jumps, the really good class accompanists find music with just the right amount of "bounce" to help lift the dancers "up." So, you see. Not easy. Maybe because I take piano, the whole thing fascinates me.

All this is going through my mind when, one afternoon, a new pianist sits down and puts her fingers silently on the keys. Madame asks for *pliés* and the music begins. Lots of rambling arpeggios. Lots of wandering melodies. Really hard to count.

"Play Schtrauss!!!" rings out in that Russian accent. Those rambling fingers freeze on the keys. Suddenly, the studio is filled with the strangely-comforting strains of the *Blue Danube* waltz.

When the *pliés* are over, it is time for *tendus*. Madame asks for a polka. Again, the music begins. More arpeggios.

"Play Schtrauss!!!" rattles the rafters. Is there a pattern here? Time for *rond de jambe par terre*. Madame asks for a waltz. Yup. Arpeggios, galore. "Play Schtrauss!!!"

In that class, I learn that "*Schtrauss*" even works for *frappé* and *grand battement* … and everything else.

(Years later, I am tasked with creating performance pieces for varying levels. I have not yet taught these students for a full year. Not yet sure what they can or cannot do, I choose a different "*Schtrauss*" Waltz for each level. Problem solved.)

Madame's "tough hand" with pianists does not stop with class. Sometimes it extends into the realm of performing. One performance, in particular, is pretty hard to forget.

Madame has choreographed an ambitious *Sleeping Beauty* suite for a student performance. It opens with that well-known Garland Waltz from Act I. Act III excerpts include the *Bluebird Pas de Deux, Puss-In-Boots,* and the *Wolf and Red Riding Hood.* Of course, Princess Aurora and her Prince perform their famous *Wedding Pas de Deux.* (This prince has many names, depending on which story you're reading or ballet company you're watching. *Désiré*? *Florimund*? Walt Disney weighs in with the rather predictable *Phillip*. Take your pick.) A rousing *Finale* brings the performance to a close.

Did I mention that our musical accompaniment will be played by one of the usual pianists from the School? The one who can eat an egg salad sandwich while playing, and never miss a beat. She keeps the melody going with her right, while grabbing a bite with her left. Amazing to watch. Madame never says a word. She's well aware of just how hard it is to find a class accompanist (cf: "*Schtrauss*").

Unfortunately, Miss Egg Salad is not too familiar with the *Sleeping Beauty* score. To keep a watchful eye on her, Madame has placed the upright piano in the middle wing on stage right. Hopefully, out of sight for at least most of the audience. Things seem to be progressing smoothly enough. Until the *Wedding Pas de Deux*.

The generic *pas de deux* in classical ballet has four components: the partnered *adagio*, the male solo, the female solo, and the *coda*. Introductions are generally four beats. (Hence, the familiar "a-five, six, seven, eight.") In this case, Tchaikovsky has shortened the introduction to the Prince's solo. It's three counts. The "6&, 7&, 8&" is played by the usual two chords for each beat. But then the next count of "1" happens to repeat that same exact chord from the introduction … before the melody starts.

Apparently, repeating that same chord is too much for our pianist. The "sameness" triggers something in her brain, and she just keeps on repeating the intro. And repeating the intro. And repeating the intro. The melody just never begins. Our dear Prince is posing upstage left, making one false start after another. Finally, Madame reaches back and lands one loud slap on the pianist's back. Like food dislodged from a Heimlich maneuver, the melody immediately comes flying out from those fingers on the keys. The Prince is finally dancing. All is well.

Musicians, of course, aren't the only recipients of Madame's tough ways. It is obvious that she plans to "toughen up" her students, too. The life of the professional ballet dancer is hard, and she wants to make sure we're up to the task. She makes us take class in heavy wool unitards over our leotards and tights. I call it, "The Ballast Theory of Ballet." We load ourselves down with 100 percent thick-yarn wool unitards throughout the week. When we shed them for Friday's Pointe Class, we'll feel light as a feather.

For that Friday Pointe Class, Madame also requires pink tights, only. No extra wool layer on the leg. No extra wool around the ankle and Achilles tendon. All of these layers help keep us warm, but can also hide a less-than-straight knee or a less-than-pointed foot. Our legs must appear the way they will be seen onstage. Completely exposed and available for correction. Yikes.

Mind you, we are *en pointe* two more times each week. Once for *Variations* (*repertoire*) class. Once for *Pas de Deux* (partnering) class. Still, that's not "tough" enough for Madame. So, in every Technique class, you must race to change into your pointe shoes after you've completed the Center Adagio, two times through.

My group (the first group) has until the rest of the class finishes that Adagio the second time through. By then, you not only need your pointe shoes on. You need to have warmed up your ankles and toes on your own. Madame doesn't want the *demi-pointe* (soft shoe) students waiting around, while she gives the pointe people their own warm-up.

Everyone in class will continue to do the same combinations, whether you're in a pointe shoe or not. And that first combination after our pointe shoes are on is always a doozy. No easing into things for us. Going up on pointe on one leg, then down on the same leg (*relevé*), right away. *Pirouettes* (turns on one leg), right away. The next combination is always a *petit allegro* (small jumps). You guessed it. If there's no special ankle warm-up for pointe, there is *certainly* no special ankle warm-up for small jumps. Everyone learns early on that "prepping" is our responsibility.

(Today, some students taking ballet at the college level have a different idea. They will let you know if they feel you haven't warmed them up sufficiently. Once, in a pointe class, I remember an unhappy college student with quite the specialized complaint. She's upset because my first combination in the center requires a *retiré* [toes touching the opposite knee]. She feels the lower *coupé* [where the toes touch only the opposite ankle] would be more appropriate.

Me: "What is your issue with the *retiré*?"
Student: "We need to do the lower *coupé* at the ankle first. To better prepare our hip alignment."
Me: "But you've just done an entire *barre* with all sorts of *retirés* up at the knee."
Student: "But the *barre* was offering support. Now the anatomy has to adjust to standing on its own."

Hear that low rumbling noise? It's Mme. Swoboda, turning over in her grave.)

The "toughening" continues. For instance, making us practice those dreaded *fouetté* turns to a slower waltz, rather than the usual sprightlier *coda*. Her theory? If you can manage them at the more challenging slower tempo, they'll be a breeze onstage to that quicker *coda*.

Neither does Madame allow you to start class in those "soft" ballet slippers. Too easy. You must remove the shanks (those stiff cardboard strips that add support) from your worn-out pointe shoes. These old pointe shoes become your new ballet slippers. Complete with elastics and ribbons.

It makes perfect sense. From the beginning of *barre*, your ankles are now getting used to the more "confining" feeling of those elastics and ribbons. Your foot is also working so much harder to "point" in that more cumbersome (albeit, shankless) pointe shoe.[14]

* * *

No one knows me better than Mme. Swoboda. That makes me very lucky. Her reputation is well-known throughout New York City and beyond. Even champion ice skaters seek her out for private lessons. That's how I get to see Olympians Dick Button and Carol Heiss at the studio. Carol sometimes shares her privates with her skater sister, Nancy.

Now that Madame has sold her School, there are "famous" dancers all around me, all the time. (To this 12-year-old, every Company member is famous.) I also get to mingle with a lot of former stars, who are teaching some of the classes. Now, they *really* are famous. Pinch me. I remember taking a pointe class from Mia Slavenska. Her makeup, her hair. So glamorous, she could be a movie star. Then there is gorgeous Kazimir Kokich, who teaches *Pas de Deux* (partnering) and *Caractère* (folk dance). Who doesn't have a crush on him?

Madame is also busy accepting invitations for her students to perform, like this request from Macy's department store. They want an Easter-themed children's show every day for the week leading up to Easter Sunday. On a tiny little stage with no wings, we put on an original skit, *Alice's Unbirthday Party*. With a script that takes *many* liberties. And we don't just dance. We have small speaking parts, too.

There is, of course, the Easter Bunny, played by talented Ballet Russe dancer, Lois Bewley. With apologies to Lewis Carroll, we add a benevolent Fairy Godmother in a long pink tutu, complete with magic wand. She is played by another lovely Ballet Russe dancer, Valerie Smith. Valerie hails from the Deep South. I have never heard such a beautiful southern accent before. I begin practicing immediately.

Funny. I have no memory of who plays Alice. Most likely because she never dances. Just sits in the front row and applauds a lot. The rest of us play an assortment of Dolls, eager to entertain Alice on her "unbirthday." Already with a Can-Can solo under my belt from last year's Junior High School Talent Show, I naturally portray a Can-Can Doll.

Since there are no wings, we all sit on the floor in front of the stage and get to watch the show right along with Alice and the children seated behind us. When it's your turn, you just pop up in place, turn around to face everyone, and introduce yourself. Then you run up these little steps onto the stage. Someone pushes "start" on the reel-to-reel tape recorder … and you dance.

Before *I* dance, I get to announce myself in a French accent, no less. No surprise that I've also been practicing this like crazy: *"I am zee Can-Can Doll, and I have come to dance zee Can-Can for you!"*

Lots of "firsts" for me in this six-day "engagement." First time dancing the same show every day, for a week. Worries that I might get bored evaporate into thin air. First time anyone asks me for my autograph. After one of the shows, a little girl does just that. I'm so nervous that I drop the pen. After another show, a woman comes up to tell me she really liked my performance. I can never forget what she asks me next: "Tell me, dear, where do you 'ballerine?'"

During the week-long Christmas break, we are allowed to take Madame's Professional Class. Pinch me, again. I'm actually in the same studio, at the same time, with those very same Company dancers I've been admiring onstage. Can you be terrified *and* exhilarated? In Madame's class, there are two kinds of dancers. "Old ladies" and "Babies." In other words, the professional Company dancers, and us.

Remember, the center combinations always travel forward the length of the studio. Naturally, the professional women lead off, followed by the men. We "babies" bring up the rear. Wait. Did Madame just forget about us? Forget that it is finally our turn to dance?

Yes, she often does. She starts to show the next combination. The professionals interrupt her, reminding her that we haven't danced yet. Then her Academy-Award performance begins: Walking backwards and bowing with both hands on her chest.

"Begging you pardon. Begging you pardon. How forget guest artists?" (I can't wait to be an "old lady.")

* * *

Time seems to fly by. All of a sudden, it's March of 1956 and I've just turned 14. The School is absolutely abuzz. There are going to be auditions for full and partial scholarships. If I win a scholarship, maybe my dad will start acting happier that I want to be a ballerina? The pressure's on. It's exciting. No, wait. What if I'm awful?

At the Scholarship Audition, some of those same former stars we mingle with every day are now our judges. Ominously seated across the front of the studio. Since only one student gets to go in at a time, it's only when we compare notes later on that we realize the "luminaries" have been taking turns giving the steps. Who did *you* get? Who did *you* get?

It's my turn. I go in. Seated in a horizontal row in front of me are Frederic Franklin, Leon Danielian, Alexandra Danilova, Tatiana Grantzeva, Nathalie Krassovska, Mia Slavenska, James Starbuck, and Igor Youskevitch.

Frederic Franklin: His warmth and charisma shine in so many roles with the Ballet Russe de Monte Carlo: from the Prince in *Swan Lake*, to a cowboy in Agnes de Mille's *Rodeo*, to Stanley Kowalski in Valerie Bettis's *A Streetcar Named Desire*. Choreographic geniuses Massine and Balanchine readily embrace this dancer, who learns steps instantly and has infallible musicality. Franklin's quick mind and innate theatricality make this unmolded clay ideal for leading roles in *Seventh Symphony* (Massine) and *Danses Concertantes* (Bal-

Arabesque at thirteen years old on the front porch of our New Rochelle home.

anchine). From his iconic partnership with Alexandra ("Choura") Danilova to becoming Artistic Director of the National Ballet of Washington (his own gem of a ballet company), in the years to come he will cast a striking presence in the American ballet scene. Performing Witches and Tutors and Charlatans well into advanced age, he tops it all off with Friar Laurence (in ABT's *Romeo and Juliet)* in his mid–90s. But to me, he's just the genius I've been told can sing a whole piano concerto, and know every step that goes with every note.[15]

Leon Danielian: "Known for his remarkable bravura and flair," in virtuosic roles such as the Bluebird in *The Sleeping Beauty*, the Harlequin in Michel Fokine's *Carnaval*, and the Peruvian in Léonide Massine's *Gaîté Parisienne*.[16] But to me, he's just the nice man who's taken time to speak with me for a 9th-Grade interview assignment with Someone Who Has Achieved Success in a Career of Your Choosing.

Alexandra Danilova: Only her friends can call her "Choura." A star ballerina of the Ballet Russe for years, she is equal parts intense stage presence and gorgeous legs and feet. Glamour isn't her only calling card. She gravitates toward experimental and avant-garde ballets, from choreographers such as George Balanchine. According to her, these ballets increase her artistic development more than a steady diet of *Swan Lake* and *Giselle*.[17] But to me, she's just the angel who has shown me how to sew a 1-inch-wide elastic strip at the very edge of my pointe shoe vamp. Now, I can keep wearing my shoes, even if the shanks are a bit broken.

Tatiana Grantzeva: While performing with the Ballet Russe, an audience favorite as the Street Dancer in Massine's *Le Beau Danube*.[18] Boarding the morning bus in her obligatory white turban, abulge with hair rollers stuffed inside to ensure flowing hair onstage that night. But to me, she's just the one who is refused entrance to the posh Neiman Marcus rooftop restaurant on tour, because of that bulging white turban.

Nathalie Krassovska: Best known for her portrayal of the title role in *Giselle*. A principal dancer with the newly-founded Ballet Russe de Monte Carlo in 1938. Performing both standard 19th-century repertory and ballets by 20th-century choreographers, Balanchine, Fokine, Nijinska.[19] But to me, she's just someone explaining why she carries those dinner rolls onto the bus every morning in her fishnet tote bag. Yesterday's restaurant. Today's breakfast.

Mia Slavenska: Most famous role: Blanche DuBois in the aforementioned *A Streetcar Named Desire*, for the short-lived Slavenska-Franklin Ballet.[20] But to me, she's just the sorceress who can teach an entire pointe class while wearing pointe shoes with neither ribbons nor elastics. No. They *never* do.

James Starbuck: Hollywood choreography: *The Court Jester*, starring Danny Kaye. Broadway choreography: *Oh Captain!*, featuring a show-stealing number for Alexandra Danilova. Television choreography: Sid Caesar's *Your Show of Shows*, featuring funny ballet satires for Imogene Coca.[21] But to me, he's just the celebrity we're whispering about, because we hear he works in television.

Igor Youskevitch: Combining outstanding technique with a dignified air as a regal cavalier. His legendary partnership with Cuban ballerina Alicia Alonso (especially in *Giselle*), gracing the stage for both Ballet Russe de Monte Carlo and Ballet Theatre (now American Ballet Theatre). But to me, he's just the dreamboat I've had a crush on for years.[22]

But, I digress. Back to the audition. While I may not remember where he is sitting, I definitely remember how Mr. Franklin practically springs from his chair to teach me an *adagio*. There is a moment in the sequence where I must *promenade en attitude* (revolve slowly on one leg with the other bent and lifted behind). This requires repeated nudging of my heel in one direction or the other, depending on the direction of the "revolving." That's the problem.

Thinking I have chosen the *correct* direction, I begin to revolve. Suddenly, and ever-so-subtly, Mr. Franklin sends his eyes in the other direction along with an almost imperceptible tilt of his head. I stop on a dime. I *reverse* my nudging heel, successfully completing the *adagio* and earning a full scholarship. How could I know that this moment is but the beginning of a long and beautiful mentoring story?

* * *

A few weeks later, Company First Ballerina Nina Novak teaches a Variations class. This is our chance to learn smatterings of the classical repertoire performed by the Company. Today's "adventure" is the famous Four Little Swans *(Les Quatres Cygnets)* from *Swan Lake, Act II*.

Nina watches as we line up, shoulder-to-shoulder. Each of us confidently crosses our own arms before holding hands with the dancer right next to us. She smiles demurely without uttering a word. Nodding to the pianist to begin, she watches in amusement as we try to execute those first famous traveling *emboités* (repeatedly changing feet), while hopelessly intertwined. It feels like trying to dance in a straitjacket. Tired of lurching out of control, we finally stop and let go.

When our laughter subsides, Nina quietly instructs us to stand shoulder-to-shoulder. Next bit of advice: Raise both arms sideways, about 45 degrees. Lo and behold. There's an available hand to clasp. But it belongs to *every other* girl. Not the one right next to you. (Each end girl bends her elbow, to clasp the hand in front of her.)

In another Variations class, I remember attempting the little solo of the Two Big Swans in the Act II Waltz. But, I am having a lot of trouble. My arms and legs refuse to work independently. Every time I *relevé* (rise) onto pointe on one leg to execute the *rond de jambe en l'air* (little circles in the air) with my other leg, my arms start waving in little circles right along with my leg. Mortifying, but I guess a little funny.

You never know who you're going to pass on your way to the studio. Like Lee Remick, who goes on to become an Academy Award–nominated movie star. (*Anatomy of a Murder. The Omen. Days of Wine and Roses.*)[23] Or Raven Wilkinson, who becomes the first black dancer to be hired by an American touring ballet company when she joins the Ballet Russe in 1956.[24]

One day, Madame announces, "*Time you do solo en pointe in classical tutu, Dearie.*" I had just danced *en pointe* as a wooden Toy Soldier for *this* year's junior high school talent show. But that doesn't count. A "classical ballet" solo? Exciting, but terrifying.

Madame takes me into the small studio. She has invited two talented 16-year-olds who just got into the Ballet Russe. Eleanor D'Antuono and Rochelle ("Chellie") Zide are waiting for me. They will show me two variations from Act III of *Coppélia*. I get to choose the one I'd like to perform.

Eleanor is up first. (Pardon the baseball lingo.) Her strong jumps are on display, as she demonstrates *Dawn* (*L'Aurore*). Then comes Chellie's effortless lyricism, as she demonstrates *Prayer* (*La Prière*). But the two of them aren't just "demonstrating." It looks like they're really performing, as if they're on stage.

I remember feeling so honored that these two beautiful dancers are doing all this for me. I also remember thinking that both solos are amazing, but … no contest. I quickly choose *Dawn*. Rather not tackle all those *bourrées* in *Prayer*. They look like they can really hurt. And besides, I *love* to jump.

I make two lifelong friends while studying with Mme. Swoboda. Phyllis Rosenberg (now Constan) and Judy Mack (now Saffer). Judy and I often have sleepovers on the weekends. I remember one, in particular. I might still be a legend for the amount of grilled steak I managed to eat at her Aunt's barbeque on Long Island.

As "regulars" in Madame's classes, Phyllis, Judy, and I escape the dreaded "nickname." For instance, when a student whose name Madame does not know comes late to class, she's instantly "Sleeping Beauty." Or, if another no-name non-regular happens to be wearing a blue hair ribbon, she is forever "*Blue Rooobon Girl.*"

But, wait. I speak too soon. Even her "regulars" can fall into the nickname trap. Take Charlotte. Madame insists on calling her Charlena. "Charlena" likes it so much, she eventually legally changes her name.

I make a third lifelong friend from Mme. Swoboda's class. Shirley Weishaar (now Brink). For the life of her, Madame cannot pronounce Shirley's name. Shirley quickly becomes "Charli." Madame never quite understands our giggles when innocently asking, "*Where's Charli?*" (*Where's Charley?* was a long-ago Broadway musical hit starring Ray Bolger.)

One day, the "re-named" Charlena and Charli team up with another similarly-named student, Sharon. This lineup (baseball, again) practically begs for shenanigans. They hatch a plan. The next time all three are in class together, they mischievously stand right next to one another at the barre.

We lose count of the number of times Madame tries to correct one of them. Because they're standing so close together, she simply cannot manage to spit out the right name.

"*Sh... Sh... Ch...*" happens over and over again. Finally, with a wave of disgust in their direction, Madame turns her back and walks to the other side of the studio. Do we get in trouble for laughing so loud? I can't remember. I've blocked it out.

Mr. Denham eventually moves the School further downtown. From 54th and Seventh, to 30th and Madison. The new building is called the Seven Arts Center. No more endless staircase. This new building has six floors. *And* an elevator. The office, dressing rooms and a smaller studio are on the 6th floor. The main, much larger, studio is on the 2nd floor. You ride the elevator a lot.

I love that elevator. Once, I ride it all the way from the lobby with Paul Newman. He is rehearsing Tennessee Williams's *Sweet Bird of Youth* on the fifth floor.

That second-floor studio is an immense space. Larger than any studio I've ever danced in. It has a long balcony on the side opposite the mirrors. Accessible by pressing "3" on the elevator. Trouble is, anyone can wander in off the street, take the elevator to the 3rd floor, enter that balcony, and watch us in class. Mme. Swoboda is not happy.

One day, an unsuspecting adult male appears

Early adventures *en pointe*—first as a soldier...

on the balcony during class. Madame stops in her tracks. Her head snaps upward.

In that shrill Russian accent, she demands, "*Who you belong to?*"

No answer. Probably paralyzed by fear. She promptly changes her tone and demeanor to charming. And a little flirtatious.

"*You don't belong to nobody? Is very sad.*"

He turns and flees. Mission accomplished.

* * *

It's now summer. Finally, I'm allowed to stay home from camp and study ballet. Since I've just won a full scholarship, I think it's sort of expected. (Thank God.)

I am so excited about summer ballet classes. This means I won't feel so horribly out-of-shape in September. I won't feel like September is only about

...**and then as "Dawn" in** *Coppélia*.

getting my turnout back to where it was. And my extensions. And my pirouettes. September will finally be about trying to get better. Instead of just catching up.

But, studying in New York in the summer has its challenges. New York summers are hot and humid. Great for the muscles. Not so great when the perspiration runs down your legs into your ballet shoes. Squish. Squish. Maybe the summer heat and humidity will help me lift my legs higher?

I know one thing, for sure. My 1954 Mount Washington calamity is in the rear view mirror. Ancient history, right? A whole two years ago. I'm 14 now, and completely in charge of my destiny.

But as my sister Stephanie likes to say, "Not so fast, chickie." Read on with trepidation. And don't try this at home.

Since Mt. Washington, the outsides of the fourth and fifth toes on my right foot are permanently numb. But, hey. When dancing *en pointe*, you're supposed to avoid those two toes anyway, right? And all my other toes seem fine. So, good to go.

True, for these eight weeks, I'll be dancing *en pointe* more than ever before. True, the New York humidity (no studio air conditioning) is bound to turn my pointe shoes to mush, more quickly than ever before. But, hey. I'm tough.

Sure enough, after about four weeks, the glue on the tops of my pointe shoes has really melted a lot. Mush. Is it possible the frostbite incident left me with inferior circulation in all my toes? Could this be why, with four weeks still to go, both my big toenails fall right off? Yes. The complete nails. All in one piece. Off.

The tragedy happens when I'm taking off my tights at home. I'm staring at two nailless big toes. I actually have to fish the nails out from the feet of my tights. I guess the tights were holding them in place? Thank goodness no one else is around.

I know. I know. No warning at all that this was going to happen? W-e-l-l, my big toes *have* been getting more and more sore. But this is my dream summer. Nothing can keep me off pointe. It's so obvious. If I "tell," I won't be dancing *en pointe* for the rest of the summer. Not an option.

My bedtime ritual is easy:

1. Remove toenails behind locked bathroom door. Toe beds can then "air out" overnight.
2. Place toenails belly-up (so *they* can "dry out") out of sight under my bed.
3. In the morning, re-tape toenails onto toes.
4. Repeat steps 1 through 3, religiously.

I somehow make it through those remaining four weeks. The rest is a bit hazy. I believe tears and a confession are involved. And a hastily arranged trip to the podiatrist. There is a vague recollection of my nail beds resembling "rolling hills."

The verdict: no pointe work. Until the nails grow back. Bumpily. And definitely ingrown. As I said earlier: "Don't try this at home." My dad says I got off cheap. I guess he means it could've "cost me" a whole lot more. Like, some of my toes?

As I start high school with all ten of them, I'm feeling kind of lucky. That's when I read about a huge coincidence. When Mickey was in high school, a football injury caused a dreaded bout with osteomyelitis. A bone infection that could've cost him his leg. He was lucky, too. I guess we both "got off cheap."

Another milestone. That summer, Madame wants me to take classes with *another* teacher. Edward Caton. He's the first teacher other than herself that Madame insists I study with. I can see why. It's like he casts a spell, and you're completely under it. He makes you do things you didn't know you could.

Mr. Caton and Mme. Swoboda were childhood ballet students together in Russia. I remember him as a tall man. Even through his loose-fitting trousers, you can see long, gently-hyperextended legs. Definitely, "ballet" legs. And he has natural turnout when he demonstrates. What a dancer he must have been. But you also have to work very hard to understand him, because has no larynx. He has to grunt each word. Separately and slowly. Is he forcing the air up from his stomach to make each sound? Now, if that doesn't cast a spell, what does?

Edward Caton's clear blue eyes, alabaster skin, and rosy cheeks make me think he must have been an adorable little choirboy as a youngster. And he always wears the same dark blue woolen cap covering much of his wispy white hair. For every class. Even in all that heat and humidity.

One particular day is burned in my memory. He has just shown us the center *adagio* combination. It's time to do it to the music. I am in the front line of the first group. We are all standing in the best 5th position we can muster. I *think* I am breathing. Can't be sure. Then, our worst nightmare.

Instead of music, we hear forced-air grunting, one ominous word at a time: "I… LOOK… AT… YOU… AND… I… CANNOT… TELL… IF… YOU… ARE… A… BOUT… TO…DANCE… OR… HAVE… A… TOOTH… PULLED. PLEASE… LOOK… LIKE… YOU… ARE… A… BOUT… TO… DANCE!"

We actually giggle. We can't help it. Then we try our best to look like we are "about to dance." The music begins. Mr. Caton is smiling. Just a little.

One more unforgettable Mr. Caton class. It starts out the same as usual. At the barre. Mr. Caton shows each exercise. We do each exercise to both sides. First, holding the barre with our left hand. Then, turning to face the other way, and holding with our right. *Grand plié, tendu, dégagé, rond de jambe par terre, frappé, grand battement, fondu & adagio, serré & battu, rond de jambe en l'air.* Some exercises are slow and controlled. Others are quick and feel like brainteasers.

After forty minutes, the barre is over. Now that we are warmed up, it's time for center combinations. But Mr. Caton does not seem pleased. We soon know why.

More forced-air grunting, one ominous word at a time: "WE… WILL… NOW… DO… THE… BARRE… AGAIN… IF… YOU… MAKE… MISTAKE… WE… DO… IT… AGAIN." And so we start from *grand plié* and do the whole barre again. All forty minutes.

Two more forced-air grunting words: "THANK… YOU…." And he's gone. Out the door and down the stairs. Wow.

Even so, classes with Mr. Caton are never a negative experience. Nothing is further from the truth. You are focusing harder than you've ever focused. Maybe because it takes so much concentration to understand him? But you are also completely drawn in by the sheer force of his personality. It wills you forward. It makes you work even harder. I feel like I can do anything in his class. His is a totally mesmerizing presence.

(Years later, Mr. Caton magically resurfaces during my D.C. years with the National Ballet. I fall under his spell once again, as he helps me recover my technique after a serious Achilles tendon injury.)

* * *

Summer, survived. (More or less.) A miracle is about to take place. Madame is preparing a small performance (she calls it a "concert") at the *Rodina* in Lakewood, New Jersey. *Rodina* is the Russian word for "homeland." The Russian *émigrés* living in Lakewood decide that should be the name of their community center.

The program will be *Les Sylphides.* But *Les Sylphides* with a twist. You see, currently studying at the Ballet Russe School is 10-year-old Maria Youskevitch and 12-year-old Leon ("Lorca") Massine. You heard right. Maria is Igor Youskevitch's daughter and Leon is famed choreographer Léonide Massine's son. Madame is nobody's fool. She knows that the names of two such famous Russian ballet luminaries are pure gold for their compatriots back in Lakewood. She decides to star the young Maria and the young Leon in the iconic *Les Sylphides Pas de Deux*. That's all they'll do. Nothing more. Except, of course, run on for the final pose at the end.

Because the *Rodina* stage is so small, the *"corps de ballet"* will be performed by eight *bona fide* Ballet Russe de Monte Carlo professional Company dancers. No, no, no. Seven, plus me. You heard right. *I'm* going to get to learn the Romantic style of Michel Fokine's masterpiece. It was this very style, this very ballet, that so enchanted me when I was four years old. It's why I immediately knew this was what I wanted to be when I grew up. Now I will be "inside" the enchantment.

The rehearsals feel like heaven. The Chopin music. The Fokine choreography. The Company dancers, teaching me and helping me. I'm dancing alongside Dorothy Daniels, Hester Fitzgerald, Josephine Jeffers, Susan May, Libby Salerno, Andrea Vodehnal, and June Wilson. June adds "chix" to everyone's first name. (A term of endearment she picked up from the Russians?) I'm Roni-chix. It makes me feel like one of the girls. Well, almost.

Why would these seven professional dancers all agree to perform in this *Sylphides-with-a-twist* for Madame? Why would they "agree" to pose in the background, like furniture, while two children dance a very simplified version of the iconic *Pas de Deux*? (10-year-old Maria won't even be *en pointe*.) What's in it for them? Well, they're all currently still in the Ballet Russe *corps de ballet* on the professional stage. In Madame's version, they get to perform those beautiful solos. The Waltz, the Mazurka, and the Prelude. You already know what's in it for me. Only Nirvana. That's all.

The performance goes well. Nirvana doesn't disappoint. All those solos, danced beautifully by the Ballet Russe company dancers. All receive warm, enthusiastic applause.

But, then it happens. Maria and Leon barely step out onstage from the wings. Thunderous, tumultuous, everlasting applause. They haven't even done one step yet, but it sounds like they are already bowing at the end.

Performing at the *Rodina* always feels a little like I'm in a movie. The audience seems to be made up entirely of elderly Russian men and women who look and dress as if they are still living in the early 1900s in their mother country. There's always a small reception afterwards, complete with accordion-playing musicians. I am blissfully eating *pierogis*. (Every culture has its "blintz?")

Suddenly, I see a gentleman approaching me from across the room. "Gentleman" can be the only word for him. He is an elderly Russian with a yellowing white mustache. Completing this perfect picture, he is even missing some of his brownish teeth. Also detectable, the whiff of someone who smokes a lot of cigars?

Nevertheless, he is resplendent in the military finery from his days in the Tsar's Army. Bowing stiffly from the waist, he extends his right hand. When I give him mine, he promptly kisses it. Then, with so much charm that I nearly faint, he extends both arms toward me. Palms facing upward, like an "invitation."

Did I mention that I am 14? I remember thinking, "Thank God this is a lively polka … and not something slower." He is surprisingly agile. I, just as surprisingly, am enjoying myself.

After this performance, I spend the weekend at Madame's house in Lakewood. I'm not exactly sure when she and Mr. Swoboda bought it. Judging from old photographs, sometime in the 1930s. I remember two stories of gray clapboard, and red shutters. The house seems overwhelmingly cluttered with books, photographs, figurines. It also has that slight "old lady" smell. I notice no screens on the windows. Maybe she never opens them? I secretly promise myself that this will never happen to me.

Madame has prepared an amazing seafood salad. It must have beets in it, because it has a reddish tint. I can't get enough of it. Speaking of beets, there is also borscht. Yum! Cold borscht, with that dollop of sour cream in the center. Madame's borscht is more pink than dark purple. I suspect some heavy cream is involved. Did I remember to mention the homemade baklava?

It feels like Madame is always cooking. And always serving. That includes daily fresh oatmeal for the gorgeous large koi in the backyard pond. It also feels like I am constantly eating. All weekend long. Then, back in class I hear, "*Dearie. I tink maybe you gain little bit weight.*"

Two years later, when I'm 16, Madame decides it's time for me to perform a *Pas de Deux* at the *Rodina*. I've been taking *pas de deux* class with Mr. Kokich for almost two years, but I'm terrified. *Pirouettes* with your partner? *Promenades* (revolving on one leg) with your partner? But then I find out my partner is Perry Brunson. The sweet, and very patient, Ballet Russe *corps de ballet* dancer.

We're performing the *Wedding Pas de Deux* from Act III of *Coppélia*. The only tutu Madame can get her hands on is a red and black one from *Don Quixote*. The absent bridal white doesn't bring bad luck. Perry's gentle tutoring gets me through without embarrassment. I'm forever grateful.

A year later, it's Ballet Russe soloist Eugene Slavin to the rescue. Perry had been such a good teacher, I figure I have nothing left to learn. Wrong! We're performing another "Wedding Pas de Deux," this time from *Sleeping Beauty, Act III*. Much more difficult. But at least I'm wearing an appropriately pink tutu.

To Be… Or Not to Be

During high school, my ongoing tug-of-war between academics (which I love) and ballet (which I can't live without) continues. But now, it's become the agony of being forcefully pulled in opposite directions. Then, when the opposing forces lose their grip. Boom. Boom. Boom. Explosions, as my two worlds collide.

My parents aren't helping. They're all for my taking as many ballet classes a week as I'd like. They brag to anyone who will listen about the full scholarship I have just been awarded. But they are also demanding that I maintain my "A" average. Boom. And insisting on eight hours of sleep. Boom. What about my homework? The collisions keep coming.

* * *

In the 1914 silent film "The Perils of Pauline," you meet an adventurous young woman with a wide streak of independence. In 1956, meet a sophomore at New

Rochelle High School who is determined to get to her afternoon ballet classes in New York City.

New Rochelle High is a French-Gothic style structure, set back from the street by a large lake. A grass-lined pedestrian causeway over the water connects the school to North Avenue, one of New Rochelle's main thoroughfares.

They say the causeway is a mile long. Not sure, but it feels like it when I'm running to make the bus. The bus that's my Cinderella coach. Whisking me the fifteen minutes down North Avenue to the 12:40 train to Grand Central station. All this, to get to ballet class on time. A full-scholarship student can't afford to be late.

I've already grabbed my coat and dance bag from my locker before my final class. When that bell rings, I'm ready to start running. Thank goodness I'm pretty good friends with the bus driver. He's well-aware of my "mission." Every day, he waits patiently at the curb with his doors open. Watching me run. The minute I slow to a walk to catch my breath, he closes the doors. I can almost hear him chuckling as I break into a run again. He reopens the doors. I must be quite a sight. Dance bag bouncing around. Two nearly-even piles of books clutched tightly to my chest. Running. Running.

The New Haven Railroad train tracks are way, way below the street. Two consecutive, outdoor wooden-slat staircases are the only way down. Scary. Sometimes, when the bus driver lets me off, the train is already in the station. The doors stay open, as I navigate those scary steps. Is that conductor holding the train for me? Good to have friends in high places.

One Peril down; two to go. Next up, the Wardrobe Challenge. Putting on my pink tights and black leotard under my dress. (It's the '50s.) A must, before starting homework. Instructions inspired by Superman:

Step 1: Choose a seat as close to the Lurching Lavatory as your sense of smell can stand.
Step 2: In this seat, immediately remove socks. Stuff sticky feet back into loafers.
Step 3: Be ready to swoop into Lurching Lavatory the minute it's unoccupied.
Step 4: Lock Lurching Lavatory door.
Step 5: Lean against available wall (not the window, not the door, not the toilet).
Step 6: Tuck left leg of pink tights into anything at your waist, because tights must never touch Lurching Lavatory floor. Scooch both thumbs down as close to toes of right leg of tights as possible.
Step 7: "Unstick" right foot from right loafer.
Step 8: Balancing on left leg, lift right knee as high as possible. (Ballet makes you flexible.)
Step 9: Wait until Lurching Lavatory is not lurching so much. Stuff right foot into tights.
Step 10: Scooch tights up to right mid-thigh.
Step 11: Lowering leg, place foot on top of empty right loafer.
Step 12: Repeat Steps 7, 8, 9, 10 & 11 for left leg.

Step 13: Scooch tights all the way up to your waist.
Step 14: Balancing on left leg, insert right foot through right leg hole of leotard.
Step 15: Repeat Step 14 with left leg.
Step 16: Writhe and wriggle leotard up and over the boobies I don't yet have, in case you forget Step 4.
Step 17: Wriggle out of dress sleeves. Toss as much of dress as possible behind you, hanging backwards from your neck.
Step 18: Wriggle into leotard sleeves or straps. Wriggle back into dress sleeves.
Step 19: Use your right toes to pry up the smashed loafer top you've been standing on. Reinsert right foot.
Step 20: Repeat Step 19 with left foot.

Thanks, Superman. (Friends in high places.)

Final Peril: the Homework Challenge. These train trips into the City and back are 35–40 precious minutes each way. Every sliver of homework I can cross off my list is heaven. Trying to read what I have written on the train is not. The curse of cursive is that the pen never leaves the paper. Disaster on a lurching train.

Okay, Mother Necessity. Time to invent. Introducing Ronnie-Write: ⅞ printing; ⅛ cursive. I don't plan it. My pen and my brain have concocted this on their own. Take the word "with." The "w," "i," and half the "t" are printed. The crossing of the "t" is connected to the "h." My teachers demand an explanation, because the Cursive God is worshiped in school. I plead my case. They acquiesce.

* * *

Redemption is like cuddling a warm, fuzzy puppy, while she's licking your fingers. It feels so good. My Yankees not only face "Dem Bums" in the '56 World Series. We beat them. And my Yankees not only beat the Dodgers. My dad even gets us tickets to the Sunday Game Four. And Mickey plays. *And* he hits a home run. We win the game, 6–2, and even the Series at two games apiece.

Ask me if I'm looking forward to going back to school after *this* game? Forget being an ostrich. I'm practically peacocking. And did I mention it's Monday, October 8, 1956? I don't know it yet, but it's a day about to go down in baseball history.

Here I am, basking in the glory of *my* Game Four victory. Giving eyewitness details to anyone who will listen. Definitely Queen for a Day. But not for long.

I'm racing to get to an afternoon class. Are the Yankees ahead? Here comes my World History teacher, Mr. Joe Katz. A transistor radio glued to his ear. Another Yankee die-hard.

ME: "What's the score?"
MR. KATZ: "We won! It's over! Larsen pitched a perfect game!"[25]

A perfect game? No runs, no hits, no errors? No, that's just a mere no-hitter. A *perfect game* doesn't even have any walks (bases on balls). "27 up, 27 down," as the sportswriters like to say. And, Yankee pitcher Don Larsen's perfect game is the first perfect game ever pitched in World Series history.[26] (To date, make that "the only...")

Mickey's biggest contribution? Not his home run. No. It's his sixth inning lunging catch, running at breakneck speed, of a Gil Hodges ball hit to deep left center field. The perfect game is still intact. Mickey gets sweet revenge against Sandy Amorós, for his catch last year in the game that broke my heart.

My life can get complicated, when it comes to baseball in the Fall. Crucial games *must* be listened to. But there's always something in the way. High School classes? Ballet classes?

A few years later, it's the final game of the '58 Series. We promise Madame Swoboda that, when Pointe Class is over, we'll practice our *Sleeping Beauty* solo variations by ourselves. Madame leaves the studio to teach another class. Look at us. We lied. We are, instead, sitting spread-eagle on the studio floor. Crowded around my transistor radio, listening to that seventh game. Oh, well. At least we're stretching.

No conflicts in the Fall of 1959, because we don't make the Series. On to 1960. I will not be discussing the 1960 World Series at this time.

* * *

The collisions keep coming all the more frequently in my Senior year. That's when the family moves to an apartment in Riverdale, three months before graduation. Dad will now be driving us the twelve or so miles to school, on his way to work. This means out the door "at 6:40 sharp." My father's exact words. Can you tell?

I quickly come up with a plan. I kiss my parents goodnight at ten o'clock. In their minds, I can now get up at 6:00, to leave for school at 6:40. Voilà. The requisite eight hours sleep.

Fact: my two sisters and I share a bedroom, and I can't keep them awake. Solution: Under my covers with a tiny lamp, doing homework until my eyes fall out of my head. If I haven't finished, I set my alarm for four o'clock and do another two hours undercover.

I can still see it. Our elevator is directly across the hall from our wide-open apartment door. Dad is in the elevator, impatiently holding down the "open" button. I'm racing from room to room. Lunch. Dance bag. Suddenly, a bellowing voice even the neighbors can hear.

"Dammit, young lady! All you have to do is get up five minutes earlier."

Graduation is approaching. I adore my high school academics, but ballet is my oxygen. When the two pursuits collide, no-brainer. I choose breathing. And that's how come I end up turning down the coveted 14th Annual Model United Nations conference. This year, it is in D.C. *Problems in American Democracy* is one of my favorite classes. Ray Ducharme is one of my favorite teachers. He tells us the first conference was held in 1946, after the ratification of the UN Charter.[27]

Mr. Ducharme is well aware of the potential impact of this once-in-a-lifetime experience. Imagine performing an Ambassador role in a simulated General Assembly, or maybe even the Security Council? Too bad imagining is all I will ever do. I am still that full-scholarship Ballet Russe student. I've recently been tapped to dance the lead role of Princess Aurora in all upcoming student performances of *The Sleeping Beauty, Act III*. Traveling to D.C. is not to be.

I am also four days late turning in Mr. D's one required term paper. It will be a substantial part of our grade. He had informed us of the due date months in advance. He has also clearly stated that we will lose half a grade (A+, A, B+, B...) for each day the paper is late. I've known for two months that Princess Aurora has first dibs on my upcoming weekends. Mr. Ducharme, though, has firmly stated that he will not entertain any excuses. I don't make any.

My chosen topic is *John Dewey and the American Education System*. I've done my research. I have copied and organized reams of longhand notes onto lined, 3×5 index cards, the suggested step before attempting a first draft. I have every intention of turning in this term paper on time. My last weekend (before the Monday due date) is spent scribbling my first draft from that stack of 3×5s. All while riding a bumpy station wagon to different nearby cities.

I am finally back home Sunday night. Two performances and one blister later, I actually start trying to proof my first draft. Success meter: Zero. I suddenly have a solution. I like this paper on John Dewey, and I like my conclusions. I want to do them justice. I will forgo as many ballet classes as it takes this coming week, to write the paper I *want* to write. Even exchange? Yes. Lower grade? Never mind. At least I know Mr. Ducharme will take the time to leave his comments. I love to write. His comments will matter more to me than the grade.

A box inside the classroom door, labeled "Term Papers," greets us on Monday. Maybe Mr. D will not notice that I'm paperless. The bell finally rings. I'm almost out the door.

"Ronnie." (So close.)

Mr. D: "No paper?"
Me (turning around): "You said no excuses."
Mr. D: "Tell me, why?"
Me: "Two cities. Two ballet performances. Ballet Russe powers-that-be evaluating from the audience."
Backing up toward the classroom door while I'm talking. Making a run for it as soon as I finish.

Back home, I glue myself to my typewriter. That's where I stay. The rest of Monday. Now it's Tuesday. John Dewey is batting cleanup. Princess Aurora is on the bench. Tuesday turns into Wednesday. Still typing.

Wednesday, May 20. I remember the date because the Yanks fall into the American League cellar. A 13–6 loss to the Tigers at the Stadium. First time in last place since 1940. Turns out, I'm having a better week than my poor Yankees. I finish my paper Wednesday night. They're still in the cellar.

On Thursday, I place John Dewey on Mr. D's desk as I'm leaving class. Thankfully, he's talking to another student and doesn't notice. Oh, yes. And Princess Aurora has replaced Dewey in center field. Ronnie's back in ballet class.

So John Dewey? What are his stats? My paper comes back, swimming in useful suggestions. Yay. And the grade? Mr. D's formula dictates a "B+." Mr. D gives me an "A." I am actually disappointed at the special treatment. I get over it quickly, though, when I learn that my GPA has landed me Class Salutatorian.

The title of my graduation address is *Tolerance*. I've never actually liked the word. To me, if you tolerate someone, you begrudgingly allow them to exist. I would like to replace "tolerance" with "respect." Granted, it's asking a lot. But aren't we 17-year-olds supposed to be idealistic?

I almost don't get to make my Salutatorian's speech. When the Faculty hears that I'm choosing ballet dancer over full-time college student, they're divided over whether or not to let me speak. They relent. I speak.

The male Valedictorian, Henry Clay Moses III, gives your standard "standing at the threshold of our future" address. My friends think I win, hands down. Chalk one up for the girls. Even some teachers are congratulating the kid who isn't going to college. Guess the naysayers decided to "tolerate" me, after all.

* * *

Academics vs. ballet: difficult, but obvious. But, ballet vs. ballet? Honing your technique further through intense study versus finally starting your professional career? Definitely less clear-cut.

Full-scholarship students at the Ballet Russe School are pretty much expected to audition for the Company right after high school. I've graduated, and I'm only three months past my 17th birthday. Am I really ready to begin an 18-week cross-country bus tour of mostly one-night stands? I just survived a senior year of four hours sleep a night. Of burning the candle at both ends. Can I please have a year to take ballet without being sleep-deprived?

Madame and I have been going around in circles about this for months. An insistent rumor of Ballet Russe's money troubles has been circulating at the same time. There are whispers that this upcoming 1959–60 season might be the last.

MADAME: *"Maybe join. Or miss only chance, dance with Company."*
ME: "I guess you're right."
MADAME: *"Need more technique to be good professional. Stay, take class."*
ME: "I guess you're right."
MADAME: *"Miss chance with Company. No good."*
ME: "I guess you're right…"

Yes. No. Yes. No. Not at all like the last time I had an opportunity to join the company. That's right. Two whole years ago.

I was 15 and in 10th grade, standing in the dressing room. And *that's* when lead ballerina Nina Novak decides to invite me to join the Company. Maybe because no one else is in there? Only Madame Swoboda.

The Company? Me? Now? I am too stunned to speak. In a panic, I stare at Madame. She flashes one of her "Cheshire Cat" grins.

Then, in a syrupy-sweet voice, through a big toothy grin, she replies, *"Thank you, but we finishing high school."*

But two years later, I'm done with high school. And expected to join the Ballet Russe. Now. Still, and without Madame's "help," I've decided I want to take that year off and polish my technique. *Without* being so sleep-deprived. What to do? Easy. Immediately take two weeks off, for sunbathing and swimming. My cunning plan: miss the Company Audition. Take weeks and weeks to get back into shape. Start with a Beginner class on my first day back.

Too bad the Company audition is also on my first day back from sunbathing and swimming. Even worse, it's in the same studio. The audition's finished. I'll bet I can sneak past all these sweaty dancers, leaving in droves. Not so fast. Nina has spotted me.

She grabs my wrist. She leans her face in, inches from mine. Her dark eyes are piercing.

> **NINA (thick Polish accent):** *"Where were you?"*
> **ME:** "I'm not in shape."
> **NINA (eyes widening, voice hissing):** *"If you want to come, I will take you. But you must tell me right now."*

Nina's grip tightens on my wrist. My searching eyes find Madame Swoboda. Smirking. She's been standing behind Nina the whole time. Saw the whole thing. Rescue? Not this time.

> **ME:** "Thank you, Nina. But I really want a year to study, without the pressure of high school."

There. Now, was that so hard?

* * *

And that's how come, one sunny Saturday morning in June of '59, Mom, Dad, and I are sitting in the Office of Admissions at Sarah Lawrence College. My parents have called ahead for an appointment, and we're sitting across from a very warm, very understanding woman.

I explain that I've been invited to join the Ballet Russe de Monte Carlo, my dream since childhood. But, I've decided to delay that for a year to fine-tune my ballet technique, while enriching my mind at Sarah Lawrence. With the help of a partial National Merit Scholarship. And, hopefully, morning Sarah Lawrence classes and the Ballet Russe School by 1:00 p.m.

Apparently, warmth and understanding only get you in the door. Attending only morning classes requires special permission. And that permission cannot be granted to this incoming freshman. Ouch.

However, our admissions lady does gently suggest something really sweet and conciliatory. Turning to my parents, she proposes that I "be given my head in ballet" for now. Sarah Lawrence will welcome me with open arms, and honor my partial scholarship, should I wish to enroll at a later date. I guess she understands that "my head" right now is filled *only* with ballet.

(Not until the mid-'60s do campus sit-ins demand, among other things, more flexibility in scheduling. God bless sit-ins. Today, a dancer need not choose between college and a professional career. Wonderful alliances exist. Among them, New York City Ballet with Barnard College and Alvin Ailey with Fordham University. Professional company dancers now arrange their academic schedule around their performance schedule.)

On our way home, my father announces his Dreaded Invisible Two-Year Clause. His words burn into my brain:

"Bust out of the *corps de ballet* within two years, young lady, or you have to go to college."

The hierarchy in a ballet company is, from top to bottom, Principals, Soloists, and *Corps de Ballet*. Anyone who knows *anything* about ballet knows that "new girls" don't just "bust out" of the *corps de ballet* that easily. It takes three or four years.

The 2nd- and 3rd-year girls not only torment the "rookies." They believe they have a stranglehold on the handful of available *demi-soloist* roles that are the "baby-steps" on your way to real soloist roles. I try in vain to explain this to my father. He won't listen:

Dad: "Never mind, kid. If ya' got it, you'll get it!"

I'm definitely doomed. I hate this feeling, but it's not the first time my father and I have butted heads. I didn't take Calculus in my senior year. I'm not *interested* in Calculus. I love French and Creative Writing. My dad tells anyone who will listen that I'm wasting my mind studying French and Creative Writing. But, I'm *interested* in French and Creative Writing. Dad wants me to be an atomic physicist. I want to do what I love. The back-and-forth goes like this:

Dad: "I didn't do what I wanted to. I did what I had to, to provide for your Mother and you girls."
Me: "What would you have done instead of going into business?"
Dad: "I love nature and airplanes. I could have been a forest ranger. Flying around in a small plane. Inspecting trees."
Me: "We would have been living someplace rural. I might never have even heard of ballet."
Dad: "Nah! The cows woulda' danced!"

An acknowledgment of the Inescapable, perhaps. But not the slightest hint of Approval, from the man whose life choices have riddled him with ulcers. He's not the best advertisement for Plan A. I choose Plan B. Years later, I overhear my parents talking. The disappointment persists:

Dad: "She will never be able to make a decent living. I should never have let her take ballet when she was six."
Mom: "It was her dream. You weren't God."
Dad: "Dammit. When she's six years old.... I AM God!"

(The jury will disregard the last statement.)

* * *

Why am I feeling depleted? It should be just the opposite. I've told Nina Novak I want to spend a year just taking ballet classes, before joining the Company. Proud about that one.

Still, I guess four hours of sleep a night, to maintain an "A" average, can drain you. The dictionary says depleted means emptied out. Guess it's time to fill me back up again. First, sleep. Then, as many ballet classes a day as this eager body can take. But that's just afternoons into early evenings.

What about the mornings? All that time I won't be taking courses at Sarah Lawrence? It's time to fill that up. Somewhere in New York City must let you take college courses in just the mornings. Ask around enough, sooner or later you get answers.

Say hello to Creative Writing at The New School on 12th Street, between Fifth and Sixth Avenues. I sign up for the Fall of 1959. My own personal Sarah Lawrence.

Getting there from Riverdale: a piece of cake. A bus to the IND subway. The express to Columbus Circle. Change to the local. Then hop off at 14th and Sixth. Walk two quick blocks. Voilà.

It's so perfect to be taking Creative Writing. For as long as I can remember, I've been writing down my thoughts. Who knew it had a name? There's form, structure, style, tone. An actual technique. Like ballet. I can't get enough. One of my favorite assignments is writing a monologue.

Granted, I like to talk, but a monologue is "structured" talking. I welcome the challenge. What I find out most about myself in this writing class is how much I welcome criticism. I love learning that something I thought was pretty good actually needs a lot of work. I feel like an empty glass. Fill me up. This is great.

But Ronnie's "personal Sarah Lawrence" would have courses in Creative Writing *and* French. Okay. One down, one to go. I see that The New School has a Fall '59 course named Conversational French. How fast do I sign up for that?

What else, besides The New School, can "fill me up?" Not what else. *Who* else. Sol Hurok, that's who. Yes, the noted arts impresario. Because it's Hurok who, after 35 long years, finally brings Russia's famed Bolshoi Ballet to the United States for an eight-week cross-country tour. New Yorkers are going to see "the Bolshoi" perform at the "Old" Met.[28] The original Metropolitan Opera House on Broadway and 39th Street.

Does this mean I get to see Galina Ulanova in person? I *have* to. I just have to. You see, I've been enchanted by her … there's no other word for it … for the past three years.

That's right. Three years ago, my Grandpa and his excited 15-year-old granddaughter went downtown to Radio City Music Hall, where they were showing a film of the Bolshoi Ballet performing their entire production of *Romeo and Juliet*, which first premiered in 1940. This performance was filmed onstage during an actual performance in their historic Mariinsky Theatre in Moscow. The music? Famous Russian composer, Sergei Prokofiev. The star? Galina Ulanova, as Juliet.[29]

I'm transfixed. Seeing Ulanova dance for the first time, I can't believe my eyes. She is 45 years old, but she doesn't look a day over 14. I swear. It's unbelievable. You'd have to see it for yourself. She's a curious kitten one minute, a mischievous pixie the next. And so light on her feet. Sometimes they seem to move as if in a blur. And she makes you really believe that Romeo is her very first love, ever. Then, there's that smile. l can never forget her smile. It seems to light up her eyes.

That was 1956. Now it's 1959, and Galina Ulanova will be appearing in the flesh, dancing *Giselle* with the Bolshoi. Right downtown. She was 45 when she transformed herself into the 14-year-old Juliet. Imagine getting to see her as this 16-year-old peasant girl?

My ballet school pal, Naomi Richardson, and I agree. We must see Ulanova dance *Giselle*. It's this Friday night, and it's sold out. They're saying even Standing Room is in doubt. We devise a cunning plan. Daring. But worth it.

Naomi and I already have Balcony tickets for Friday. It's the very same day, but we're going to the matinee. A mixed bill. Four short selections. The Bolshoi calls it a "Highlights" Program.

Now the basics. The Met has six levels. The first five: Orchestra, Parterre Boxes, Grand Tier, Dress Circle and Balcony. The tippity-top, sixth level above the Balcony is called the Family Circle, but better known as the "nosebleed section." Our plan goes into action right after the matinee curtain comes down, and it goes like this:

1. Casually wend our way to the Balcony Ladies Room.
2. Linger and loiter until we are the only two left.
3. Begin occupying two non-adjacent stalls.
4. Break out sandwiches and assorted munchies. (Dinner.)

And so begins our stakeout. The goal? To ever-so-casually emerge from our stalls (one at a time) like strangers, about forty-five minutes before curtain. Exiting the Ladies Room, we'll blend in with the Balcony crowd. Ever-so-patiently we'll mingle and descend. Mingle and descend. Mingle and descend. Eventually arriving on the main floor. Eventually, watching from Standing Room at the back of the Orchestra.

Well, *that* bubble certainly bursts. About an hour before curtain, ushers come into the Balcony Ladies Room to check for stowaways. So our plan's not that cunning? Or original?

I have no idea what Naomi does. I make sure my stall door is locked. I scramble to sit on top of the back of the toilet, hiding my feet. Maybe the Stowaway Cops won't try the door? My pursuer is smarter than that. A terrifying flashlight is suddenly aiming down at me from above the stall next door.

The jig is up for both of us. I guess Naomi agrees, because she's slowly slinking out of her stall. The spacious elevator feels like it's in no rush. Dress Circle…. Grand Tier…. Parterre Boxes…. Orchestra. Now, the final blow. Crossing this large, very crowded lobby to get to the street. I'm not in handcuffs, but I might as well be. And our Stowaway Cop is relentless.

"Keep moving. Keep moving." Her *sotto voce* nudging is driving me crazy. Relentlessly urging us past women dressed to the hilt. Of course. Ulanova's first *Giselle* is exactly like another Opening Night. The jewels. The fur. The stares. And I'm this crumpled mess, looking like the stowaway I am. What if one of my mother's friends recognizes me? Can't I just crawl out on all fours?

The agony ends. We're back where we started. On the sidewalk, and desperate. With time running out, Naomi and I do the only logical thing. Food. Corner coffee shop. Pineapple pie *à la mode*, with vanilla ice cream. Wolfing it down, we hatch Plan B.

Plan B: Walk around the corner to a nondescript door, way down the block. *That's* the entrance for ticket holders to the Metropolitan Opera House Family Circle. The notorious "nosebleed section." Our only hope. If there are *any* unsold seats, that's where they're going to be. And they have to be the ones with the most obstructed view. Who would want to sit in them? We would.

In the nosebleed section, there are only four rows of seating. That shrinks to only two rows, as the "horseshoe" gets closer to either side of the stage. Dreadful sightlines aren't the only slap in the face. There, in a teensy-weensy lobby, is one teensy-weensy elevator to the very top floor.

The ignominy of it all. As Naomi and I squeeze in, I go over my "lines" in my head. We go straight to the sixth level in record time. None of those pesky stops on fancier floors. Fortunately, the postage-stamp of a Family Circle lobby fits perfectly into our plans. Ticket-taker and ticket-holder mingle in easy earshot of one another.

It is now twenty minutes before curtain. Now or never. We begin "lurking" and audibly discussing how our mothers are "driving in from Brooklyn with our four tickets" and should be "arriving any minute." The rest is not difficult to imagine. At the ten-minute mark … at the five-minute mark … our "concern" for our still-absent parents deepens. Traffic? A fender bender?

Folks with tickets begin to sympathize. One sweet lady even offers us a single ticket that she isn't using. We thank her, certain that our Moms are "arriving soon."

Finally, there's no one left in that lobby except the ticket-taker, Naomi, and I. The applause for the Maestro can be heard faintly through the closed double doors. I actually begin crying. Not over my missing Mom. Over missing Ulanova's performance.

The ticket-taker, bless her heart, finally asks us where our seats are. I blurt it out through sobs. "The four closest seats to the stage … in the second row." Obviously, I am naming the four worst seats in the house. You see only half the stage.

Then she asks the dreaded question, "Which side?" Dear God. Help me now. Wild-eyed, I practically shout, "Left!" The usher is opening the left door to peek in. The overture is suddenly blaring.

It's a miracle. Those exact four seats *are empty*. The Lord must be an Ulanova fan. Our ticket-taker is beckoning. We get to "our seats" as the overture is ending. Right on time for "curtain up." Is this real?

The eeriest part is looking across the house and seeing people sitting in our "opposite" seats. What if I had blurted out, "Right!" instead of, "Left!"? Don't think about it, Ronnie.

There's that thunderous applause. Ulanova must have just come out of her house. At least I think so. I can't really tell, because Giselle's house is on stage right. The part of the stage we can't see from our very, very, very downstage seats on the left. Never mind. I've seen enough Giselles. I know what she's doing. She's making her circle and I can see her now. I am seeing Ulanova dance. I say it to myself, again. I'm seeing Ulanova dance.

I finally notice my right fingernails digging into my left wrist.

* * *

If all goes as planned, I'll be auditioning for the Ballet Russe in the Fall. That means being away from home for a little more than four months. On Tour. There *is* something a little bit scary about that, knowing I'm only 18. But, hey. I'm starting to feel grownup enough. Eighteen is a big deal. The government thinks I can drink and vote. I should be fine.

Let's do the drinking part first. Can't wait to get to a Yankee game. Finally, old enough to order a cold beer with my hot dog. I hook up with Shirley ("Charli") Weishaar, my Hoosier friend and fellow Ballet Russe student. She's ready, and so am I. We're headed straight for the Bronx.

Have I mentioned that I am still very short for my age? Back in the seventh grade, all of 4'8". A rousing 5'2" by the time I graduated from high school last June. Yes. I go by "twerp." Never mind. Nobody's calling me twerp today.

You have this beautiful spring day. You have this gorgeous Yankee Stadium. You have Charli and me, screaming at umpires. All while holding frankfurters from Hot Dog Guy. Beer Guy is getting pretty close.

"Hey, getcha cold bee-ah! Bee-ah hee-ah. Getcha cold bee-ah!" My face lights up. I pop out of my seat. Miss curly-hair-cherub-face-dimples-5'2" is waving down Beer Guy.

I'm screaming, "Over here … cold beer … over here!" Beer Guy takes one look at me. His "nah!" gesture crushes me, instantly. So does his, "Don't bother me, kid."

Obviously, I'm now waiting for Soda Guy. That's what we New Yorkers call a carbonated drink. Shirley calls it a "phosphate!" They say phosphate in Indiana? "One cherry phosphate, please?" I love this country.

Aside from seeing Mickey play, I don't remember anything about the game. Not the other team. Not the score. Guess being waved off by Beer Guy is still on my mind. Don't worry. There's a happy ending to the Beer Guy Tragedy. That evening, Charli comes home to dinner with me. Steaks are on the menu. Even better. A couple of well-chilled Heinekens, straight out of the bottle.

Wait a minute. What else can you do in New York, after turning 18? Besides yelling for Yankee Stadium Beer Guy? You can vote. It's 1960. My first presidential election, and I get to vote for John F. Kennedy. Beyond delirious.

My ballet school pal, Judy Mack, turns 18 in June. We immediately hatch a plan. On Election Day, vote separately. For everything else, we'll stick together. Like glue. Taking ballet classes. Riding the subway to Sixth Avenue and West 4th Street. Watching the election returns and sleeping over at Judy's.

Judy's "Village" apartment is a few steps away from the subway. Yes, "Village." Only tourists say "Greenwich Village." Judy lives right above the Italian butcher. "Half a pound of ground round, please."

Now we're racing up one flight of stairs. Got to watch those returns. The polls have just closed. Plenty of time to broil two hamburgers, defrost a box of frozen string beans, uncap two bottles of Coke. I don't know about Judy, but I'm feeling completely grown up. I remember thinking I was all grown up at 16. But this? *This* is real.

The election is a nailbiter. A little after 1:00 in the morning, Judy and I give up and go to sleep. Guess what? We don't miss a thing. My eyes pop open. It's now 6:00 in the morning. Turn on the TV. No decision yet. Judy wakes up a little after 7:00. We are both watching when Kennedy is announced the winner. Wow, 1960. You're turning out to be quite the year.

* * *

When I open my eyes on Thursday, October 13, 1960, I'm thinking, "Thank God this is not a Friday. I need all the luck I can get." Today is the day I audition for my first professional job, a *corps de ballet* position with the Ballet Russe de Monte Carlo. If you want to be really dramatic, you can argue that my entire life has been building toward this one moment.

But, as significant as Audition Day is, it's going to have to share the spotlight. For the uninitiated, October 13, 1960, is also a very big day in baseball. My beloved Yankees face the Pittsburgh Pirates at Forbes Field in Pittsburgh, for the *rubber* (final, seventh) game of the 1960 World Series. What's a girl to do? Bring her transistor radio to the audition, that's what.

Now, about this audition. Exactly how is it going to work? It seems all the dancers are to be taught the same sequence of steps. In this case, a *grand allegro*. That's a combination made up of many large jumps and leaps. Then we're randomly paired off for our appearance before the judges. Everyone waits in a large anteroom just outside the Studio, to be called in, two at a time. Once again, I am sitting on the floor, pretending to stretch while glued to my transistor radio.

Pirates are up 4–0, after four. Finally, the Yankees wake up and score a run. Then another. Okay, 4–2. By now I'm biting my nails. Any pretense of stretching has vanished long ago.

Holy mackerel! With two on, Yogi smashes a 3-run homer. The Yanks are ahead, 5–4. I'm trying to stifle my shriek, when I hear, "Ronnie Mahler and…." I kid you not. *Now* I have to audition? I'm too excited to remember any of those steps they taught us. Okay, calm down. Think of Yogi's go-ahead homer as a favorable omen. This is good. This is good.

As I enter the Studio, I try not to look so deliriously happy. I hardly acknowledge the other girl. I'm almost feeling giddy. Too many emotions at once. Is there such a thing as too much adrenaline? Calm down, Ronnie. Calm down.

The pianist plays the obligatory 5 … 6 … 7 … 8 …. My audition partner and I begin to perform our *grand allegro* combination. In the middle of the sequence, I goof up. I do an *arabesque* two counts too early. Too much adrenaline? Oops. Time to smile and improvise. I do an extra *arabesque*, this time on the correct music.

Disaster averted. No more hitches. Sadly, not so for my audition partner. She gets rattled by my mistake and stops in her tracks. I feel bad for her. If only she'd kept on dancing.

As okay as things have just gone inside the Studio, that's how "not okay" they have been going in Pittsburgh. A 5–4 lead when I went in to audition has turned into a 9–7 deficit after eight. I'm going to make the rest of this as quick as possible. It still hurts.

We tie it up in the top of the ninth, as everybody in the studio heads upstairs to wait for the posting of "The List." Suddenly, my friends are jumping up and down and pointing and screaming, "Ronnie, you made it! You made it!"

I, however, am ten feet away from the bulletin board, curled up on the floor, sobbing, "I don't care. I don't care." Bill Mazeroski has just hit a walk-off home run to give the Pirates the Series.[30]

* * *

It's really happening. I sign a contract with the Ballet Russe de Monte Carlo. I'm now officially a member of the *corps de ballet*. Company director Sergei Denham thinks the name Ronnie "looks too much like a boy."

Former Ballet Russe star Frederic Franklin stares off into the distant horizon and proclaims, "Rah-NEE! Rah-NEE!" Spelled "Roni." We're back to spaghetti.

Too bad Rice-A-Roni had to come out on the market two years ago. Now, all I'm hearing is "Row-nee."

Prologue

(In 1969, when I'm signing a soloist contract with American Ballet Theatre, Director Lucia Chase wants me to change Roni back to Ronnie. She thinks, on the program, "Roni Mahler" will look too similar to Danish ballerina Toni Lander. I refuse.)

First Intermission
Life Lessons

Madame's School of Hard Knocks

Glass #1...

Maybe I need to learn humility? You see, I love to talk in class. If it's in my head, it's out my mouth. Difficult to go undetected, when your voice is so low.

I can practically hear Madame in my sleep: "Basso profondo ... *shut up!*" Finally, I guess Madame has had enough. She throws me out of class. I have to apologize to get back in? Too stubborn. The standoff lasts maybe three days. This is only hurting me. I fix things.

Glass #2...

Maybe, punctuality? When trying to get to class, not allowing time for the elevator can be a mistake. (Today, they call it "time management." Back then, "shaving it a little too close." Either way, I'm not good at it.)

Pointe Class starts at 3:00. I walk in with less than five minutes to spare. That, after being in the dressing room for an hour. Once again, Madame has had enough. It's 2:57. She can see me getting off the elevator through the open studio door. She starts class early, making me late. I try to plead my case. She narrows her eyes and walks away. You can be innocent of "A," while the issue is "B." (Infuriating, but instructional.)

Glass #3...

Maybe, responsibility? This glass might be the hardest to swallow. Madame is putting on a huge performance at Philadelphia's Convention Hall. To fill the 75-foot-wide stage, she is combining students from her New York and New Jersey schools. A pretty good-sized group. Performing to Johann Strauss II's *Voices of Spring*.

Madame is finally notified that the stage is available to us. There is a hugely-important ten o'clock rehearsal on Sunday morning. Onstage.

I'm 19 years old and Madame has put me in charge. The doors will be locked. She has entrusted me with the only key. I calmly arrive at 9:30. In front of me, an ocean of dancers camped out in front of the entrance. Almost spilling into the street. Many are on the pavement, stretching. All are waiting for me. Guess who didn't think this through? By the time everyone files in and finds a dressing room, it is time to start rehearsal. Obviously no one, on pointe or off, has had time to warm up. Not good.

Did I mention that Madame has also been waiting outside, along with everyone else? She half-hisses, half-growls in my ear: "IF YOU WANT TO BE FIRST... YOU HAVE TO BE FIRST!" Not easily forgotten.

Glass #4...

Survival? I have just signed my first professional contract. Madame and I both know that this is the year I'll be joining the *corps de ballet* of the Ballet Russe de Monte Carlo.

One day in class, something happens. To be honest, I never know what that "something" is. Nevertheless, all corrections stop. Abruptly. Madame will not even *look* at me. If she is walking past my line, she shuts her eyes when she gets to me. She reopens them when she is in front of the next girl. The exercises go by. Not one correction. I feel invisible. The next class is the same story. And the next. And the next. You get the picture.

Days. Weeks. A month. Not a peep. I run the gamut of emotions. Guilt. (What did I do?) Shame. (I'm in the doghouse.) Victimized. (Poor me.) Anger. (What right has she?) Resignation. (This is not changing anytime soon.) Survival. (What can I do?)

Ah, yes. Survival. The most important piece. Here is what I can do. I can scour my brain for every correction Madame has ever given me. *Chin sticking. Fingers sticking. Back like Mack Truck. Shoulders. Legs higher. Feet.* I can correct myself.

New Ritual: Right after class, I check out the small studio right off the waiting room. Yes! It is free. I dart in there, pointe shoes still on. I work on the steps I just had trouble with in class. I'm in that little studio anywhere from 5 to 15 minutes. Depends on how bad a class I think I just had.

I accept this new life. I finally feel like I am improving on my own. One day, I am practicing especially hard after a very struggling class. Trance-like focus. This may even turn out to be a 25-minute day.

A shrill voice suddenly pierces the air. *"Chin! Fingers! Back! Shoulders! Legs! Feet!"* Without averting my forward-focused gaze, I attempt to visibly address each correction. Without acknowledging the source of that voice in the studio doorway, I know corrections will be raining down again. The drought is over.

That was tough. And possibly cruel. But also smart. Thinking about it, I bet Madame is just trying to make me more independent. She's not going to be around to correct me, when I'm out on tour for 4½ months. If I can't correct myself, how can my technique survive? 250 miles a day on a bus. No daily Company class. Not even an organized pre-performance warm-up. That will be tough, but now, so am I.

(One year later, my first Ballet Russe tour is behind me. I'm back in class. By now, I'm well-aware of how unpredictable Madame can be. But this might eclipse them all. Out of the blue, after class one day, the following brief exchange.

MADAME: *"You never show you first contract."*
ME [incredulous]: "But you always mocked professional dancers to me. You said they thought they had 'arrived?' You said they thought they had nothing left to learn?"
MADAME: *"But you first contract. I never see."*

Go figure. Suddenly getting all maternal on me. Could this have been the reason for the cold shoulder last year? Her feelings were hurt? I'll never know. I will never ask. Better off not knowing.)

Madame Knows Best

Madame Swoboda never announces that she's about to teach you a very, very important lesson. Things just happen, and suddenly you realize you've learned a basic truism of life that you will remember for all time. Here are a few Swoboda pearls of wisdom:

Pearl #1

Yes, Madame is once again correcting me in class. But, with only three months left until my first tour, she decides it's time for another kind of toughening. What I've come to call her Laboratory Classes. Private lessons that make me feel that my technique and I are under a microscope.

Once a week, I come to her tiny second-floor "efficiency" apartment on W. 58th Street, between Seventh and Sixth. Forget the elevator. I walk up the one flight of stairs. (Warm-up?)

Before each lesson, Madame has me roll up the area rug in her "postage-stamp" of a living room. Because there is no music, she simply counts from, let's say, 1 to 16. Very often, she pauses her counting to deliver a lengthy correction. Then she resumes counting, from wherever she thinks she maybe left off. I can recall some v-e-r-y l-o-n-g e-x-e-r-c-i-s-e-s!

I wear no tights, no ballet shoes. She says this allows her to see exactly how I'm standing on my foot on half-toe. Or how my leg muscles are working. These laboratory lessons are so valuable. I suspect she knows that.

One of the perks (or bummers) of working with no tights is realizing how often your thigh muscle (quadricep) isn't really as "pulled up" as it should be. Horror of horrors. You can be standing on a seemingly straight leg, and your quad can be sagging. Well, if not exactly sagging, at least not on "high alert." Obviously, it's by no means an "automatic." You're in charge. You must make it happen.

I quickly learn that a pulled-up leg is my best friend. Everything is easier, stronger, better. Balance. *Adagio. Pirouettes.* A new day has dawned. And all because Madame is insisting on no tights, so she can see my bare legs.

Pearl #2…

This story starts off as kind of a feather in my cap … until it isn't. I'm not exactly what you would call a "natural dancer." Don't get me wrong. I have two natural gifts:

jumping and *port de bras*. They're important, and I'm grateful. What I don't have is natural turnout, beautifully curved insteps, or high extensions.

Mme. Swoboda was born with all of these. That's how I know she's a really great teacher. I think it's easy to teach the things you yourself had to work for. Not so easy to build, in someone else, those things that came naturally to you.

She has naturally gorgeous feet, with very high insteps. Don't get me wrong. I have a high arch underneath my foot. When I get out of the pool, my wet footprint has a nice big space between the ball of my foot and my heel. But the *top* of my foot (instep) is completely flat. My foot is still strong enough for pointe work. It just doesn't look as pretty as someone whose instep looks more like a banana.

I'm, therefore, truly amazed when Madame comes up with a series of exercises to build my instep. I am 12, and I pour my heart into them.

Yikes. Am I going to need a lot of patience and perseverance. These foot exercises don't work their magic quickly. But three years later, wow. What a difference. I've actually managed to re-form the bones on the top of my foot. They now have a slight arc to them. Not exactly a banana, but there *is* a curve. Pretty.

Madame also comes up with an exercise to help build my left leg's extension *à la seconde* (to the side). It's definitely not as high as the one on my right. I see this as a great chance to even things up. What I *don't* see is that yellow caution light, urgently blinking away in my mind. Apparently, in the pre-teen years, your hips can fall victim to overwork.

Madame's strenuous "extension exercise" goes like this. First, I hold onto the marble countertop in front of the mirror, at the dressing table in my mom's huge bathroom. Then, I slide my left foot up my shin bone, until it's under my right kneecap. With my bent left knee now out at the side, this is called *retiré*. Then, removing my left toes from my right leg, I hoist my left thigh up as high as possible. I hold this agonizing position for maybe ten seconds, to build strength. Then, the unthinkable. With my thigh still raised, I attempt to extend my left toes upward, into a now much-higher *développé à la seconde*. Then, I hold *that* for a second or two.

I practice this exercise "with a vengeance" and, apparently, way too often. My left hip is now injured. To hear the doctor explain it, I have overstretched the ligaments and tendons attached to my femur head. Or something like that. I'm not allowed to lift my left leg higher than 45° *for a whole year,* or I'm in danger of forever walking with a slight limp. (It's a great exercise. Just don't overdo it.)

I'm always slightly annoyed when I hear, "Every cloud has a silver lining." What could possibly be the silver lining for this awfully dark cloud? It turns out, Madame is a genius when it comes to finding the benefits of keeping my left leg low for the next twelve months. What I can't practice in height, she helps me gain in strength and control and balance. Lightbulb Moment: Working with your leg low can be just as difficult and agonizing as trying to lift it higher. It never once felt like a wasted year. Genius … definitely.

Pearl #3…

It is 1958. I am a Junior at New Rochelle High. Madame has choreographed a hauntingly beautiful piece for her advanced dancers. Three short movements to an excerpt from Christoph Gluck's *Orfeo ed Euridice*. The occasion is a Youth Concert accompanied by the legendary Philadelphia Orchestra at the historic Academy of Music. Associate Conductor Maestro William Smith will conduct.

This *Orfeo ed Euridice* excerpt is really different from Madame's 19th-century classical suite from *The Sleeping Beauty*, which we've recently performed. This time, we're wearing soft ballet slippers. The choreography requires parallel feet. Not a turned out leg in sight.

Think Isadora Duncan. Our flowing tunics evoke the Three Graces from Greek mythology. Our moves and our poses pay tribute to the spirit of those graceful figures.

Madame has had to choreograph in linear rather than circular patterns. We only travel back and forth. That's because the Orchestra will be onstage behind us. These steps and patterns have been created with limited space in mind. I, for one, love this departure from traditional classical technique. I feel very versatile.

The performance is at nine o'clock in the morning. We get to the Academy of Music very early, because there is a seven o'clock rehearsal onstage with the orchestra. Because Maestro Smith, our conductor, is not yet in the theater, the Concert Master is temporarily in charge of the Orchestra.

One look at how the orchestra chairs have been placed on the stage, and I know we're in trouble. The strip of stage left for us to dance on is wide enough, yes. But the depth is only maybe four feet, at best.

I see Madame approach the Concert Master. She is asking for a little more depth. The Concert Master is shaking his head, "No." Madame turns and walks back to us with the news. I am surprised that she seems to have given up so easily. We struggle through our rehearsal as best we can, in such limited space.

Around eight o'clock, Maestro Smith arrives. Okay. It's time to "watch the master" at work. No, not him. Madame. She approaches the Maestro and introduces herself. I have seen her turn on the charm before, whenever she wants something. Her performance now leaves all others in the dust.

Right there. See. That's the hint of compelling artistry. And right here. Watch. The brief flash of her irresistible smile. And always, just the right touch of obsequiousness.

Maestro listens intently. He speaks. They laugh together, softly. They seem to be hitting it off. He suddenly motions to one of the stagehands. Chairs begin to move. And, presto. Just as suddenly, we have gained nearly another three feet. The performance goes well. Everyone is happy.

Later that day, I can't resist:

> **Me:** "Madame. What's your secret? How did you get us the extra space?"
> **Madame:** *"Dearie. Always talk to big man. Little man waste you time. Try be important. Big man already important. Always help."*

Philosophy 101

After a while, I get pretty good at imitating Madame's favorite sayings, with an accent, to boot.

If you're upset and having a bad class: "*Cry but try, Dearie. Cry, but try!*"

If your raised leg in back is not in line with your spine: "*You tink is arabesque? Is you imagination.*"

If your turns need more practicing: "*You have to do pirouette left, right, day, night!*"

When we're talking too much in class: "*What you tink? Is tea party here?*"

When she wants us to divide up into two groups, three syllables: "*Spleet na heff.*"

When you fall down, trying to do a difficult step: "*Dearie. I buy you ice cream!*" (Never happens.)

When a student returns after missing a few classes (while faking a "bow"): "*We have guest artist today.*"

If your arms and head are not "coordinating" with your legs: "*Car-dination, Dearie. Car-dination.*"

"*Fingers sticking. Fingers sticking.*" Referring to too much tension in my fingers. (Her only comment, after I pull off six *pirouettes en pointe* right in front of her.)

When she thinks it's time for a no-frills class with relentless work on alignment and balance and turnout and higher *développés* and *attitudes* and *arabesques* and *grand rond de jambe en l'air* (whew), she announces, "*Today, we do geem*" (short for "gymnasium").

When it is the start of Yom Kippur, and you're planning to take the train straight home from ballet class, but suddenly the School has an extra ticket for tonight's performance of *Giselle*, starring Alicia Alonso and Igor Youskevitch at The ("Old") Met: "*God forgive you, Dearie. God understand.*"

Years later, when she does not like my boyfriend: "*Dearie. Is so inappetizing.*"

Even more years later, when she is watching *me* teach: "*Dearie, you talk too much. Shut up. You tell them what to do … every meee-NOOT!*"

Even lots of years later than that, when a Kansas State student reporter asks her to agree that classical ballet is the only "real" form of dance: "*Dearie. Only two kinds dance. Good dance and bad dance.*"

Act One
Ballet Russe and National Ballet

Ballet Russe de Monte Carlo

My First Year in Ballet Russe

1960. What a year. Beer, despite Beer Guy. College courses. Voting for President. Successfully auditioning to get into the Ballet Russe. Attending the exciting first day of rehearsals? Wait. This last? Easier said than done.

As it turns out, Mount Washington isn't my only encounter with frostbite. Now, it's nearing the end of the second week of December. Sunday the 11th. And it has started to snow. And snow. And snow. What would one day be referred to as "The Blizzard of 1960" has begun.[1] Why do I remember the exact date? Easy. On Monday, December 12, the Ballet Russe de Monte Carlo begins rehearsals for its 4½-month-long winter tour that opens in Los Angeles.

Long before the snow, December 12 has been burned into my consciousness. This is the day that will decide which "new girls" get cast in which ballets. Now, in spite of the snow, I'm determined to show up. The night of December 11, I can hardly sleep. I'm eyeballing the damage as soon as the sun comes up.

Yup. A winter wonderland. How can something so picturesque be such a pain in the neck? We're in our apartment in Riverdale, in the northwest corner of The Bronx. The part that curves westward over the northern tip of Manhattan. One of the highest elevations in the five boroughs of New York City.

Back up. Back up. "Highest elevations?" Highest elevations … as in "last to be plowed?" Sadly, yes. Oh, dear. So the bus (just a block away) won't be taking me to the subway? Okay. I'll walk.

> **MOM:** "You can't go out in this. You'll never make it."
> **ME:** "I can't miss my first day of rehearsal."
> **MOM:** "They'll understand."
> **ME:** "I won't be put in any of the ballets."

Mom can't talk me out of it. On go an extra pair of black tights over my pink ones. On go the tallest rubber waterproof (alas, unlined) boots I own.

I fearlessly chart my course: I'll walk along the bus route down to Broadway. Take the Broadway IRT to 125th Street. Walk east on 125th Street, across town.

Seventh, Sixth (Lenox?), Fifth, and Madison. Turn right on Madison. Walk downtown four blocks to the Russian Orthodox Church at 121st Street. (They're giving Mr. Denham the ballroom, rent-free.)

Okay. Task One: Getting to the subway. I leave my apartment building with no idea what "unplowed" really means. If the streets are level, the snow's knee-deep. If I'm walking downhill, sometimes mid-thigh. Who knew snow could be so heavy? Dragging one leg forward and then the other. Is this what "trudging" means? Seeing the elevated tracks getting closer, I make a bad call. I'll just cut across the grass here, and get there sooner. Not smart. Snow deeper.

I have no idea how long I trudge. Or how long I wait for a train. I do know that my toes are starting to hurt and go numb at the same time. Is that even possible? No wonder. That deep snow has fallen inside my not-quite-tall-enough boots. My feet are literally packed in snow.

Task Two: "Unpack" my feet. Once seated on the train, I manage to remove my boots. Shaking doesn't work. Snow clings. So I'm scooping the snow out of each cold and wet boot, before putting my foot back inside the same cold and wet boot. At least my feet are no longer packed in snow. But now my hands are colder than ever. Can *fingers* hurt and be numb at the same time?

Task Three: Walking to the Russian Orthodox Church. Renewed sense of purpose and fortitude. I feel reborn.

Rebirth doesn't last long. Even though 125th Street is not in Riverdale, it hasn't been plowed either. This snow, too, manages to pack inside my boots. Unevenly, in fact. A glance downward shows me walking on the outsides of my feet. If they weren't already numb, if I could feel my ankles, they'd feel like I was spraining them.

The answer. Don't look down. Whatever you do, *don't stop*. Losing my balance. Steady, Roni. Steady. Now limping has joined trudging. Trip. Fall down. Maybe I'll just stay here? What if nobody finds me? I start to cry. No one to hear me. I stop crying and get up. Limp on.

Believe it or not, after turning right on Madison Avenue, I come across the Hospital for Joint Diseases at 123rd Street. This time someone *would* find me. Maybe I'll just curl up inside those double glass doors… Snap out of it, Roni. Just two more blocks. Do what you came to do.

The ballroom of the Church, where we will rehearse, is on the 2nd floor. It has its own side entrance. But the long, outdoor staircase hasn't been shoveled. Too dangerous. It's back to the heavy, formidable, medieval front doors. Once inside, pretty creepy. And pretty dark. Except for the daylight coming through the stained glass windows. I walk toward the altar, unaware of the female corpse (in the open coffin) in front of me. I've been only looking down, limping forward on my twisted feet. Feeling like the hunchback of Notre Dame.

Suddenly, there she is. The corpse. I'm beyond screaming. Lurching backward, I see a makeshift sign pointing up some back stairs. Am I finally here?

In the ballroom, I see only two other dancers. Andrea Vodehnal and Richard "Dick" Tarczynski. Andrea walks over. Dick is joking about how I'm the last person they expected to see.

She's saying, "Hi, Roni." I can't speak. Tears running down my cheeks. Just like in the movies. She's already walking me to the dressing room. Tights are coming off. Both feet puffed, eerily white, from the ankles down. A sight one never forgets.

"Dick!" He rushes in. Takes one look. Rushes out. Returns with a bucket filled with snow.

"I'm from Chicago" is all he says, alternately rubbing each foot vigorously with that snow. It seems like forever. Most likely just ten minutes. Then he waits (I don't know how long) and does it again. And again.

Believe it or not, enough people eventually show up, and we manage to get in some rehearsing in the afternoon. Oh, no. My feet are so swollen, only half of my foot fits into my ballet slipper. Tarczynski to the rescue again. Yes, Dick has an extra pair of shoes. His feet are much, much bigger than mine. Today, they're a perfect fit.

We begin rehearsing *Swan Lake,* Act II. I'm assigned my slot for the first, single-file Entrance of the Swans. Just one of the girls. Feels amazing. My toes are beginning to really hurt now. At least the new choreography is keeping me busy. Less time to think about my toes, which are in agony.

Okay. First entrance is done. Now, we're re-entering for the famous *Pas de Deux* danced by Odette and Prince Siegfried. Trouble is, no new steps to learn for now. Just posing in two vertical lines on either side of the stage. Our feet are required to be in a position referred to as "B+" or *attitude a terre*. On stage left, you stand on your right leg. Your left leg is bent in back. Your left knee is touching your right knee, and your left toes are pointed and resting on the floor diagonally behind you. Kind of like a bike stand.

Well, the toes of my standing right foot are killing me. I surreptitiously lift my left toes off the floor behind. Bringing my left foot around to the front, I place my left heel on top of my right toes and really press down hard. And press down hard, and press down hard. The pain of standing on my toes is better than the pain of the frostbite. All this time, I'm so very carefully maintaining my required upper body position. So I can blend in.

Nina Novak is running the rehearsal, and she'll never notice that my left foot is out of position because it's standing *on top of* my right one.

"*Rah-nee. Po-si-tion.*" I can't believe it. She's making me hold my position, even if I'm not missing any dancing? Even though she knows my feet are frozen? Has she no compassion? Shut up, girl. You wanted this. Now take it. I dutifully put my left foot back in place. Suddenly remembering kneeling on that left knee scab eleven years ago.

I stay in town with my friend, Margery Lambert, for the next two nights. Over the following three days of rehearsal, I am cast in every ballet. Just as I had hoped. Yes, I wanted this. Plus, I'm chosen as one of the Six Princesses in *Swan Lake*, Act III. One could even say that it's a tiny, little *demi-soloist* role. Yay. On my way.

But, try as I might, I still can't shake the horror of seeing both bare feet swollen and absolutely white from my ankles down. Did I just narrowly escape disaster? What was I thinking? Was it worth the risk? Most likely not. But knowing me, I guess it was inevitable.

If I had missed Monday, would Nina have still put me in the ballets? Most likely my spot in the *Swan Lake corps de ballet,* yes. But would I have been chosen as one of those six Act III Princesses? I doubt it.

(Funny. Writing now about being frozen then, it makes me feel all that pain over again. Yes, Dad. You were right about the toe nails incident. So, I "got off cheap" again.)

* * *

"The Day" has finally dawned. December 26, 1960. At last, I'm a *bona fide* member of the Ballet Russe de Monte Carlo. Today is the day my first tour begins. In Los Angeles. And this New Yorker has never been west of New Jersey. (Four years ago, I took my first airplane trip to Miami Beach, but that was south.)

This new schedule is pretty tight. I'll get used to that. We land. We check into the Clark Hotel. It's a couple of blocks from the Philharmonic Auditorium. We open tomorrow night.

Oh, and we say goodbye to airplanes. For the next 4½ months, it's all bus. But, first, it's five enchanting performance days at the Philharmonic. Yes, your math is right. The fifth day definitely does fall on New Year's Eve. And how do we celebrate? By dancing a Matinee and Evening.

On Opening Night, the first ballet is *Les Sylphides*, Michel Fokine's breathtakingly beautiful evocation of a Poet, alone in the woods with his thoughts. Represented here by Sylphs, and performed to the immortal strains of Frédéric Chopin.[2] This was the first ballet I ever saw when I was four years old. I was enchanted then, and I'm enchanted now. But, now I'm *in* the forest. A circle, come full 'round?

The Nocturne. The Waltz. A Mazurka, or two. A Prelude. A *Pas de Deux*. A grand finale. This is more than perfect.

December 27, 1960. Onstage has been called. A lot of milling about. A lot of soft murmuring going on. I am one of 19 Sylphs and one Poet, amid a sea of long white tulle skirts and fluttery sleeves. All, in a poetic pale blue light. This is so other-worldly. No other way to describe it. I mean, we're wearing wings. That's right. In the back. At the top of our bodice hooks.

It feels kind of intimate, with the curtain still down. It's like we have a secret the audience doesn't know yet. I'm transported. I blurt out, "This is like a dream."

> **The Poet:** "Just wait till you've been doing it for a couple of months."
> **My Silent Thought:** "Go away. You're not in my dream."

And, you're also wrong, you silly man. I'm performing night after night, and it still feels like magic. Like living on a new planet. Unfamiliar, but intriguing. Everything I do, I'm doing for the first time. And I'm not just talking about dancing all these ballets.

My mind goes back to when I was nine and met Mr. Danielian and Mme. Danilova at the Roosevelt Hotel. I was told the Ballet Russe was important and famous. Now I'm hearing people say it's "legendary." (Twenty-one years later, *New York Times* dance critic Jack Anderson calls it "The One and Only."[3] My first professional job was performing with the "one and only Ballet Russe." Who knew?)

I love checking out the costumes hanging on the racks in Wardrobe. You find the inner grosgrain waistband. There, in indelible, sweat-proof, black marker, is the name of every dancer who's ever worn this costume. A costume that's been handed down from dancer to dancer. You can read each name, now crossed out. Wow. Gertrude Tyven. Norma Vance. Two of Madame's former students. Crossed out. Only the name of the dancer wearing the costume now doesn't have a line through it.

Here's another major "first." I call it "from pillar to post." When the curtain goes up, I'm in the dreamy, blue-ish light of a *Les Sylphides* forest. The next minute, I'm in a Sultan's harem in Ancient Persia. *That's* a first. Not exactly a Sylph. It's still Michel Fokine's choreography. But this time I'm a Slave. In a ballet called *Schéhérazade*.

Schéhérazade

In 1910, *Schéhérazade* debuts in Paris, starring the vibrant and unequaled Vaslav Nijinsky as The Golden Slave.[4] *Schéhérazade's* main characters also include The Favorite Wife (Zobeide) and The Eunuch. In Fokine's scenario, the Sultan suspects Zobeide is being unfaithful. He conspires with his brother to pretend they are going off to war together.

The Female Slaves convince The Eunuch to unlock the Male Slaves' quarters. Straight to the Harem they go. The Golden Slave falls in love with Zobeide. The ensuing orgy is interrupted by the Sultan's unexpected "return." Things do not end well for The Favorite Wife.

I can thank famous Russian artist and designer Léon Bakst for the lush sets and costumes. Muted plums and pinks. Gold tassels everywhere. Is it in a program note that I read he's known for viewing "performance as escape?" Funny. That's how I feel. Performing takes me away to a land of make-believe. Except when my role requires me to handle a prop. Like, a buckle and a strap. Total nightmare. Those things come easy to lots of people. Not me. All thumbs, every time.

We haven't talked about the "orgy" yet. When the Eunuch lets the Male Slaves into the harem, the orgy begins. Its centerpiece is a sultry, lustful *Pas de Deux* (dance for two) for The Golden Slave and The Favorite Wife, who have fallen madly in love. But a steamy dance for two does not an orgy make. Let's count: 3 Odalisques (concubines), 4 Pink and 4 Green Females Slaves. Eleven women. There's a male slave for each of us. Okay, 22. And the principal couple. This orgy can now boast a respectable 24.

As we "couple off," Mr. Fokine thankfully gives us Slaves some moments for a little get-acquainted choreography, before getting "down to business." It happens when we "Pink" slave couples form a shallow diagonal, fairly close to the footlights. I remember this moment for two reasons. One, because I get to use my arms in a really memorable *ports de bras* sequence. The second, because thanks to this shallow diagonal, I'm close to the orchestra pit. So, out of the corner of my left eye, I can see the idle male timpanist enjoying watching me.

Back to the diagonal. My partner is kneeling in front of me on his left knee, pressing forward on his right front leg. His arms are down at his sides, with palms facing upward. Indicating submission. I am standing close enough in front of him that my outstretched arms can almost touch his face. My legs are in what I have dubbed my "Harem 4th position." Standing on my bent left leg in *demi-plié*.

My straight right leg is extended forward, balancing on the ball of my foot like a bike stand. The violins are playing that hypnotic Rimsky–Korsakov theme. I am moving my arms in the most exotically graceful *port de bras* sequence I've ever known.

Extending my right arm and shoulder forward, the palm of my hand imitates caressing the left cheek of my partner's eagerly uptilted face. My left arm and shoulder quickly follow suit, reaching toward the right cheek of his face. What happens next defies description, but I'll try:

    1. Both hands "corkscrew" upward, till my palms clasp each other overhead.

    2. Only to immediately "uncorkscrew" them down again, to press both arms down and back at my sides.

I think the other Pink Slaves are doing the same thing, but I'm not sure, because I'm too absorbed in this flowing sequence. My most favorite moment of the whole ballet.

When the acquaintance dance is over, that's when my nightmare begins. Everyone has the same job. To lie around, lounging among all those tasseled pillows at the back of the stage. And not just lie there. We must imitate an orgy. Ballet is family entertainment, so the operative word is "imitate." Only make-believe caresses are permitted. We must only play at acting lustful and steamy. Fake stroking of arms and legs. No touching.

In fact, Wardrobe has threatened fines if the women's costumes are returned to the racks bearing tell-tale smudges of the men's body makeup.

My partner is not very good at make-believe. I just can't keep his pancaked limbs (and paws) off my chiffon. Plus, he has bad breath. Thank goodness *Schéhérazade* is the last ballet. Here I am, trying to scrub off "Romeo's" body makeup at the same dressing room sink where my friend is waiting to wash her face. Have I mentioned the slightly disgusted looks from Wardrobe, when I'm turning in water-splotched pantaloons?

Back to the dancing. I love the choreographed mayhem we have to create. The slaves' quarters need to look abuzz with frantic fun, so the Sultan has something to "angrily interrupt."

Okay, here goes frantic fun: My arms are down. One is close by, in front of me. The other is behind. My elbows are straight, and my downward-facing palms are flat, with stuck-together fingers. All this, while doing these adorable prancing steps, with a flexed front foot, that are snaking around the stage, here and there, in single-file. Don't forget the constant, sharp "about-faces," changing direction. Chaos is fun to perform. Fear is fun to project. *Not* being a Sylph? Not bad at all.

So, Michel Fokine makes up steps to beautiful music, and I get to perform them. *Les Sylphides, Schéhérazade*. Nice job for an 18-year-old "first-year-girl."

But *Schéhérazade* isn't the only story ballet I get to dance, where the characters are people instead of Sylphs or Swans. And Fokine isn't the only great choreographer who enchants me. It's like a magic carpet is flying me across time *and* geography. New destination: Paris in the late 19th century…

Gaîté Parisienne

And whom can I thank for that voyage? The inimitable Léonide Massine. He choreographs and performs in his own ballets. And this one is called *Gaîté Parisienne*.

In 1938, as the Ballet Russe de Monte Carlo prepared to celebrate its inaugural season, the idea for *Gaîté Parisienne* comes from Comte Étienne de Beaumont, a French aristocrat and life-long patron of the arts. His concept, and ultimate libretto, is a ballet about café life in late 19th-century Paris. Massine is so intrigued that he agrees to choreograph to the endearing music of Jacques Offenbach. Beaumont designs the strikingly colorful sets.[5] The same can be said for his costume designs, which are then faithfully executed by future–Oscar-winner, Barbara Karinska.[6]

At the naive age of 18, my view of this new ballet is definitely egocentric. Ergo, I'll talk only about *my* Can-Can costume. It is one of 16, representing a rainbow of colors. Mine is plum. Standing around in it, I'm not very exciting to look at. It's just an unadorned satin, sleeveless, ankle-length dress. But when I reach down toward my toes, grab the hem of that skirt, and take it with me as I stand up again. Wow. That's another story. And I'm not just talking about the opaque black stockings held up by garters. I'm talking about fuchsia ruffles everywhere. Row upon row, upon row of them.

You're wondering, what's the big deal? Didn't I already wear a Can-Can costume for the Albert Leonard Junior High School Talent Show when I was 12? No comparison. Only knee-length, with a much smaller full-circle skirt. This full circle is so big, it could easily cover my face. And underneath, lots more fuchsia ruffles. Lots and lots more fuchsia ruffles. "Working" this skirt is a full-time job. Time for a glossary:

1. "The Windshield Wiper," side to side. Most common.
2. "The Elevator," up and down.
3. "The Rustle," quick-and-tight shake-n-bake moves from side-to-side. Not to be confused with the slower side-to-side of "the windshield wiper."
4. "The Billboard." One hand holding your skirt up under your chin. Pretty easy.

But the other hand? Not so much. That's because you can't let the satin side of the skirt "flip over" and interrupt that continuous fuchsia circle. If you grab the satin too far from the skirt's edge, it flops over. All-ruffle effect? Ruined.

When you're posing in billboard position, your elbows are close to you. The rest of the time, you're holding your skirt about sixteen inches away from your body. Better be pressing your shoulders down. Otherwise, your upper arms really start to hurt.

I love my Can-Can getup because it makes me feel like I'm at the *Moulin Rouge* in a Toulouse-Lautrec painting. Especially because of those black opaque stockings held up by garters. Top it all off with high, fingerless black gloves and a black velvet choker. Even a fuchsia "pouf," worn at a jaunty angle on my head. Too bad I have to pin on a small cluster of really fake-looking curls, for bangs. Ugh.

Although Mr. Massine is not in rehearsals when I am learning *Gaîté*, I can almost feel his presence. You see, I've danced for him before. Five years ago.

It was a Christmas Show in the children's ward of Roosevelt Hospital. And take my word for it, you can "feel it," when Massine is in the room.

I definitely could. And so could his son, Lorca. He and Maria Youskevitch were dancing together again. This time, poor Lorca spots his father in the audience, freezes, and runs right off the stage. Little Maria is left alone to improvise. And she pulls it off.

Now it's five years later. Pinch me. I'm actually performing in *Gaîté Parisienne* with the Ballet Russe de Monte Carlo. Mr. Massine is watching again, but only from the audience. Never in the rehearsal studio. Thank God.

(Fast-forward a decade. I'm dancing with American Ballet Theatre, and the Company is reviving *Gaîté*. Massine, himself, is overseeing this restaging of his wildly popular ballet. Our paths cross once again.)

* * *

Gaîté also demands the added excitement of a quick costume change *within* the ballet. To understand this, you need to know the character I portray earlier in the ballet. I am a "Cocodette" (according to one synopsis, a "flighty young woman of questionable virtue").

We six Cocodettes enter on each arm of three handsome Billiard Players. Wearing snug, spaghetti-strap bodices and swirling skirts, we end up flirting with The Peruvian and the Soldiers. True to our reputations.

But where's that climactic Can-Can? Well, not before a harrowing 4½ minute costume change. The other six Can-Can dancers have been patiently awaiting their entrance, partially lined up in the wings. Suddenly, six Cocodettes dash past them to the quick-change room, unpinning their Cocodette headpieces on the run.

Before *Gaîté* began, we each brought down our Can-Can costume to the changing room. We pre-set a chair with our accessories: Rolled-up long, black fingerless gloves. Black velvet choker. Fake curly bangs next to six bobby pins and a small mirror. Hair pouf. Luckily, we've been able to "underdress" parts of our Can-Can costume. The garter belt, black stockings, and ruffled trunks. No. Never visible during the Cocodette choreography. Same shoes.

Dresser quickly unhooks you. One Cocodette costume, dropping down at your feet. Dresser "pools" your Can-Can costume on the floor next to you. Step out of one swirly dress and into another. Dresser pulls up the Can-Can costume. She's zipping you up, as you're pulling on your gloves. She's tying your choker as you're pinning your curls. Last three pins for your Can-Can pouf. Done. Get in line. Catch your breath.

Now the Can-Can, itself. Meredith Baylis, the Lead Can-Can dancer, does two circles of leaps, before hopping on one leg with the other out to the side. Then crashes into a split for her eye-popping finish. She brings down the house every time. What a crowd-pleaser.

Did I say crowd? Oh, yes. I almost forgot about all the applause. All that cheering. All that rhythmic clapping during the familiar Can-Can melody. No one tells you about that in rehearsal. I've never danced in front of so many people before. Wow.

Now, the amazing Can-Can choreography. We 16 Can-Can dancers are lined up offstage. To this day, it is seared into my body. And my brain. All those years that I was dreaming about becoming a ballet professional? Not once do I imagine dancing something as energetic as this. As adrenaline-pumping as this.

Here goes. We're lined up offstage, two-by-two, shortest-to-tallest. We're awaiting our musical cue to enter through the upstage center archway. Our skirts are ready, as described. We begin "counting" the music before our entrance. At the same time, we're feverishly doing "The Rustle," those quick shake-n-bakes with our skirts. Get that energy level up. Get it up, now.

Unison performing trick: Even those who won't be first "out of the gate" will be imitating the choreography in place, while inching forward. That's the only way to be doing the correct step on the correct foot, when you finally burst onto the stage through that upstage center archway.

All this time, we've been counting….

* (& 8 &), 1 & 2 & 3 & 4, & 5 & 6 & 7 & 8, & 9 & 10 & 11 & 12 & thir-teen, four-teen…. Go!
* ("The Billboard") Step, Hop, Step, Hop
* ("The Windshield Wiper") Lunge, Lunge, Lunge, Lunge
* ("The Billboard") Step, Hop, Step, Hop
* ("The Windshield Wiper") Lunge, Lunge, Lunge, Lunge
* ("The Billboard") Step, Hop, Step, Hop

All the above, while making a counter-clockwise circle around the stage and letting out intermittent shrieks at the tops of our lungs. Who knew that, one day, I'd be allowed to shriek at the top of my lungs onstage?

We end up in four horizontal lines of four dancers each, standing on our left leg, with the right leg bent and the right foot posed "turned in," next to the arch of the left one.

I'm in the second line, so I get to do a cartwheel. I've been practicing for this moment since I was eight years old. Can't believe I'm getting to do one of my beloved cartwheels onstage, during the Can-Can.

Wait a minute. Did I say, "Standing on our *left* leg?" Oh, no. That means my cartwheel has to be to the *right*? But I only cartwheel to the left. Oh, well. Here goes. My right cartwheel is a disaster. Butt sticking out behind. Legs barely at ten o'clock, when they should be at high noon. Or at least 11:57?

At our first Gaîté rehearsal, I immediately blurt out, "I'll work on it. I'll work on it. I promise. I'll have it by next time." Ten years of relentless practicing, down the drain. But, I work and work to redeem myself. By the next rehearsal, I have a passable cartwheel to the right. You could say that my cartwheels have become "ambidextrous." Or, "ambiguous," as Yogi Berra would say?

The "Classical" and Other Hurdles

Being on tour means setting up my "theater place" for the first time. Like a calming ritual. Really, really important. When you're 18, and on the road for 4½ months, homesickness is always lurking. Your theater place is like a little bit of home. Like a bedroom, maybe. And just like your bedroom, you pick your color. Mine? Every possible shade and hue of green. Calm. Regeneration. Growth. Pretty.

First up. General hygiene. Dressing rooms in old theaters aren't the cleanest places in the world. Under your feet, a white hand towel from the hotel (returned after the show) does nicely for carpet. On to the table, itself. The "area rug." My forest green place mat. Its woven pattern ends in fringes around the edges. My two-sided makeup mirror sits smack dab in the middle. As if she's a queen, holding court. One of her ladies-in-waiting is a green-themed, fabric-covered box. The other is a chocolate-brown tin, saying HERSHEY'S in big block letters, with a snap-up, attached lid. One of my prized possessions. Looks exactly like the chocolate bar.

These two steadfast Ladies-in-Waiting are the keepers of all manner of makeup and its paraphernalia. Blush. Several shades of eye shadow. A tube of theatrical eyeliner paste that I "cake on" with tiny strokes from a very fine brush. Theatrical lip color, applied with my trusty, retractable lipstick brush. False eyelashes, glue, curler. Mascara. Ready to serve Her Majesty in the blink of an eye.

But where's the all-important "foundation?" Because I sweat so much from my scalp, I can't use a liquid base. Or even liquid eyeliner. Everything just streaks down my face. I have to use Max Factor's dry pancake base. That familiar flat circle with the screw-top lid, applied with a slightly damp sponge. Let me introduce you to my small, pale-green, condiment dish. The kind that might hold jam on the breakfast table? Now, it's my cherished water bowl to wet the sponge. Filled halfway and sitting right at my theater place. Beats having to stand at the sink.

Then there's the green-themed theater robe, draped over the back of my chair. A definite fashion statement. But, why? Well, the *corps de ballet* dressing room is most likely too small to hold all the costumes. Makeup applied. Hair done. Headpiece affixed. Pointe shoes on. Theater robe on. Walk down the hall to Wardrobe. Get into costume.

Make no mistake. Performing all those magical ballets onstage is its own kind of heaven. But backstage is another show of its own. We "new girls" usually dance in the *corps* of every ballet, every night. So, only a short intermission for makeup and hair changes. Max Factor No. 21 pancake for *Les Sylphides*. Cover that with Max Factor No. 24 pancake, plus blush, for *The Nutcracker, Act II*. False curls to imitate bangs, for *Gaîté Parisienne*. Altered eyebrow shapes for exotic *Schéhérezade*.

* * *

My Ballet Russe de Monte Carlo touring life isn't complete without mentioning mastering the "Classical." Our word for that signature 19th-century female hairdo. Queen Victoria comes to mind. And all those famous ballerinas of the 1800s. (George Balanchine, the noted choreographer and co-founder of New York City Ballet, has nudged the needle by scrapping the "classical" hairdo, in favor of a high bun and no center part.)

So, how hard is making this "classical," anyway? Here's the painstaking truth. Very hard. At least for me. Despite dying for long hair growing up, my mom has always kept it short to keep its natural curl "under control." I've only finally grown out my hair this past year, knowing I'd have to master the "classical."

The ingredients are pretty straightforward: bobby pins, hair pins, 2 hairnets, about 18 inches of ¼" grosgrain ribbon. (Satin can knot too easily.) Begin with a center part, separating the hair down either side of the face. Secure hair behind your ears. Then place the center of the ribbon three fingers–worth behind your hairline. After also tucking the ribbon behind the ears, tie it underneath all the hair in the back.

On one side, bring forward one inch of hair, in front of the ribbon. Wind a pretty large pin curl (the larger, the better) directly above the ear, secured by crossing two bobby pins in an "X." Repeat with hair on the other side. Take some hair from behind your right ear and bring it forward to cover the pin curl, using small hair pins to secure everything in place. Repeat with hair on the other side. Cover everything with two fine hair nets.

Then, somehow fashion a low, oblong-shaped bun at the back of your neck. Take these instructions with a barrel of salt. I'm definitely a rookie, when it comes to long hair.

Did I mention that I'm a terrible head-sweater? Under all those lights, my hair doesn't stand a chance. It's soaked halfway through the first ballet. You know that classical hairdo that curves the hair gracefully around those just-above-the-ear pin curls? Well, those gracefully curved edges are ungracefully "scalloped" on my "curly classical." Naturally curly hair: a curse, as well as a blessing.

* * *

I love this new world of daily performing, but it boggles my mind. It's like living on another planet. With a separate reality. If there's a Matinee and Evening, I can be in the theater literally from noon until nearly midnight. And incredibly busy every moment.

Yet none of it relates to my real life. I go practically nonstop all day and night. Suddenly, I am done. I leave the theater and check my life's to-do list. Not a thing has been crossed off. Excruciatingly busy for almost twelve straight hours. No errands run. No letters written. Laundry still not done.

I sleep. I wake up. My busy, make-believe life starts all over again. My To-Do-List is on the back burner, again. Sorry, List. They're waiting for me in Never, Never Land. Difficult? Maybe. But kind of thrilling.

Yes. I am thrilled to be performing. But let's face it, I'm only 18. And my family is 3,000 miles away. In the theater, everything is perfect. The blues only start when the magic ends. Every day. Back at the Clark Hotel. "Homesick" doesn't begin to describe it. Luckily, solace is just a half a block away.

The corner coffee shop. It's called Googie's and it never closes. *And* their nesselrode pie is advertised as "mile-high." That can go a long way to soothing a homesick teen. (Years later, I learn that Googie's is iconic. Who knew?)

After a "double show" day on New Year's Eve, I bid goodbye to 1960. You were a great year. Except, of course, for that World Series walk-off home run by a Player-Who-Shall-Remain-Nameless.

On the morning of January 1, we're boarding our buses. One for dancers, one for musicians. Destination: San Diego. Thank goodness it's a short trip. We're scheduled for our second Matinee and Evening in a row, at the Russ Auditorium. Happy New Year, Roni!

Kind of like my theater place, the dancers' bus is also a slice of "home away from home." For the next 4½ months, anyway. The dancer seated next to you, your bus mate, is crucial. I'm truly blessed. My bus mate wins the Miss Compatibility contest, hands down. I give you the inimitable Carolyn Martin. (Soon to become Carolyn Santonicola, when she marries Frank French Horn…. I mean … Santonicola. I've renamed all our musicians by their instruments.)

Carolyn is the ultimate Southern belle, especially to this dyed-in-the-wool New Yorker. Polite. Easy-going. Humorous. All delivered in the sweetest Southern accent I've heard since Valerie-from-Savannah, who played our Good Fairy in *Alice's Unbirthday Party* at Macy's. And Carolyn is a fellow Pisces, to boot. Our birthdays are just five days apart.

BALLET IMPERIAL

Poof! Did a whole day really just go by? This matinee-and-evening itinerary stop is done in a flash. San Diego is now in the rear-view mirror. Were we even there? Our buses head north. Destination: San Francisco. Three days of performing at its historic War Memorial Opera House, which opened in 1932 with a performance of Giacomo Puccini's *Tosca*.[7]

The War Memorial Opera House and I are about to meet. My arms are tingling with anticipation. I enter the Stage Door, walk into the wings backstage, and finally make my way out onto the stage itself. And almost fall down.

This spanking-new wood floor may be beautiful. But it is treacherous. As in, slippery. Almost like ice. *That* slippery.

(We later hear that the Soviet Union's famed Kirov Ballet, who performs right after us at the Opera House, actually refuses to dance unless the floor is fixed. The 1961 iteration of the Ballet Russe de Monte Carlo doesn't have that kind of clout.)

We are closing the program with George Balanchine's *Ballet Imperial*. I really love the tutu I get to wear. The thing I most remember is the deliciously soft hue of my baby-blue satin bodice. Choreographed to Tchaikovsky's *Piano Concerto No. 2*, it is one of my favorite ballets.

Back in 1941, Mr. Balanchine choreographed *Ballet Imperial* for American Ballet Caravan, the predecessor of his New York City Ballet. The tutus and scenery harken back to the traditional grand Russian Imperial style. Hence, the ballet's title and the tutu I love so dearly.

(In 1973, Balanchine decides to honor Marius Petipa as "the father of classical ballet," and Tchaikovsky as his greatest composer. He renames his ballet *Tchaikovsky's Piano Concerto No. 2*. Gone are the tutus and scenery. Chiffon skirts by noted ballet costume designer Barbara Karinska now adorn the dancers and grace the stage.)[8]

Here's the breakdown of *Ballet Imperial*. Six tall *corps* girls perform in the First Movement. Six not-so-tall *corps* girls (don't call them short) dance the Second Movement. We're all on stage together for the Third and final Movement.

I'm cast as a tall girl. My memory of the First Movement is crystal clear. *Ballet Imperial* is, after all, the first time I get to perform the genius of Mr. Balanchine's choreography on a professional stage.

There is definitely a section in the First Movement that stands out for all time. It's the 7½ minute *Pas de Deux* danced by the Principal couple. And we six tall girls are onstage during the entire 7½ minutes. In a gentle semi-circle, splitting the stage. Three standing on our left leg. Three standing on our right.

I'm the middle girl on stage left. So, while standing on our left leg, our right leg is bent with a pointed toe in back, knees together. Mr. Balanchine calls it B+. Obviously, the majority of our body weight is on the standing left leg. (We'll come back to that later.)

Our arms are held in a position known as *demi-seconde*. This finds them out at our sides, while curving gently downward with elbows really lifted and palms facing down. All this time, your sternum is held high, while your shoulders are down, to accentuate your long and graceful neck. You heard right. Elbows lifted, shoulders down, sternum lifted. For 7½ minutes.

Sometimes, after a while, your elbows can't help but begin to sag. Maybe just a tad (as my bus mate Carolyn would say). But if they do, you can be sure there's a sharp rebuke after the show from the Ballet Mistress. Especially when this Ballet Mistress is the female Principal performing right in front of you onstage.

Can we discuss the pain that begins to radiate along your arm, from the shoulder on down toward the wrist? We six tall girls devise a plan. Don't they say that desperation is the mother of invention? Something like that. Roughly halfway through the 7½ minutes, at a certain moment in the *Pas de Deux* choreography, twelve elbows *imperceptibly* lower a sixteenth of an inch each. Twelve lungs silently and imperceptibly exhale. Mission accomplished.

And remember how most of our weight is on our left leg? Now, at the end of you-know-how-many minutes, we patient tall girls finally get to move. By having to immediately execute a very strenuous hop on that poor left leg. But this is no ordinary hop. This is a *cabriole*. A hop high enough to beat your two straight legs in the air, before landing again on that poor left leg. Mr. Balanchine. How could you?

I'll spare you the rest of the steps that follow the infamous *cabriole*. I'm happy to report that we six tall girls soon get to leave the stage for a welcome rest. Albeit short.

The First Movement is almost over now. Time to go back onstage for the final entrance. My partner in both the First and Third Movements is my friend, James (Jimmy) Capp.

Jimmy's right hand is lightly around the back of my waist. I am holding his outstretched left palm gently with my left hand. We are poised and ready in the stage right wings. When our familiar musical cue is heard, he calls me by my first and middle name.

"Let's go, Roni Joan." (Jimmy is imitating my mom, when she wants me to hustle.)

On the first musical phrase, we three Stage Right couples run onstage first, posing upstage right. On the next musical phrase, the three Stage Left couples run into place, posing upstage left, from the opposite wing. After a 1-count *fermata* (pause), the music becomes much faster. Mr. Balanchine's choreography obliges with a burst of steps requiring quick changes of direction. Eight people fall during our performance that night. (Only one doesn't get up.)

Whoosh. I'm on the floor. I hear, "Get up, Roni Joan. Get…." Next thing I know, Big Jack, our largest and sweetest stagehand, is carrying me to a chair backstage. I don't remember being scooped up from the stage. I'm just in his strong and gentle arms.

I *do* know that my left elbow and the outside top of my left thigh are killing me. Because they're hurting so much, I'm leaning completely on my right side. So, everybody assumes I've sprained my left ankle. The clock is ticking, while they're needlessly trying to take off my left pointe shoe. With my breath knocked out of me, I'm mouthing, "Elbow…. Elbow." But no one can hear me.

The not-so-tall girls are already dancing the Second Movement. There's not a lot of time to get my costume off me and onto my replacement for the Third Movement. Thank goodness Principal Dancer Paula Tennyson was still in the theater, as an understudy for the Lead Ballerina role. If I have the biggest rib cage in the world, Paula Tennyson has the smallest. She *is* tiny. I can still see our Wardrobe Mistress, Cornelie (Corrie) de Brauw, overlapping all that extra beautiful baby-blue satin from one end of Paula's back across to the other, before stitching her up.

I don't remember anything about getting back to the hotel. Then, I suddenly remember that my Aunt Phoebe (Mom's sister) is driving down tomorrow to see the evening show. All the way from Davis, California. I should call her to tell her I'm not dancing. Save her the trip. It's too late. I'll try her early in the morning. I set my alarm for 6:30. The piece of paper they gave me last night says, "X-rays at (hospital name). 7:15 AM." Why so early?

I open my eyes for the umpteenth time. It's finally morning. Just lying there, without moving, and *everything* hurts. My left arm is still bent at 90 degrees. It's so swollen, there's no way I can straighten it. When I try to walk, my left thigh is killing me. I find a spot that's sore to the touch.

How I manage to get dressed and get a cab to the hospital, I'll never know. The nurse is very matter-of-fact. She directs me to place my arm on the X-ray table. I grit my teeth because my upper arm has been pinned to my side since last night. Just lifting it onto the table is agony. I manage somehow, but only my upper arm is on the table. My lower arm is sticking straight up at a right angle. She says, "Straighten your arm, please." I say, "I can't."

What happens next is like out of a horror movie. That evil nurse forces my hand down flat on the table. Then, she adds a sandbag for good measure. I shriek only once. She won't care, anyway. Is this the 20th century? It feels like the Middle Ages.

The verdict: Nothing broken. Just terribly bruised. She gives me a sling and "something for the pain." Still so matter-of-fact. In the taxi back to the hotel I remember that I never called Aunt Phoebe, to tell her not to come. Oh, dear. Too late now.

I lie down and fall asleep for I-don't-know-how-long. The telephone wakes me up. It's Aunt Phoebe, in the lobby. I don't tell her over the phone. Better in person. When I open my hotel door and see her standing there, I burst into tears. I'm so homesick, and she and my mom look so much alike.

In between sobs, "Oh, Aunt Phoebe. I forgot to call you. You made the trip for nothing. I'm so sorry. And the X-ray nurse was so mean." I can't stop sobbing. Aunt Phoebe doesn't say a word. All she does is hug me and rock me side to side. It feels so good. For the first time, I think maybe it's going to be okay.

I'm finally calm again. Aunt Phoebe asks what happened. I can hardly speak. My voice sounds like it's not coming from me.

"I fell in the performance. My elbow and thigh. My left arm is pinned to me. It hurts so bad if I try to move it. Could you brush my hair and hook my stockings?"

(Nine years later, Aunt Phoebe makes the trip again. This time, she sees me dance Queen of the Wilis in *Giselle*, as a soloist with American Ballet Theatre. Same beautiful War Memorial Opera House. Better floor. I don't fall down.)

I'm happy to report that, after about a week, I'm slowly able to move my left arm away from my torso. Straightening it? Not yet. The good news is that I can get back onstage.

In Act I of *Giselle*, Bathilde is the beautiful aristocrat who is engaged to Albrecht. Lucky for me, Bathilde is a non-dancing role. Perfect.

When I'm finally back on pointe, it's in the *corps de ballet* of *Giselle, Act II*. The reason is really funny. Credit the stylized *ports de bras* of the Ballet Russe Act II choreography. In classical ballet, the usual "high 5th" arms are overhead, framing the head like a cameo. With the hands opposite one another.

In the Ballet Russe *Giselle*, the Act II "high 5th" for the *corps* is *not* symmetrical. The middle finger of the left hand gently touches the right forearm, about a third of the way toward the elbow. It's actually very pretty. It feels pretty, too. The best part? My left elbow doesn't have to straighten as much as my right. (Lemonade, anyone?)

Touring Nuts 'n' Bolts

A word about my roommates on the tour: Roberta ("Bobbi") Berson and Shirley (who prefers "Charli") Weishaar.

Bobbi and I have been studying together since we were six or seven at the Swoboda School of Ballet. She has the best sense of humor. One night on tour, she has us in stitches. She runs out of the shower, towel-less, and poses in front of the mirror like those Swans being frightened by the Hunters in Act II of *Swan Lake*. Complete with bulging eyes and sucked-in cheeks.

Charli is part of what I call the "Indianapolis Clan." A bunch of great gals, all fulfilling dreams of studying ballet in New York City. Linda Phillips, Suanne Shirley, Carmela Martinelli. Charli's Mom makes her a deal. Go to college for just one year, and I'll support you in New York after that.

Charli spends one year as a dance major at Butler University with George Verdak, himself a former Ballet Russe dancer (1943–1952). Then, it's off to the Big Apple. A year of study with Mme. Swoboda lands her a spot in the Ballet Russe *corps de ballet*.

To hear Charli tell it, her audition was not without its own touch of drama. Madame was seated in that imposing, horizontal line of folding chairs. The one that stretches the width of the studio, in front of the mirror.

A mainstay of many auditions is those infamous *fouetté* turns. That's where you complete one turn, 16 times, while going up and down on one pointe shoe. Hopefully, "on a dime." When Charli begins her 16 consecutive *fouetté* turns, she (sadly) begins drifting to the right. (A common occurrence.)

Watching this, Madame Swoboda begins leaning so far to *her* right, she could fall out of her chair. Through pure grit, Charli stops traveling and finishes the last bunch of the fouettés on that dime. The Folding Chair Brigade apparently notes the strength in her impressive recovery. Charli makes it into the Company.

Charli and Linda and Suanne and Carmela all end up sharing a huge apartment on Riverside Drive. They are such a fun-loving bunch. Adventurous. Great senses of humor. (Do I recall a cat named "Dammit"? Who doesn't want to scream "Dammit, get outta here," now and then?) A new moniker is definitely in order for this quartet. With a nod to Gene Kelly's 1957 Broadway hit, I re-dub them "Les Girls."

These "transplanted" New Yorkers at the ballet school all seem like warriors to me. Working day or night jobs, just to pay rent and take class. Makes me feel almost guilty for being a native New Yorker. I get to live at home. Free room-and-board.

You can count "Les Girls" among the "warriors." Linda ends up working with Jerome Robbins and later becomes Assistant Business Manager of Harkness Ballet. Suanne is a Jack Cole dancer on Broadway. Carmela, "Cami," dances with both Ballet Russe and Pennsylvania Ballet. Successful warriors, if you ask me.

* * *

Following our three days in San Francisco, the one-night stands kick in. We typically pull into the next city around 2:00 p.m. Michael Subotin, our tour manager, handles the check-in. My nickname for Mr. Subotin is the Ghosting King. Ghosting, you ask? "Ghosting" is the art of cramming four dancers into a hotel room meant for two. So, only two girls are legitimately checked into the double room. The other two girls just waft in like ghosts.

Needless to say, the Ghosting King has it all figured out. He pre-divides the 18-or-so touring weeks by four. He registers each of us for four-and-a-half-ish weeks. We each have that many receipts for Uncle Sam. Only several weeks into the tour, Santa Monica gets the prize: $1.13 per person for the night.

Enough with the bookkeeping. After getting a key from Mr. Subotin, I dump my bags in the room and make a beeline for the dining room. My task: eat as much as I can, as slowly as I can. It's roughly 2:30 in the afternoon, and this meal has to last until curtain down at 11:30.

Eating now always feels like breakfast, although the food choices say "dinner." 7:00 a.m. was so long ago. My "orange juice" is a small house salad with Thousand Island dressing. My "cornflakes" is a large ground-beef patty with two vegetables. And don't forget raspberry sherbet with lots of coffee creamer poured on top. Yes, at *this* "breakfast," there *is* coffee. Lots of coffee. None at 7:00 in the morning. Needed to sleep on the bus. Did I mention the couple of Almond Joys thrown in my purse, for "emergencies?"

I walk through the Stage Door around 5:00 p.m., 3½ hours for class, makeup, hair, headpiece, tights, pointe shoes, costume, and "Places." Wait a minute. Back up. Did I say class? There *is* no Company Class. No organized warm-up.

Yikes. How on earth am I ever going to stay in shape? Keep my technique sharp? Practice those gnarly nuggets of choreography that give me trouble every night? For the first time, I might finally be understanding what Mme. Swoboda may have meant when she said, "*Steeck with the Jeem! Steeck with the Jeem!*"

"The Jeem" is my friend Jimmy Capp, a dancer (late 20s?) who fought in the trenches in the Korean War. He has already been with the Company for a couple of years. "Jeem" knows the ropes.

More importantly, Jimmy is very disciplined. Sometimes, unnervingly so. (The army?) I ask him about Korea only once. Staring straight ahead, he says, "It wasn't pretty." Sometimes I see a look in his eyes that seems to confirm that. I never ask him again.

Jimmy is an amazing "tour buddy." He always finds a space backstage to lead me through his own barre and center exercises. He doesn't sing, but he counts. It's from Jimmy that I learn the art, and value, of counting an exercise. And, of course, counting eventual music. Jimmy not only helps me warm up for every show, but also helps me stay in shape. He knows all these "strengtheners" that really sharpen my technique. I definitely *"steeck with the Jeem."*

Right up there with "theater place" and "theater robe" is your theater *case*. A ritual all its own. It holds absolutely every single thing you need to get yourself onstage: makeup, hair paraphernalia, pointe shoes, rehearsal clothes, theater robe and theater slippers (forgot to mention the slippers). Everything.

Your theater case is the one piece of luggage you don't need to schlep around the country. In every city, the stagehands unload all the theater cases just inside the loading dock. You do have to push it (too heavy to lift), from the loading dock to your dressing room. (Hopefully, a nearby male dancer will take it up the stairs?) We've already covered the unpacking process of setting up your theater place. Obviously, after the show, it's got to all fit back in there. Eeek.

Your theater case is a two-piece affair: a black fiberglass bottom, with a matching black lid that fits snugly on top. Two black canvas straps are secured with leather and rivets, underneath the bottom half. You refill this bottom half after every show. My, that pile is looking really high, now that everything's back in.

The moment of truth has arrived. You place the top half on top of the really high pile. Can the lid squish that pile down far enough? Will those two canvas straps be able to meet on top to hold the lid in place?

It's time for my "Little Mermaid Moment" (as in the famous statue in Copenhagen, Denmark, not the Disney movie). Only instead of a waterside rock, I'm kneeling on the lid of my theater case, with both knees planted on that hard black fiberglass lid. My only hope of squishing the lid down far enough, so the straps can close. Little Mermaid, do your knees hurt, too?

You heard me say it. "So the straps can close." Let's hope. Thread the first strap through the serrated buckle. Now, can I yank it through far enough to catch and thread back through? Whew. Just made it. One down. One to go.

Here's my red-face moment. I return my theater case to the loading dock. There it waits, next to all these other sanely-packed types. *Their* lids are a respectable 2–3 inches from the bottom. Mine is more like 10 inches? Looking definitely "overfed."

The edge of *my* theater case lid barely covers the edge of my theater case bottom. I was never a light packer.

Curtain is at 8:30 every night, so you're back in the hotel room around 11:30–11:45. Forget an open restaurant. God bless those little cans of "fruit cocktail." Next order of business, washing your pink performance tights. No way these aching legs can stand at the sink. I sit in the empty tub, as close to the faucet as possible. Feet at the open drain. Knees up around my ears. Just me, my tights, the streaming water, and that tiny hotel bar of soap.

You'd be surprised how dirty your tights can get in some of these old theaters. Maybe you danced one of those ballets where you kneel and then get up and then kneel again and then get up again. Be prepared for grime on any part of your tights that was touching that dirty stage. Scrubbing with a nail brush might be involved.

One night in the theater, I start putting on my tights at half-hour, only to discover that I must have washed the same leg twice. I have to quickly scrub that other grimy knee and foot. Damp tights inside your pointe shoe. Ick.

So, other nightly chores: hot bath, and write your mother. Do not fail to write your mother. I learn that the hard way. If she doesn't hear from you for a few days, she calls the theater 25 minutes before curtain. The stage manager pages you on the P.A. system. "Roni. Your mother is on the phone." Ouch.

Okay. Canned fruit, tights, bath, letter. Finally, sleep. Pretty much not before 2:00 a.m. Alarm is set for 6:45. Bus call is at 8:00. My *modus operandi* is to go down for breakfast at 7:00. Avoid last-minute crush of dancers and musicians. That orange juice and cornflakes, only. No coffee. Need four more hours of sleep on the bus.

Back in my room by 7:20. Thirty minutes to finish packing. At 7:50, I'm "eyeballing" my luggage, as the driver puts it under the bus. That bus is leaving at 8 o'clock sharp. With or without you. Once, a dancer had to book himself to the next city.

The "premium" sleeping space on the bus, the overhead luggage rack, is reserved for the principal dancers. This lowly *corps de ballet* first-year girl racks out on the floor. Rest stops are every two hours. We call them "pee pee *powsers*." (The "German pronunciation!") Trusty bus mate, Carolyn, nudges me awake so I don't get trampled. I continue sleeping in my bus seat.

Confession: that's not the way things started out. The first two months on tour, I eat a doughnut at every rest stop. My waistline and I finally realize the wiser choice is to stay on the bus and keep dozing. It doesn't take me too long to learn that "routine" is the only chance I have of coming off tour "in shape." The only chance I have, at staying sort-of healthy. And injury-free. Yes, routine sets boundaries. I sound like my parents.

Boundaries are good. But, I'm eighteen and away from home for a long time. Sometimes you have to do something nuts. Like checking out this great Farmer's Market, while performing in Seattle. Roommate Bobbi and I hear it's not to be missed.

A Farmer's Market? That's not so nuts, you say. But coming back to the hotel with two hamsters? Pretty nuts. Like I said. Eighteen and away from home. How are we going to sneak them into our hotel at every stop?

We name the hamsters *Nachas* and *Tsuris* … two Yiddish words meaning "happiness" and "troubles." I am never quite sure which hamster is which. What if they die? One of them does, and we bury it on the lunch stop. We decide the deceased hamster was definitely Tsuris. Happiness lives to see another day.

Speaking of another day, it's really hard to keep track of what day it is. One-night-stands feel like Mondays, Tuesdays, or Wednesdays. One of those strings of Mondays and Tuesdays and Wednesdays goes on for twenty days. With no day off. Some days are for travel only, but those do not qualify as "days off."

What about the Union, you ask? I am just a new girl, so I don't really get all that. I do remember voting now and then to "waive" something. Everyone always votes "yes." So I vote "yes." Voting "no" never even comes up.

What about the money, you ask? Well, the paycheck is kind of small. Cue my dad's warning: "There's no money in ballet." Your poor paycheck. It also has to buy your performance tights and pointe shoes. You even pay for your own hotel room. And there's no per diem. God bless the Ghosting King.

(Nowadays, the ballet companies buy your tights and pointe shoes, and pay your hotel. And per diem.)

* * *

Red Rock, Wyoming. A "travel" day. No performance. Just get up in the morning, have breakfast, and travel to the city you'll be performing in that night. So, breakfast. It's about 7:30. Our hotel coffee shop is the only place serving breakfast, and we have an eight o'clock bus call. The grim reality: Two buses of 40 hungry dancers and musicians vs. 1 cook/server, 8 counter stools, 3-ish small tables.

Total mayhem. Not many orders have been "plated," as they say. Someone springs up, runs behind the counter, begins frying eggs. Someone else is pouring coffee. Someone else, juice. Who ordered toast? I got cereal here. Anybody ask for milk? The lone cook/server is now taking the orders. Two buses pull away on time. Forty full stomachs. Mission accomplished.

File this next nugget under "truly unforgettable." The scene: Laramie, Wyoming. Another travel day. At check-in, the hotel clerk tells us it's "15 below." Wow. Gotta experience this. I'm out the front door in a flash. My goal: half a block to the corner drugstore, and back.

I'm not even halfway to that drugstore, and I'm already racing back to the hotel. That's really cold. What was I thinking? Thank goodness we don't perform here. I instantly invent a two-part wardrobe accommodation: First, my wool scarf now covers my nose and mouth; then, it's tied behind my head, pinning the hood of my winter coat snugly to my ears. I have just learned two imperatives: (1) Feel no drafts around your head and neck, and (2) Keep the air you're inhaling warm.

Okay, 15-Below, you won't catch me off-guard again. I've got this. Set wake-up call, fall asleep, answer wake-up call. "Good morning. It's seven o'clock and 40 below." Whoa. Time for double layers of everything.

As eight o'clock nears, it's an odd sight. The lobby is still teeming with dancers and musicians. No one is on the buses. They tell us the gasoline has frozen in both tanks. Next 45 minutes: dancers and musicians, warm and cozy in the lobby. Two stalwart bus drivers doing Lord-knows-what in 40-below. How do you re-liquefy frozen gasoline?

I remember only three things after that: (1) The drivers walk back into the lobby with blue noses. I kid you not. The ends of their noses are blue-ish. (2) We board those utterly frigid buses. (3) Carolyn and I face each, sitting on each other's feet. The rest is a shivering haze.

* * *

Let's take stock so far. Thankfully, there's been only one Treacherous-And-Mortifying moment on tour. Falling during *Ballet Imperial* in San Francisco. But we do have an entry for the category of Mortifying-But-Not-Treacherous. I can't remember the city, but I'll never forget the ballet. *Giselle.*

It's Act II, and I'm one of 16 *corps de ballet* "Wilis" (ghostly spirits of jilted young maidens). We're in a semicircle, awaiting the very, very fast running re-entry of Albrecht from upstage left. There's one of us whose place in the semicircle blocks Albrecht's clear path to bolting back onstage. It's vital that this girl remember to pose a step to her left, allowing Albrecht unobstructed access to the stage.

That girl is me. Albrecht is none other than the ultra-famous Igor Youskevitch. I've forgotten to pose a step to my left. Suddenly, from behind, I'm almost knocked off my feet and have to struggle to stay upright. Not pretty.

But that's not the worst of it. When boarding the bus the next morning, Mr. Youskevitch, befitting his star status, is sitting right there behind the bus driver. I'm just about to lower my head in shame when I smell a distinct aroma.

I blurt out, "H. Upmann No. 12." Mr. Youskevitch, lit cigar in hand, snaps his head up. Looks me directly in the eyes. Then he grins that trademark grin of his, which is really a debonair half-smirk. In an instant, last night is forgiven.

MR. YOUSKEVITCH: *"How you know?"*
ME: "My dad smokes that cigar. I'd know the aroma anywhere. Back home, if the elevator smells of H. Upmann No. 12, I know my dad's home."

* * *

We're slowly threading our way up and down and across this great country. Red Rock and Laramie aside, some of these one-nighters can begin to blur together. But, hey. They're not all one-nighters.

We do get to spend two days each in Portland (Oregon), Denver, Newark, and Brooklyn. The Itinerary Gods also bless us with three days each in San Francisco, Seattle, Houston, Chicago, and Cleveland. They don't bless us with balmy weather. Much of this great land of ours is bitter cold. I remember the bleak dead-of-winter. Everything looking so gray. Always.

Now our bus is wending its way from Wichita, Kansas, to a performance in Dodge City. Flat. Endless. I've never been to Kansas, but I did see "The Wizard of Oz" when I was six.

Leaving Radio City Music Hall, I said to my mother, "Kansas is black-and-white and the rest of the world is Technicolor." Now … looking out the window … I hear those words again in my head.

"Y-Y-Y-Y-up," I say out loud. To no one in particular.

More cities. More hotels. More theaters. I hear myself say out loud, again, to no one in particular, "I have been in sub-zero temperatures for three straight weeks." I'm doing that more and more lately. Saying things out loud, to no one in particular. Eventually, I remember arriving in Des Moines, Iowa. It is five degrees *above* zero. I take off my scarf. I take off my gloves.

Swan Lake, Act II

It's almost starting to feel like the end of this tour might actually happen. The final Saturday night and Sunday matinee at the Brooklyn Academy of Music is getting closer and closer. But first, there is a weekend of performances at the Music Hall in Cleveland, Ohio. And, we have our first nomination for Most Glorious Moment on tour. Bette Davis says it best in *All About Eve*: "Fasten your seat belts. It's going to be a bumpy night."

Remember that invisible clause my dad inserted, when I was signing my first Ballet Russe contract? Two years to break out of the *corps de ballet* in a demi-soloist role. Or go to college, young lady. Hello, Cleveland.

The ballet: *Swan Lake, Act II*. The demi-soloist role: one of the two Lead Swans. Or "Big Swans," as we're unfortunately called. To completely understand the situation, we have to return to our rehearsal period before the tour.

One of the Big Swans is a "third-year-girl." She's been performing the role for a while now and arrives totally out-of-shape when rehearsals begin. Not only is she a heavy smoker. Rumor has it she hardly took class during the layoff months. The other Big Swan is the very talented and conscientious Andrea Vodehnal.

The Big Swans lead the *corps de ballet* in every entrance throughout Act II. They also dance a variation together. A real gut-buster. It's all jumps and goes on forever. Unfortunately, it also follows the utterly adorable variation for those legendary four "Little Swans." Even their moniker is adorable. *Cygnets.* And they bring down the house every time. Following them is no picnic.

Back to the gut-buster. The first time we rehearse *Swan Lake, Act II*, our out-of-shape dancer and Andrea run their variation. Guess which one collapses in pain with a knee injury? She is immediately replaced by Marina Chapman, a very talented and conscientious "second-year-girl." Marina and Andrea dance the variation beautifully throughout the tour.

Remember those seat belts? Are you buckled up? Poor Marina. Here in Cleveland, while rehearsing the Big Swans variation for tomorrow night's *Swan Lake,* an old knee injury returns with a vengeance and takes her out for the rest of the season. It's devastating to watch. There, but for the grace of God…

Everyone can finish that sentence. I've always said we dancers "dance between injuries." Just like professional athletes. Your body is on the line during every rehearsal/practice. Every performance/game. Always vulnerable to catastrophe. It sounds melodramatic, but that's the way it feels.

Nina Novak, our ballet mistress/lead ballerina, immediately turns to the original dancer, who had hurt her knee in that first rehearsal week many moons ago. Although her injury has healed, she has done precious little to get into really good shape again. Her heavy smoking isn't helping. She tries to run the gut-buster.

That Friday afternoon in Cleveland, she has neither the leg endurance nor the lung power. She breaks down coughing only halfway through. It's such a cliché, but the silence in that large rehearsal hall is deafening. Frozen faces. Stunned disbelief. In such a short time … one variation, two catastrophes.

Nina Novak's voice breaks the awful silence. "Roni, can you dance Big Swans tomorrow night?"

A "first-year-girl?!" Unheard of. A "yes" flies out of my mouth. My mother would approve. She always tells the story of interviewing for an Office Manager's job. When asked if she knew how to work the new IBM Selectric typewriter, she quickly answers, "Yes." She gets the job, goes home, and teaches herself how.

Okay. Let's talk scheduling. We are "scheduled" to dance three different programs at all three Cleveland performances: tonight, three short ballets; tomorrow night, three more, including *Swan Lake, Act II*; and a Sunday matinee, three more. Amazingly, all these ballets have to be rehearsed today. Yes, this afternoon.

Tomorrow, Saturday, is a "free day." And, no. On Sunday, there's no rehearsing before a matinee. Excuse me, you ask? How can Saturday be a free day if there is a performance that evening? Aha. Who said anything about 24 hours? Did I say 24 hours? We're "free" until 6:00 in the evening.

Our Friday rehearsal of *Swan Lake*. Priority: Getting Roni through all the Big Swans group choreography while the full *corps de ballet* is still on call. It's very, very different from the *corps* choreography I have been performing since the tour began in LA. Good thing I have all those other Swans around me, and don't have to learn this in a vacuum. Especially my new places in all those big formations.

We start with the Entrance, progress to the Waltz and then the *Pas de Deux*. We finish with the Finale and the Departure. Steps learned. Time's up. Must get ready for tonight's "mixed rep."

But, wait a minute. Wait just a minute. I haven't learned the variation. Have to remember to ask Andrea, my other Big Swan, if she has time to teach it to me. But first, I still have to go through my usual routine for tonight's performance: hair, makeup, warm-up with "The Jeem." One extra thing. Telegram to folks: "I don't have to go to college."

Guess what? Angel Andrea to the rescue. Backstage, during the show, she tells me to meet her at the theater tomorrow afternoon, and she'll teach me the variation. Even though it's her free day. I'm saved.

The next day, Big Swans Saturday, my hotel room telephone which never rings … rings twice.

The first call is Mom. They got my telegram. I fill her in on every exciting detail, especially my emphatic "yes." Channeling her IBM Selectric story. She wishes me all the best. She says my dad does, too. But he's on the golf course right now.

"Remember the little man in the balcony, dear. And your father says to keep your head down." (Advice for a good golf swing.)

The second call: Angel Andrea. The janitor will let us into the rehearsal hall at 2:00 p.m. and Company Pianist, Rachel Chapman, will be there, too. Another angel working on her free day.

Ah, Rachel. Our beloved rehearsal accompanist. R-R-Rachel wants to be called by her first name. A native Russian, she gargles the "R." The "a" is short, like "ah." And the "ch" is pronounced "sh." Rachel accents the second syllable. I adore R-R-Rah-SHEL. Definitely a force to be reckoned with.

Rachel doesn't just play for rehearsals, either. She's also Principal Pianist for the Company orchestra, gloriously performing as the Soloist whenever *Ballet Imperial* or *Bach Concerto* are on the program. When they are not, she's still in the pit every night, filling in for whichever instruments are missing.

Once inside the rehearsal hall, it feels like the North Pole. I guess they're waiting for the Company to show up before turning on the heat? Welcome to early March in Cleveland. Our feet and legs are freezing. R-R-Rah-chel's fingers, too.

Andrea proceeds to lead me through a short barre and center. Wonder of wonders. We are actually doing class to music. Rachel's familiar and soothing melodies feel like a miracle, indeed. It's been such a long time. Remember, no Company Class on tour. Just warming up with "The Jeem," who counts. Thank you, Rachel.

After about forty-five minutes, we make believe that we're warmed up. Now, onto the variation. Rachel's cold fingers have to play less than robustly. Our legs and feet won't be dancing too robustly, either. Still, we plow ahead. About an hour later, mission: complete. Choreography: learned. Fueled by human kindness instead of heat? A bit mushy, but true. Watch out, Big Swans variation. Here I come.

Andrea and Rachel leave. I stay on. Can I remember all these steps on my own? I run the variation alone. The ultimate test of any duet. Luckily, I pass with flying colors. But "sequence" is everything in a new role. I decide to start from my very first entrance. Singing the music, I mark through the entire Act in order, until my final exit.

"Mark," you ask? "Marking" is kind of like walking through it. No pointed feet. No straight knees. No actual jumping or turning. Kind of like indicating the choreography, without actually doing it. "Marking" is the opposite of "full-out." Full-out is peak energy, ultimate effort. High jumps, all the turns, lots of pointed feet and straight knees. Even when you're only in rehearsal.

A lot of dancers have trouble onstage because they never rehearse "full-out." They think they have to "save something" for the performance. "I'm storing up my energy." The exact opposite is true. The smart dancer exhausts themselves in rehearsal. Sometimes they run the whole thing one more time for endurance. My pet name for that little escapade is the Blue-Lip Special. It's often not pretty. Not your best effort. But when you have to run through all those steps only once onstage, piece o' cake.

Eventually, a friendly face appears in the studio doorway. *"Roni, you go back hotel now. Lie down thirty minutes, or legs collapsing tonight."* That soft, yet compelling, voice belongs to Mme. Sophie Pourmel. Our "Directress of Wardrobe" and another Russian émigré. Mme. Pourmel is absolutely right. It's almost 4:30 and time for me to get out of here. (In little over a year, George Balanchine, New York City Ballet's legendary Ballet Master, will make Mme. Pourmel Supervisor of Women's Wardrobe at "City Ballet.")

I immediately take Mme. Pourmel's advice. Luckily, our hotel is right across the street from the theater. Within five minutes, I am "horizontal" on my hotel room bed. Still reviewing tonight's new choreography with my eyes closed. Interrupted by that third and final phone call. I'll bet it is my dad. He'll be wishing me good luck, now that he's back in the clubhouse.

The next words I hear still ring in my ears: "Well, kid, are you coming down or do we have to come up and get you?" Yes. My folks are in the lobby. Mom had already bought the plane tickets when she was calling me that morning. There are no words…

Knowing my parents are here makes me almost giddy as I walk into the theater. That feeling is, however, short-lived. Everyone seems pretty excited for me. Everyone except those infamous "third-year girls." They know that exactly two Saturday nights from now in New York, I will be getting another shot at Big Swans. Or maybe not. The third-year girls have convinced their out-of-shape contemporary that she can return to form in time for Big Swans in the Big Apple. So, I'm sitting at my theater place. I'm putting on my makeup. And I'm listening to:

"You'll be ready."
"You can do it."
"You'll be back dancing Big Swans in New York."
"You've got two whole weeks."
"That's plenty of time."

I guess I should be grateful that I'm not finding ground glass in my pointe shoe. Who hasn't heard of that?

What to do? The only thing I can. Slowly, methodically, apply my makeup. Focus my mind on just that. Let nothing else in. Block out everything around me.

This is good. This is good. Whatever I'm doing is working. Wonder Woman. Impervious to all things negative. Enveloping myself in my pre-performance ritual: makeup, hair (classical), headpiece (non-moldy ribbon), warm up with "The Jeem," costume, onstage call. Stage left. Orchestra. Curtain up. Hunters. Prince, Odette, Von Rothbart…. S-W-A-N-S. One by one.

Entrance over. We're back in the stage left wings, until we go on again. Now, it's practically time for our running-and-flapping re-entry for the famous *Pas de Deux*.

Andrea is saying, "If I didn't know any better, I'd swear I saw your mother in the front row." A quick "yes" over my shoulder is all I have time for. Time to run back onstage. You see, we follow the four Little Swans (*Cygnets*), and they're starting to run on. Here we go, right after them. Here comes Odette. Gosh, I love this *Pas de Deux*.

The four Little Swans and two Big Swans get to exit about three-quarters of the way through. It gives us time to prepare for our variations. Thanks to Andrea's hard work this afternoon, ours goes off without a hitch. Coda. Departure. Done. Success. Ecstatic. Brooklyn Academy of Music, here I come?

Well, not exactly. Turns out, two weeks *is* plenty of time for Third-Year Girl to reclaim her Big Swans role. No demi-soloist chance for me on this final "hometown" weekend, with all my friends and family watching.

I find myself muttering, "Wait 'til next year. Wait 'til next year." And I'm not just talking about missing out on a second performance of Big Swans at the Brooklyn Academy of Music. Don't forget. My poor Yankees lost the World Series to the Pittsburgh Pirates this year.

Act One

* * *

At 19, I am a woman of the world now. I've successfully completed a cross-country bus tour with the Ballet Russe. Learned to stand on my own two feet, even when *not* in pointe shoes. So now that I'm back home, Mme. Swoboda thinks nothing of sending me on the train to Wilmington, Delaware, every late Friday afternoon. I stay overnight in the home of Catherine Streltzov, who runs a local ballet school. (Ms. Streltzov danced in the *corps de ballet* in the late '30s, when Madame and her husband were starring with the Chicago Civic Opera.)

My task on Saturday mornings is to create a student-worthy version of *Coppélia's* Act I *Thème Slave Varié* (the "Friends Dance"). I'm working with her most advanced students. Maybe five or six very eager teenage girls. The first hurdle is to find out what they *can't* do. In other words, what steps are "beyond" their current ballet technique. Then, I just back up a bit, and give them steps they can do very well. Making them look good is Job One. This is something I absolutely love doing. Turns out, I'm also pretty good at it. Little do I know that these are the first "baby feathers" of what will one day become my teaching wings.

The girls perform their *Coppélia* "Friends Dance" beautifully. Their parents are thrilled. More importantly, Mrs. Streltzov is very pleased. If I'm ever asked for "references" now, I finally have one.

My Second Year in Ballet Russe

My "wait 'til next year" prayer hits a snag. The Ballet Russe is running out of money. This is the '61-'62 season. Will there even be a "next year?" That is the question. It's a question that's been bantered about for a while now. It's what had me on the fence about signing with the Company straight out of high school.

In the end, there *is* a Company. Being a second-year girl is just as exciting. Except everything isn't happening for the first time. No, no, no, no, no. That's not true.

How about the first time being chosen to perform an absolutely genuine, *bona fide*, no "demi" in sight, soloist role? That's right. No disrespect to the Two Big Swans in *Swan Lake, Act II*, but you're looking a bit like small potatoes right now.

TRIBUTE

But how? Well, remember my scholarship audition savior, my mentor for the past five years? His initials are "FF"? Yes, Frederic Franklin has choreographed a ballet for the Ballet Russe de Monte Carlo. For only six dancers. Two side (soloist) couples and a center (principal) couple.

It's the Ballet Russe's 25th Silver Anniversary. Director Sergei Denham is commemorating this by commissioning new works by star Ballet Russe alumni.

The score Mr. Franklin has chosen for his celebratory work is the divinely-danceable *Symphonic Variations* by César Franck. The title of the ballet is *Tribute*.[9] Undoubtedly, in honor of Ballet Russe de Monte Carlo's glittering past. Twenty-five years that gave him his opportunity for a glittering career.

Tribute premieres in the summer between my first and second Ballet Russe seasons. On the shores of the Charles River in Boston, Massachusetts, no less. In a large, white, outdoor tent. Daylight, our only lighting. Matinees, our only choice.

I'm forever grateful to former Ballet Russe ballerina, Moscelyne Larkin. I can't remember exactly why she's with us on the Charles River that summer, but I do remember this. My toes are killing me. They are really, really sore. One day, she sees me tenderly examining my bare, flaming-red feet and asks what's the matter.

> **ME:** "Moscelyne, do the toes ever get tough, or is it going to hurt like this forever?"
> **MOSCELYNE:** "Please. Call me 'Moussia.' I always soaked my feet in alum. Every night. It toughens the skin. And I painted my toenails with iodine. It takes a little of the soreness away."

Forever grateful doesn't begin to cover it.

The Boston performances are exciting. But for me, *Tribute*'s real premiere is when we officially begin our 1961–62 season in Chicago. In a *real* theater. With *real* lighting. And all the dramatic effects that go along with it. This 19-year-old, in her first *bona fide* soloist role, is blissfully overwhelmed.

"On Stage" has been called by the Stage Manager. All three couples are practicing challenging moments of choreography, either alone or in small groups, behind the closed curtain, in regular "room" light.

Then we hear, "Places." Time to stop moving around and find our "marks." Another exciting first for me. "Marks" are colored, half-inch wide, small strips of glow-in-the-dark tape, strategically placed on the floor to indicate our exact opening positions. In this case, the marks are in a long diagonal from downstage left to upstage right. "Washington state to Florida."

My tour buddy Jimmy Capp (aka "The Jeem") and I, are downstage left, in "Washington." The principal couple, Andrea Vodehnal and Eugene Slavin, are smack dab in the middle of the country. "Kansas?" Side Couple Number Two, Gail Israel and Franklin Yezer, are upstage right in "Florida." It's really, really important to be "on your mark." Otherwise, you won't be in the center of your spotlight when it finally comes on.

I'm posed slightly diagonally in front of Jimmy, to his left. Our positions are identical. We are each standing on our left leg. Our right leg, bent at the knee, allows us to cross our arched right foot in front, with a pointed toe resting gracefully on the stage floor. Both arms are gently arced down at our sides, held slightly away from the body. Giving our armpits a chance to "breathe"? The chin is slightly lowered with downcast eyes. Gazing at the floor beyond our crossed foot, maybe five feet away.

That pose is emblazoned into my very soul, for all time. I can "feel" my dear friend Jimmy's presence behind me. He always makes me pose first. That way, he can mirror the exact tilt of my head. The exact angle of my arms and crossed right foot.

Then, the Stage Manager's warning. "Going to black." My heart is definitely beating faster now, as I struggle to keep my balance in the momentary pitch-blackness. (Thank you, glow-in-the-dark tape.) The curtain opens just in time, giving me some ambient light from the audience-filled "house." Whew.

And then it happens. The lighting effect that so overwhelms me. The theater is dark. The stage is dark. As the audience is hearing the first gentle strains of César

Franck's delicious score, a spotlight begins a slow "reveal" of Jimmy and I. We must remain absolutely still, in the warmth of the spotlight, as the centerstage "reveal" occurs. Then the upstage right "reveal."

You know how a kid dreams of slamming a home run in the bottom of the ninth, to win the World Series? Well, this kid has dreamed of a solo in a spotlight, on the darkened stage of New York's Metropolitan Opera House. Close enough.

One of the hallmarks of Mr. Franklin's stellar dancing career was making the audience feel *his* joy when performing. He's the same way when teaching class. He can even make attempting a dreaded double *arabesque pirouette* (revolving twice around on a straight leg, with your other leg as high up behind you as humanly possible) seem like a happy occasion.

In my mind, Mr. Franklin's choreography evokes the same sensation. It exudes joy. At least, it makes me feel completely joyous when performing it. He's often called the "dancer's dancer." He knows how to make you feel good and look good. That is, until you don't. Allow me to explain.

It all begins in Pocatello, Idaho. Things are good. For starters, we'll be performing *Tribute* tonight. Then, there's an amazing dress shop that greets us in the hotel lobby. I spy this gorgeous, maxi-length, cocoa-colored suede number in the window. Exactly my size. On sale. I buy it on my way to the hotel coffee shop for the big before-theater meal.

As great as the dress is, the coffee shop waitress is better. My roommates and I are her first customers. No one else from the Company has come into the hotel dining room yet. She obligingly serves us coffee. When I go to take a sip, my cup is stuck to its saucer. When I try to add sugar, there's a hole in the sugar bowl spoon. When I try to cut my meat, the knife bends in half.

All the while, our impish waitress is pantomiming "shhhh," pressing her index finger to her lips. Asking us to please squelch our reactions, so she can pull her antics on the next unsuspecting vict … er, customer? This jolly soul and her trick tableware have managed to jolt us out of humdrum, into hilarity. Quite the feat. And most welcome.

Not so welcome is the very slippery wood stage awaiting us at the theater. We are greeted by an ominous sight. Our Stage Manager, sprinkling the stage with Ajax, then spraying it with Coca-Cola. The Coke's acid helps break down the shellac. Apologies to my teeth? My stomach?

Although I've never tried "spraying" the Coca-Cola myself, I know it involves placing one's thumb over the bottle's hole, leaving just a sliver of space uncovered. Shaking vigorously. Covering the stage with as fine a mist as possible. No puddles, please. An art form, for sure. A little like what the Yankees do with champagne, after winning the World Series?

Back to Frederic Franklin. His *Tribute* fairly reeks of joy and exuberance. In one of the many exuberant sequences, Gail and I join Andrea in a short *pas de trois*. The end is especially fun. I'm happily spinning toward the stage right wing, only to end up flat on my face. Can lightning strike twice? First, the slippery San Francisco stage. Now, a slippery Pocatello stage. Another fall. Extremely embarrassing. Not nearly as serious.

Ever-so-close to that right wing, I begin my exultant *relevé arabesque* finish. But my right *relevé* foot slips out from under me. I belly flop to the stage floor and have to crawl into the wings on my hands and knees. In an instant, everyone is crowding around, worried that I'm injured. Should I fake it? Should I say "yes" to ease the shame of it all?

I don't get to think that for long. Wardrobe Mistress, Corrie de Brauw is standing over me. In her inimitable Cockney accent, she blurts out, "Ow, nothin's 'urt but 'er prawd!" Corrie is right. I'm not hurt. The judges' decision? More mortifying than *Ballet Imperial* in San Francisco. Much less treacherous.

The great thing about this second tour is that sometimes you're a Soloist (*Tribute*). And sometimes you're right back in the *corps de ballet*. But still having the time of your life. I'm not just talking about the *corps* of *Les Sylphides*, whose magical, other-worldly qualities have been thoroughly aired here. I'm talking about another magical Fokine ballet, just revived for this tour. I'm talking about *Les Elfes*.

Les Elfes

I'm having the time of my life dancing in *Les Elfes*. My favorite things are all coming together. First, a composer I love. Felix Mendelssohn. Add to that, I'm dressed entirely in hues of my favorite color. My theater color. Green. And I'm wearing the costume of a fairy-like forest creature. Pale green chiffon swirling around my legs. Forest-green bodice that feels like velvet. On my head, a matching green, loosely knit cap, with gold ribbon intertwining.

And, of course, my wings. I have two wings attached in back, at the top of my bodice. In my imagination, these wings are completely different from the wings on my *Les Sylphides* costume. A Sylph's wings help her waft and flow smoothly. My *Les Elfes* wings let me frolic about. Just like all those tiny forest fairies, playing in and around their oh-so-tiny waterfalls. (For the rest of my life, when I need to escape the doldrums, I envision myself back in this whimsical world.)

This ballet, first choreographed by Michel Fokine in 1924, was restaged by the Ballet Russe de Monte Carlo in 1937.[10] A ballet company traditionally rotates the selections in its repertoire, and *Les Elfes* has been tapped for revival this year.

Mendelssohn's *Midsummer Night's Dream* Overture is perfect for the First Movement. Lots of happy elves, flitting and frolicking in a happy forest. When the curtain goes up, the opening *tableau* finds all us elves in a big circle on the forest floor, sitting back on both heels with our heads to our knees. Our arms reaching out behind us, with hands "fluttering" like crazy. Tiny wings getting ready to fly?

No fluttering in the Second Movement. This is the Andante section of his Violin Concerto in E Minor, Op. 64. Now, imagine sitting serenely upright on the forest floor, as if cushioned by imaginary moss. Both legs are bent, the pointe shoe of my left foot barely touching my right knee. The pale green of my chiffon skirt draping softly around me. My shoulders and head tilting wistfully to the right.

All I have to do now is listen. Listen, as the orchestra swells with the strains of that delicious E Minor melody. Soon, sounding a tiny bit sadder, in the virtuoso hands of our solo violinist.

Are you wondering what choreography Mr. Fokine has envisioned for this heaven-sent music? To my 19-year-old eyes, it's the most poignant *Pas de Six* (dance for six) ever created. Three male-and-female couples. The men are supplying balance for the women. Now, by the waist. Now, by the wrists. The women seem to be moving in perfect time with the graceful lifting and lowering of the violinist's wrist, as bow moves across strings.

Since my early teens, in *pas de deux* class at ballet school, I've struggled with some of the same moves I'm seeing here. They look so easy when I'm watching them now. Multiple *pirouettes*, quickly revolving many times on one leg *en pointe*. *Promenade* in *penché arabesque*. Now revolving much more slowly on one leg, while leaning forward with the other leg as high as possible in back and the arched torso tilting forward. I'm watching such graceful dancing. I'm listening to such poignant music. On and on and on. All, as a fairy-like Elf in the forest. Definitely heaven.

The Third Movement of the same violin concerto is not called *Allegretto* for nothing. It definitely picks up the pace. No more watching for me. This Elf is up and dancing. *Les Elfes* is very popular with audiences, so we get to perform it a lot on tour. All the more Mendelssohn-and-green-chiffon-time for me. Bliss.

Minkus Pas de Trois

A few weeks into the tour, I see Nina Novak looking my way and then whispering to costume directress Mme. Pourmel. Looking and whispering. Looking and whispering. Finally, I find out why. It's a problem with "casting."

In a few weeks, the *Minkus Pas de Trois* (we just call it *The Minkus*), is scheduled for both a Tuesday mixed bill in Long Beach and a Thursday mixed bill in Pasadena. The Tuesday cast is okay. The usual principal dancers. But on Thursday, two of those same principals are already dancing in the three other ballets that night. They can't dance in all four.

Wait a minute. Does this mean we "*malinkis*," (a Russian term of endearment for "little ones")—Jimmy Capp, Gail Israel, and I—are being given the chance to perform *The Minkus* on Thursday? Sure, the three of us were "told to learn" *The Minkus* during the rehearsal period before the tour. That's what "understudy" means, right? Wait. Hold your horses. The *Minkus Pas de Trois* is a principal dancer role. Maybe the occasional soloist has a shot. But my name *is* up there on the call board. This must be happening.

On the program, it's listed simply as *Pas de Trois* from *Don Quixote*, with Léon Minkus as composer.[11] The music is happy and engaging. The choreography is happy and technically challenging. Because it's from "Don Q" (absolutely nobody says *Don Quixote*), the two women wear red tutus and red roses to one side of a low bun. The man is dapper in a red cummerbund and black bolero jacket trimmed in gold. His "Spanish look" is completed by ¾-length black tights to just below the knee, revealing white tights, and white ballet shoes.

Meanwhile, you would think I was getting ready for a really big date. Leading up to Thursday, I have scheduled tweezing eyebrows, shaving legs, and applying a fresh coat of colorless nail polish. Oh, the audience will be able to tell. For sure.

So, you think *this* is big news? Think again. Because the *unthinkable* happens two days before. It's around 6:45, before our 8:30 curtain. You can clearly hear raised voices coming from the stage. Something about a tutu being "impossible" to wear.

Next, those words, in a thick Russian accent, that you only hear in the movies. "*I refuse to dance!*" And one of our female principals is storming and stomping into the wings. Trouble is, *that* female principal is dancing *The Minkus* in tonight's show.

You guessed it. The *malinkis* are on. Two days earlier than scheduled. Untweezed, unshaven, unmanicured. Thank goodness I've already "chosen" the perfect pair of pointe shoes. Ribbons and elastics sewn. Broken in. Thank goodness the three of us have been rehearsing ourselves nonstop for weeks. In each and every hotel hallway on tour.

Thank goodness there's no time to think. It's makeup and hair. Now. My warm-up with The Jeem tonight actually calms me down. (God bless familiar routines.) Curtain is at 8:30, and we open with *Les Sylphides*. I never realized what a great warm-up the *Sylphides corps* can be. There's even an *adagio*, including that dreaded *penché* (tilting forward to the floor) *arabesque*. Don't forget all that *petit allegro* (small, quick hops) in *arabesque* with your leg low in back. It's like taking class onstage.

Les Sylphides is finally over. Back to my theater place. Goodbye, pale Sylph (Max Factor 21). Hello, down-to-earth Señorita (Max Factor 24). Add a little blush to each cheekbone, a brighter red for the lips, and that fabulous red rose on the right side of your bun. Who's that looking back at you in the mirror? I hardly recognize her. Now, it's into that red tutu and onto the stage.

They say it went well. Don't ask me. I don't remember a thing. Not one step. All I know is I didn't fall down, and I don't think I blanked on any of the steps. On to "Cocodettes" and the Can-Can in *Gaîté*. My kicks have never felt higher.

Of course, two nights later, we perform our already-scheduled *Pas de Trois* in Pasadena. We're veterans now. Nothin' to it.

After Pasadena, it's back to business as usual on planet Earth. Third-Year Girl has never again relinquished her stranglehold on Big Swans. Never mind. Mr. Franklin's *Tribute* is quite the step upward. I love our "rep" (short for repertoire) and I love performing in it. Even in the *corps de ballet*.

Once again, we are closing the season at the Brooklyn Academy of Music. This 20-year-old is finishing her second year of touring with the one and only Ballet Russe de Monte Carlo. Our bus has traveled from sea to shining sea. Who needs Big Swans? My folks are going to see me dance *Tribute* in my "hometown."

I've been having the time of my life in my own personal land of make-believe. The tour seems to have "flown by." Well, a tiny sliver of exciting reality did manage to puncture even *my* dream-like bubble. Toward the end of February, John Glenn completed three orbits of the Earth in his Mercury spacecraft. I guess that's one way to "fly by."

Am I on top of the world, or what? "Not so fast, Chickie." Is that a rug being pulled right out from under my performing feet? It most certainly is. All those relentless rumors of the Company's "imminent demise?" Those whispers of "union difficulties," making it hard to "stay afloat?" Can the rumors be true? They most certainly can.

Act One

The Ballet Russe is going to fold. Immediately. Well, almost immediately. Right after our two magical days of performing at the Brooklyn Academy of Music. Such a sad distinction for my native New York City.

By the time I'm unpacking my theater case for opening night, all of New York has heard the alarming news. They say some ballet company directors are coming to see us. Hoping to spot soon-to-be unemployed talent? Lucky me. I have Frederic Franklin's *Tribute*, a ballet for three couples, to help me be noticed.

Before you know it, the Sunday matinee is over. Now it's packing up my theater case for the last time. It feels like a miracle we get paid. The Ballet Russe de Monte Carlo is no more. The end of an era.[12]

Brooklyn Academy of Music, over. Dancing, over. It's Monday. Reality has hit with a thud.

The National Ballet of Washington, D.C.

It's still Monday. My phone suddenly rings. Edith d'Addario, Director of the Joffrey Ballet School, is calling. Her words ring in my ears to this day:

> *"Mr. Joffrey saw you perform this past weekend. He would like to invite you to join the Company, for its upcoming tour to India. He requests that you take Company class at five o'clock this afternoon."*

Dead silence. My tongue feels frozen in my mouth. A voice finally answers. It doesn't even feel like mine.

> *"Please thank Mr. Joffrey and tell him how much I appreciate the invitation, but I'm already committed to Frederic Franklin's National Ballet of Washington."*

Did I just turn down an offer to join The Joffrey Ballet? I guess so. Like Yogi Berra says: "When you come to a fork in the road, take it." Do I ever. And that "fork" is leading me straight to Washington, D.C.

You say you've never heard of the National Ballet of Washington? That's okay. Nobody has, yet. Because Frederic Franklin is still busy giving birth to it. As in, busy swooping up his four original *Tribute* dancers from the Ballet Russe, and throwing us all into his DC-bound suitcase. Andrea Vodehnal, Franklin ("Frank") Yezer, James ("Jimmy") Capp … and me. Eugene Collins replaces Eugene Slavin. Anita Dyche replaces Gail Israel. Now, *Tribute* can perform in our new home. The Capital of the United States of America.

* * *

Mr. Franklin, of course, doesn't stop with us. He has a whole new company to populate. Now he's busy contacting his dear friend, George Balanchine. They go way back, all the way to the early days of the Ballet Russe in the '40s, when Mr. Balanchine was choreographing *Raymonda* for Mr. Franklin and star ballerina Alexandra Danilova.[13] Long before George Balanchine came to be recognized as the most important choreographic influence of the 20th century.

Now, in 1962, Mr. B is offering Mr. Franklin the chance to hire scholarship students from a "special" class at his own School of American Ballet. "SAB" is the official School of his well-established New York City Ballet. The students in this special class are being groomed to join "NYCB," or "City Ballet," if you're a *real* balletomane.

Have no doubt. This class is pretty darn special. So special that it includes the young Suzanne Farrell, soon to be taken into NYCB. Also, soon to become a favorite of Mr. B's.[14]

But, I digress. Let the record show that Mr. Franklin selects five very talented dancers from that class: Evelyn Ebel, Judith Hellman, Lucy Maybury, Patricia Mideke, and Julie Rigler. (All go on to dance wonderful National Ballet roles over the years.)

Thank you, George Balanchine.

The National Ballet's First Season

In the Fall of '62, Frederic Franklin's very own National Ballet of Washington (D.C.) sprouts its wings, with the help of a grant from the Ford Foundation.[15] I sign my contract as a full-fledged soloist. The National Ballet is located at 2801 Connecticut Avenue, N.W.

Opening night will be at Lisner Auditorium on the campus of George Washington University. The date: January 3, 1963.[16] We have four months to mount three ballets.

The evening's "opener": Mr. Franklin's staging of *Swan Lake, Act II*. I'm so excited because, rather than the usual knee-length tulle skirts, every single Swan will wear a short white tutu. Not just Swan Queen Odette. Lucy Maybury and I will perform as the Two Big Swans. Yes, the same *demi-soloist* role I filled in for, in Cleveland. Now, excitingly polished with Mr. Franklin's cloth.

Second on the program, a new ballet, *Early Voyagers*, by famous dancer and choreographer, Valerie Bettis. Performed to a commissioned score by Ned Rorem. And yours truly gets to dance a leading role.

The "closer": Another brand new work, *Homage au Ballet*. Mr. Franklin's choreography to the music of Charles Gounod.[17] And every dancer will be in it. I hear talk that this full-company piece will be our "signature ballet." The staple of our repertoire?

I'm second cast for one of two couples (*demi-soloists*) on either side of the principal couple. Once again, my partner is my good friend, Jimmy Capp. *And* that role comes with its own solo. Beside myself with joy. Because "second cast" is *not* "understudy." An understudy only goes on when a dancer is either injured, ill, or out of town. The second cast has its own scheduled performances, just not the one which *premieres* the ballet.

On a personal note, Mr. Franklin thinks it is about time I start calling him "Freddie." How can I possibly do that? He's my mentor. He suggests Uncle Fred. Done.

* * *

It's our first day of rehearsal. We're all standing at the barre in excited anticipation. Dressed in our obligatory white practice clothes. Uncle Fred energetically strides into the studio to teach Company Class. Above his trademark khakis and canvas belt, a white, short-sleeve, V-neck t-shirt.

The daily company class is a compulsory 90-minute ritual to improve technique, and also warm us up for the hard work ahead. After the obligatory 15-minute break, Uncle Fred re-enters with a breathtakingly beautiful woman wearing a white leotard, white below-the-knee teaching skirt, pink tights, and pink ballet slippers. He introduces Sonja Dragomanovic. Our Ballet Mistress.

I am entranced. A seamless blend of demure Slavic charm and quiet chic. Understated gold earrings offset slightly bouffant red hair, folded behind into an obedient French twist. All this, perched atop the classic ballerina neck. Even her corrections are delivered with compassion and empathy. Sonja defines "classy."

Have I painted this portrait a tad too rosy? Guilty. Sonja is the embodiment of the elegance I one day hope to attain. (Before gaining entry to the ballet school of the Zagreb Opera House in Yugoslavia—now Croatia—eight-year-old Sonja began her training with Mia Slavenska, renowned Ballet Russe de Monte Carlo ballerina. Years later, I take pointe classes with Mme. Slavenska at the Ballet Russe School in my native New York City. Mischievous Universe. You wouldn't have it any other way.)

In those very early National Ballet days, we have to schedule rehearsals around the School classes. That means stopping at 3:30 p.m. and reconvening from 7:00–10:00 p.m. Not an easy feat, pumping the energy level back up at that late hour, not to mention after dinner. I remember one particular evening rehearsal. Just that afternoon, Uncle Fred finished setting *Swan Lake, Act II*. So naturally, at 7:00 p.m. he wants to see a run-through.

Swans and Hunters groan in unison. Not possible. Too tired. Pick something else. At which point, Uncle Fred says, "Okay. We'll just do the Coda and the Epilogue." When we finish that, he asks if Odette would like to run her solo variation. After that, Big Swans. And why not have a go at your "Cow Hop?" (His term of endearment for our ooom-pah-pah waltz.) Would the Cygnets care to go through their little ditty? Just for stamina. Okay, ladies. "How about Rosie O'Grady?" (His term of endearment for the *Corps de Ballet* waltz.)

You're getting the picture, yes? Then the Entrance of the Swans. "Finally," the Hunters entrance which always begins the ballet. The entire ballet, in reverse. Uncle Fred. What an imp.

* * *

I can't believe I have such an important role in *Early Voyagers*. Valerie Bettis, our guest choreographer, and Uncle Fred have an interesting history. Back in 1952, Valerie choreographed *A Streetcar Named Desire* for the recently-formed Slavenska-Franklin Ballet.[18] She cast her friend, "Freddie," as Stanley. He was leery of playing so "against type," but Valerie convinced him she could draw it out of him.

Now, ten years later, history seems to be repeating itself. This time, Valerie is choreographing a dramatic role for me: a "Tomboy," engulfed in adolescent angst, who reluctantly dons a dress (and pointe shoes) to attract a boy she likes. When I confide to Uncle Fred my fear of playing such a dramatic role, he reassures me. "Don't worry. Valerie will draw it out of you."

The tomboy character feels pretty close to home. Boys always just think of me as their "buddy," because I can talk baseball with them. But the tomboy choreography? That's another story. This is not classical ballet vocabulary. I'm rolling around on the stage one minute. Executing a musical theater "Over-The-Leg" jump the next. The floor is bruising every inch of my body. But I'm in heaven.

Valerie is blessed with an infallible "eye." She sees the tiniest choreographic insecurity I might be trying to gloss over. She senses a moment's hesitancy, if I'm struggling to interpret a new choreographic phrase. I learn that term from Valerie. "Choreographic phrase." I also learn, "For the nonce." (For the time being?)

All the tutus for *Swan Lake* and *Homage* will be made onsite. Classical tutus, made especially *pour moi*. That will be a first. *My* last name will be the only name in black marker on the inside grosgrain waistband. Not the last in a string of crossed out names. The "magician" who measures me and sews my tutu-to-be is May Ishimoto. I learn patience from May. The sweetest, calmest, most soft-spoken person I've ever known. May teaches me the Zen-like art of Standing Absolutely Still for a Very Long Time. Otherwise, you're not going to like the way your tutu fits.

* * *

Portraying "The Tomboy" in Valerie Bettis's *Early Voyagers* at the National Ballet of Washington premiere in January 1963 (Photographer unidentified. Courtesy DC Public Library, The People's Archive).

Opening Night, January 3, 1963, is finally upon us.

Swan Lake, Act II: Lucy and I pull off our Big Swans variation without a hitch. I feel like my "nerves of anticipation" help me jump even higher. Judging from the audience applause, the *Pas de Deux* and *The Four Cygnets* must've gone great, too. They brought the house down.

Early Voyagers: It's not conventional ballet choreography, so I honestly can't tell if I pulled it off, or not. But, the audience loves it (13 curtain calls!), and Valerie is pleased. What more can you ask?

Homage au Ballet: This one I can tell you all about, because I'm not in the opening-night cast.

Voyagers bows over. Race to dressing room. Take off makeup. Throw on street clothes. Make it out front before the *Homage* curtain goes up. See the ballet just like the audience does. Strange, but still exciting. I, and the audience, think it's a hit.

We get a favorable review from Jean Battey, Dance Critic of the *Washington Post*. We immediately begin expanding our company repertoire, by working on Uncle Fred's staging of Michel Fokine's famous *Les Sylphides*.

* * *

An out-of-town performance magically pops up when the Philadelphia Academy of Music has a cancellation on its subscription series. Rehearse our opening night program again. Board the bus to Philly. This time, the second cast is dancing *Homage au Ballet*. I'm "on"!

After the "transformation." The satin dress and pointe shoes say it all—the "Tomboy" days are over.

Built in the style of Milan's La Scala, the gorgeous Philadelphia Academy of Music theater opened its doors in 1857.[19] The stage is gently raked (slanted), ensuring that the upstage voices of a milling opera chorus can be heard. It also ensures that a dancer (me) who tends to be too far "back" on her leg when attempting to hold a pose *en pointe*, is now completely and effortlessly "on balance." If only for one night. Some dancers are "natural balancers," and the rest of us are not.

With a little help from that raked stage, I manage to do a triple *pirouette* in my *Homage* solo, which is rare for me. Then, for the big finish, I complete an athletic combination of jumps and turns, and balance on one pointe shoe for what seems like forever. I'm ecstatic. I exit stage right to sustained applause. Is this what "on top of the world" feels like?

After the performance, I'm feeling a bit satisfied with myself. As I'm sitting at my theater place peeling off false eyelashes, there's a knock on my door. It's Valerie-Of-The-All-Seeing-Eye, and this infallible eye doesn't stop at her own choreography.

I wish someone could've taken a picture of my face, when I hear what she has to say: "I thought it looked a little *under* tonight." In Valerie-speak, "under" means flat. Fewer bubbles. Less effervescing. Here I am, basking in the glory of feeling so "on balance" throughout my solo. But Valerie is sensing the lack of electricity she is used to feeling when I perform. Can it be that "on balance" for me feels a little like "complacent" to the audience? When I'm on an un-raked stage and every fiber of my being is straining to hold a balance, am I, perhaps, radiating an exciting aura of urgency? Maybe balancing *isn't* everything.

A few weeks later, I'm walking toward 2801 Connecticut Avenue to take company class, when I hear, "*Ronaldo! Ronaldo!*" That's Uncle Fred's pet name for me.

I see him, running down the sidewalk toward me, holding a newspaper. "*Look! Look!*" He's waving a review of our recent Philadelphia Academy of Music performance. It's from noted dance critic P.W. Manchester, in the March 1963 issue of *Dance News*.

Describing *Homage au Ballet*, Ms. Manchester writes: "All the soloists were excellent, but Roni Mahler stood out by taking the stage as if by divine right, that touch that marks the special ones."

Holy mackerel. This 21-year-old is seeing her name in professional "print" for the first time. Exhilarating and dizzying, all at once. Uncle Fred is thrilled for me. But with a hint of warning in his voice he says, "Enjoy it. The fun is in the getting there." I'll keep this in mind.

Season Two: Enter George Balanchine

It's September of 1963 at the headquarters of the National Ballet of Washington and its School of Ballet. What a memorable season I'm about to have.

Last year's Opening at George Washington University's Lisner Auditorium was (dare we say it out loud?) a hit. The question on everyone's lips now: "What's next?"

Can this ambitious band of youthful dancers keep the excitement going? In which creative direction is Artistic Director Frederic Franklin aiming this time? One sure to raise his dancers to an entirely new level? Yes. Because Mr. Franklin has George Balanchine up his sleeve. Balanchine is giving the National Ballet three of his signature works: *Serenade* (Tchaikovsky), *The Four Temperaments* (Hindemith) and *Pas de Dix* (Glazunov). They will be performed as an All-Balanchine program in February.

And there's more. Mr. B is also lending us his esteemed Ballet Master, Una Kai. During the months of her "residency," and under her expert guidance, we'll learn all that famous choreography.

Una Kai is quite the story. First, she performed with Balanchine's New York City Ballet for twelve years. Then, she's invited by Mr. B to become the Company's Ballet Master, while still performing. She continues as Ballet Master, after her performing career ends.[20]

Una Kai is a virtual encyclopedia of Balanchine choreography. Two nice touches: She asks us to call her "Una." We also learn that nobody who's *anybody* says, "*The Four Temperaments*." It's "Four T's" from that moment on.

But, Ms. Kai is not only staging the three Balanchine works. She's also teaching a lot of Company Classes, which precede every five-hour rehearsal day. That daily, mandatory, 90-minutes of laborious exercises. First holding onto the *barre*. Then, in the "center," holding onto absolutely nothing. Except your spine and your muscles and your tendons and your sinew.

Rudyard Kipling intones in his poem *If*:

> *If you can force your heart and nerve and sinew*
> *To serve your turn long after they are gone,*
> *And so hold on when there is nothing in you*
> *Except the Will which says to them: 'Hold on!'*

Those choice Kipling words *really* do apply to the ballet dancer in Company Class. And in performance, too.

Good thing Ms. Kai is teaching all those Company classes. Her exercises begin to subtly school us in the unique technique and style of Mr. Balanchine's ballets. This is where I'm all of a sudden learning some gems of "Balanchine technique." Some examples....

The slower-paced *glissade* is replaced with the sprightlier *precipité*, transforming a two-part traveling step into only one lightning-quick move.

The *changement* is revisited. I'm used to starting in 5th position and simply jumping in the air to land with the other foot front in 5th. Now, I change the other foot front *on the way up*, before I land. It makes me feel much lighter on my feet.

It's the same for *assemblé* and *petit jeté coupé*. I jump off the standing leg and my legs hit their required position while I'm *still going up* in the jump, instead of on my descent. So much prettier to watch. So much more fun to dance.

I'm euphoric in Una's Company class. Jumping (*allegro*) is my favorite thing, and Mr. Balanchine has made it even more fun than before. When you're doing small jumps, it's called *petit allegro*. But the same "Balanchine rules" apply even when you're jumping as high as you can (*grand allegro*). Whee!

* * *

The months fly by. It's now forty-eight hours before we open. Mr. B arrives at the National Ballet studios at last. This is the day we've been waiting for. He will watch us run through all three ballets. Then, he will coach us and polish every step he sees us dance. After all that time in rehearsal, are we ready? We've learned the choreography. We've learned the formations. We've learned how to "count" the music. Una Kai has masterfully brought us to this moment. We are primed. I hope.

Yes. Mr. Balanchine, himself. Can you imagine? I can't. I'm beside myself with fear, cloaked in excitement. What if he's mean? What if he hates everything I do? What if? What if? Can you tell I'm only weeks away from my 22nd birthday?

Pas de Dix

On the first morning, we begin with *Pas de Dix* (dance for ten). This choreographic gem is an excerpt from the full-length *Raymonda*, with music by Alexander Glazunov. Marius Petipa is credited with the first full-length production of *Raymonda*, which premiered in 1898 in St. Petersburg, Russia.[21]

In Mr. Balanchine's *Pas de Dix*, there is one Principal Couple and four soloist couples. The ballet opens with an *Entrée*, followed by an *Adage*. It ends with a *Coda* and a *Galop*. In between, there are solos for the Male Principal, the Female Principal, and each of the four Female Soloists. (I am one of those.) The four Male Soloists have a group dance.

Our *Pas de Dix* run-through for Mr. B is going along smoothly enough. A different angle of the head, here. An altered *épaulement* (carriage of the shoulders), there. *Entrée*, over. *Adage*, done. Next up, all those solos.

My variation comes first. Mr. B polishes my *Czárdas*-flavored *ports de bras* (arms) and all-around flair.[22] Under his guidance, I learn to be energetic, yet elegant, at the same time. This feels so good!

Moving right along. Second Female Soloist variation passes muster. So does the dance for the four Male Soloists. Now, we arrive at the third Female Soloist variation. This is where I have an epiphany. A "teachable" moment that doesn't even involve *me*, but speaks to the heart of what makes a really great choreographer.

This variation requires hopping on one foot *en pointe*. Lucy Maybury, the lovely dancer performing this variation, is blessed with beautiful hypermobile feet that arch gorgeously when she's standing on pointe.

Alas. That hypermobility is a blessing and a curse. Looks beautiful. Makes hopping *en pointe* really hard, because you have to be able to *not use* your completely arched foot. Some dancers can hop *en pointe* right away. Others can master it after a while. For still others, it's never possible. To her credit, Lucy has worked hours, trying to make these hops happen.

The first two-thirds of Lucy's variation is beautiful. Mr. B seems to be enjoying watching her. Then come The Hops. Lucy tries and fails. She valiantly tries a second time. Before she is halfway through failing again, he's springing to his feet.

The next thing you know, Mr. B is standing beside Lucy with a reassuring look on his face. Before she can begin to say she's sorry, he's already creating an alternate step that accentuates her beautifully arched feet and the strength of her effortless *relevés* (going up and down repeatedly on the same leg).

I can't believe that such a renowned choreographer is willing to accommodate the dancer standing before him at this very moment. His ballet steps may be precious to us, but they're certainly not precious to him. Another choreographer might refuse to make such an accommodation. Not George Balanchine.

Who knows? Maybe when Mr. B originally choreographed those hops *en pointe*, the dancer in front of him could do them in her sleep. His way of showing her off? Now, this dancer has different skills. He simply molds the willing clay of the moment into a different design.

(Years later, I'm invited to be a guest instructor at an out-of-town dance studio. I'm teaching pointe students this same solo in a Variations Class. Their usual teacher is observing. When some of the students have trouble hopping *en pointe*, I begin to teach the alternative choreography.

USUAL TEACHER [shaking her head]: "But that's not Balanchine."

A-c-t-u-a-l-l-y…)

The Four Temperaments

One ballet down; two to go. Now, Mr. B wants to see a run-through of "Four T's." In ancient Greece, Hippocrates alluded to the four humors of temperament: Melancholic, Sanguinic, Phlegmatic, and Choleric. Mr. Balanchine bases his ballet upon these, to the commissioned Paul Hindemith score.[23]

The ballet follows this structure. The initial "theme" is depicted in three short *pas de deux*. The "variations" are then presented in four movements, each led by principal dancers. A male for Melancholic, a male and female for Sanguinic, another male for Phlegmatic, and a female for Choleric (my role).

Following the run-through, Mr. B begins by "cleaning" the three short *pas de deux*. Then it's on to those four "temperaments."

Mr. B watches "Melancholic." When it's over, his first comment, to the Male Lead, will echo in my head forever: *"Don't show me you melancholic, because you lose dog or wife. Show me how limbs melancholic."*

Dog before wife? Mr. B certainly has a sense of humor. I think I get what he's after. *We* are not melancholic. Our *bodies* are. This is the first time I've ever heard of making your body look sad. Not your face. I am, at once, puzzled and intrigued. It's on to "Sanguinic" and "Phlegmatic."

At long last, the final temperament, "Choleric." When Ms. Kai was teaching me this solo, she explained that "choleric" means ill-tempered.

One thing's for sure. It'll be easy for me to avoid "looking" angry. Who has time? The explosive choreography for my entrance is much too fast-paced. It's like learning a whole new language and being far from fluent. And it's absolutely the first time I've been asked to move so angrily.

The steps seem like words spewing forth in a tirade. Spinning. Kicking. Crouching. Hurtling. "Throwing a tantrum" with my body. Defiance and freedom, all rolled into one. Almost therapeutic.

Like being naughty and not getting punished. Oh, the times I "blew my top" (my parents' words) when I was little, and got sent to my room. Now, will I get applause for doing that? Is this the role I was born to dance?

I think back to when I was six years old and the School of American Ballet wouldn't enroll me because I wasn't seven yet. I grew up thinking I'd never dance for Mr. Balanchine. Who knew?

All I can think about is how this was Tanny's role. Tanaquil Le Clercq. Her Dad named her after the Etruscan Queen.[24] ("Tanaquil" means a wise reader of omens.) When I was ten, my mother took me to see NYCB at New York's City Center. And guess what I saw? Tanaquil Le Clercq dancing "Choleric" in *The Four Temperaments*. Those legs. Those long, long legs. That supple, supple body. Tanny. Polio may have you in a wheelchair now, but you're still my inspiration. (Tanaquil tragically contracted polio on the company's European tour in 1956 and remained paralyzed from the waist down until her death in 2000.)

Snap out of it, Roni. Uncle Fred is asking if you're ready. I'm nodding a frantic "yes," as my music begins. I dance my entrance solo. The start of the Finale must wait. First, Mr. B wants to "clean" the solo I just showed him. I'm too excited to be nervous.

I can't put my finger on any one set of instructions, on any one descriptive gesture. But, only five minutes under Mr. Balanchine's barely audible tutelage, and… Are those *my* limbs? Moving like *that*? Then stopping? Then moving again? All around the studio in that peripatetic, start-and-stop way? I don't even feel like myself. It's like I'm someone I've never met. I like this me. She's exciting! And to think, I wasted energy fearing this rehearsal. Does Mr. B have this effect on everyone? A little voice inside me figures he does.

Mind you, not every moment of "Choleric" feels like you've been shot out of a cannon. There's a fleeting, slow-moving *adagio* phrase where things do calm down a bit. But it ends up making me feel a bit "inadequate."

The moment comes early in the Finale. Four men enter from the wings, approaching me from the four corners of the stage. The Melancholic male lead, the male of the Sanguinic lead couple, the Phlegmatic male lead and a fourth male dancer. Four guys and a gal. So much help. What could possibly go wrong?

From the kneeling position ending my solo, I step onto pointe with my leg behind me in a high *arabesque*. I'm immediately held on balance by two of the men, each holding one of my wrists. The third and fourth men are supporting my raised arabesque leg high behind. I'm supposed to rotate one full circle, as the men slowly pass me around while staying in place. Mr. Balanchine wants my *arabesque* leg above my waist. (No problem.) But he also wants *my torso held practically upright.* (Problem.)

"Stop, stop." Mr. B's voice is softly emphatic. The pianist immediately stops playing. My four "cavaliers" stop their "passing around" duties. My full *promenade* circle is nowhere near completion. If a proverbial pin drops now, it'll sound like a thud.

Mr. Balanchine walks slowly toward me. Apparently, he is not pleased with my torso. Apparently, it's not "upright" enough.

In theory, one's *arabesque* emanates from the rotated femur (thigh) in one's hip joint. The body remains upright, while the flexible hip joint allows the *arabesque* leg to barely affect the upright torso.

My anatomy has never been able to achieve that kind of textbook *arabesque*. Sure, I can get my leg up plenty high in the back. Well above my waist. But, my lower back is not all that flexible. My lower (lumbar) spine doesn't really have that lovely gentle curve of a backwards letter "C." Nor does my upper (thoracic) spine have that lovely gentle curve of a front-facing "C." My thoracic spine is kind of straight, like a yardstick. (Over the years, I've been told that my arabesque gives off an air of "authority." Perhaps because it's so busy trying to defy nature? In this case, my own anatomy.) To put it bluntly, my *arabesque* looks like it's coming more from the back of my waist, than emanating from the hip socket. Hence, not a lot of "uprighted-ness" in my torso.

Picture this: The four men have me frozen in this "supported" *arabesque* for what seems like a really long time. All the while, Mr. B is walking his own slow circle around this specimen of a "supported" *arabesque*. And he's also doing a lot of that double-sniffing. I guess he finally surmises that there are no "movable parts" here, that can be cajoled into a different shape.

One last double sniff and he sits down. The music continues. The *promenade* circle is completed, and on we go.

Terrified? Mortified? Traumatized? Pick your adjective. No hole in the floor to swallow me up. Thank goodness School of American Ballet wouldn't take me. My *arabesque* would certainly have become an "issue."

I do manage to crawl back into Mr. B's vision of things. It involves mastering the signature Balanchine Forward Pelvic Thrust. This "look" is a bit easier to achieve. For one thing, it allows for the bending of the front knee to send the hips in a forward direction. Eventually, Mr. B seems pleased.

Turns out, Mr. Balanchine isn't scary after all. He is clear when telling you what he wants, but never makes you feel inadequate. He is patient, if extremely particular. And I love that little quick, double-sniff of his, when he's thinking.

Serenade

A little history. *Serenade*, George Balanchine's first major ballet choreographed in the United States, begins as a student workshop project for his fledgling School of American Ballet. Mr. B wants to teach the students how to be onstage. The resulting piece debuts June 9, 1934, at the White Plains estate of Felix M. Warburg.[25] Mr. Warburg has built a makeshift outdoor stage for the occasion.

(Years later, in 1981, Mr. B is about to rehearse the final *Elegy* section of the ballet. Before it's time to begin, he notices the long, beautiful hair of his three female principals, Karin von Aroldingen, Maria Calegari, and Kyra Nichols. With plenty of time before the start of rehearsal, they haven't yet put their hair up in buns. He unexpectedly asks them not to. To this day, the *Elegy* female principals perform with tresses flowing.[26])

There are three female principal roles in *Serenade*. Believe it or not, I get to dance two out of the three. Since all the *Serenade* women wear the same costume, I can perform both the Russian Girl and the Dark Angel in every performance of *Serenade*. Why? Maybe because the National Ballet has so few principal women? How lucky am I?

But wait a minute. The Russian Girl and the Dark Angel *both* appear in the final *Elegy* section. As a result, I'm never entirely certain which "character" I'm dancing, as I make my many entrances and exits throughout the *Elegy*. Not important.

There's one thing I know for sure. The entire *Elegy* section begins with the Dark Angel (me) walking in that slow, possibly treacherous, diagonal from upstage left to downstage right. But not alone. I walk this endless diagonal while feeling "glued to," and covering the eyes of, "He Who Is Doomed to Never Again Set Eyes on His Beloved."

Standing behind him, my left arm is wrapped around, pressing his stomach to mine. My tucked-under pelvis is gently pushing him slowly forward. The insides of my legs are "guiding" the outsides of his legs. I have no simile to describe how *my* walk feels, with my legs so far apart.

My right hand covers his eyes. My pinkie finger, just far enough away from his face so he can see a sliver of the stage as he "blindly" walks forward. Extra challenge: the male dancer, Stevan Grebel, is about twelve inches taller than I. Reaching up to his eyes ain't easy.

As "The Dark Angel" in George Balanchine's *Serenade* with the National Ballet of Washington, alongside Stevan Grebel and Sonia Arova in Winter 1964 (Photographer unidentified. Courtesy DC Public Library, The People's Archive).

Once at our destination downstage right, I then perform the hair-raising feat of slowly revolving on one leg, while the other is lifted in *arabesque* behind. Why hair-raising? Isn't a ballerina asked to do that a gazillion times? True, but usually she's being turned by her partner's hands on her waist or both wrists. Never before is she turned *only by her partner's hands*, working miracles while they *manually rotate* her standing thigh. His hands are totally hidden from view by the Dark Angel's long, multi-layered, blue tulle skirt. So, it looks like magic. But she must keep her balance while completing one agonizingly-slow full circle. (Hello, latissimus dorsi.) Hair-raising, but exhilarating.

At some point, I start dancing as the Russian Girl, and that's when this story begins. Two things to know: First of all, Mr. B is sixty years old at the time. Secondly, the choreographic sequence in question is over almost before it starts. It's performed within just four counts of music, and then I'm gone as quickly as I arrived.

Remembering that "downstage" is toward the audience and "upstage" is toward the back, I begin standing downstage right. My partner is "upstage," on center.

This is what Mr. B *would like* to see happen: I run diagonally to my partner. When I arrive at his right side, I do a quick pivot to the right, on my right leg in demi-plié. I finish with my back to my partner, who now faces me while leaning forward slightly at his hips, with his flattened back as parallel to the floor as possible. Now wrapping his right arm around my stomach, he quickly hoists me upside down onto his flattened back, while facing the audience again. At the same time, I'm doing a *développé devant* (front) with my right leg sticking straight up toward the ceiling. He is supporting himself almost completely on a bent right leg, with his left toes touching the floor out at the side. Then, in the blink of an eye, I am back on my feet, now on his left side, and running away toward upstage left.

My partner and I try this run-and-lift sequence over and over again in rehearsal, to no avail. Suddenly, Mr. B springs up off the bench and begins sniffing his trademark sniff. The next thing I know, I am lying upside down on *Mr. B's* flattened back with my right leg in *développé*. Because his weight is almost completely on his right leg, I am lying slightly to the right of his spine with my head next to his. Because I've dropped my head all the way back, I'm now seeing everything upside down in the mirror. But, wait. There's more. What happens next is almost unfathomable.

All this time, Mr. B's right arm is still behind him, around my stomach. As I watch upside down in disbelief, I hear him say, "*She so BAH-lahnz* (balanced), *I let go.*" His right arm has left my stomach and is now reaching out to his side.

Then I hear him say, "*I stay one leg.*" Those stabilizing left toes have since departed the floor. His left leg, once outstretched, is now bent at the knee and completely off the ground. The most amazing part is that this picture is seared into my brain *upside down*: Mr. Balanchine, balancing me on his back with both arms outstretched, while standing on one leg. At sixty!

Now, I face a distinct crossroads in this weekend's performances. When it comes time for this topsy-turvy lift, I can look with dread at my partner, knowing peril awaits me if he forgets what Mr. B showed him. Or, I can simply "imagine" that it is Mr. B waiting for me every time, at center stage. Not my less-than-confident partner. Never again will I fear this lift.

For years to come, my one-of-a-kind, personal recollection piques the interest of the next generation of Mr. B's disciples.

In 2015, Sandra Jennings, a former New York City Ballet dancer, turned *répétiteur* (rehearsal master) for the Balanchine Trust, is in Las Vegas, setting *Serenade* on the Nevada Ballet. When I go to the performance, the lift is not there. I'm talking to Sandy backstage after the show:

ME: "Sandy, when I did that lift, who was I? The Russian Girl or the Dark Angel?"
SANDY: "Russian."
ME: "So, the lift's been changed?"

Imagine Mr. Balanchine's flat back instead of that desk ... and you've got the picture!

When Sandy questions *my* question, I tell her my story. Sandy says she's going to try to put it back the way it was.

Then, at Kansas State University, I'm presenting the annual Roni Mahler Award to Professor Grace Hwang for her unflagging promotion of K-State Dance. Honoring Grace's love of all things Balanchine, I add a special flourish when recounting that unforgettable lift, with the help of the desk onstage next to my lectern. At the appropriate moment, I lie down on the desk on my back, my arms outstretched and my straight right leg extended upward at 90-degrees. Oh, and I'm looking *upside down* at the audience, with my head hanging over the front edge. When I continue talking from that position, Grace's award ceremony enters the ranks of the unforgettable.

* * *

What's Mr. Balanchine like outside the studio? During his whirlwind stay in Washington, D.C., I actually get to attend a small dinner party with him.

Rehearsal has just ended on Thursday, and Uncle Fred invites Una Kai, Mr. B, and me to dinner at his place. Uncle Fred is a great cook. Mr. Balanchine is a great cook. Turns out, Una Kai is also a great cook. I don't cook, but I'm a good listener.

As you can imagine, food is a big topic of conversation. Dish after dish is being discussed in remarkable detail. Suddenly, Mr. B pops up with this gem: *"Before begin cook, always rub hands fifteen minutes lemon juice. Teach women in Company cook. More interesting than men."*

I never learn to cook.

The Camera Click

He's 19. I'm 21. I'm a budding ballerina with Frederic Franklin's National Ballet of Washington, D.C. He is a bright young photographer with *The Washington Star*. His name is Mike Mitchell.

Mike Mitchell is assigned to take the pictures for "The Article." The article that's going to be in the entertainment section of *The Star's* Sunday edition. It might even be on its front page. The reader will get the inside scoop on the years of struggle it takes to become a budding ballerina with the National Ballet of Washington. That's why Mike is following me everywhere. Documenting my day, as it were.

This "following me everywhere" situation does have its perks. The National Ballet is performing at the White House on February 10, 1964. The invitation had come from First Lady Jackie Kennedy back in early '63. By the time our February '64 date rolls around, after JFK's assassination the previous November, everything is very, very, very bittersweet. With the Kennedys gone, it's 16-year-old Lucy Baines Johnson who welcomes us to the East Room for our performance. Lucy is amazing. I can't believe how poised and gracious she is. And only 16. That's five years younger than I am.

So, what's it like, dancing at the White House? Knowing you're living a once-in-your-lifetime experience? Everything about this day is entirely unique.

Because we won't have all that much room to dance, Mr. Franklin has wisely chosen to present only the famous *Pas de Deux* from *Swan Lake, Act II*. Its choreography moves at a slow pace and can be performed in a relatively small space. Musically, it's a poignant *adagio* melody.

So, let's revisit the story of *Swan Lake*. Prince Siegfried's Mom gives him a crossbow for his 21st birthday. He and his buddies are wandering the forest, looking for something to shoot. Aiming his crossbow at an unusually beautiful Swan, Siegfried suddenly realizes he can't pierce the heart of such an exquisite creature.

Good thing. Turns out, Swan Queen Odette just looks like a swan on the outside. On the inside, she's this gorgeous maiden who has been turned into a swan by Von Rothbart, the evil man she refuses to marry.

For Prince Siegfried, it's love at first sight. But the poor Swan Queen Odette, danced by Andrea Vodehnal, is understandably scared to death. She's just constantly trying to get away from this much-too-ardent stranger.

There's a famous part of the *Pas de Deux*, which takes place exactly on center stage. Prince Siegfried has to quickly hoist Odette over his head, two times in a row, in her beautiful *arabesque*, first right and then left. Poor Odette doesn't yet trust this guy, so naturally, she's trying to "fly away" in these airborne arabesques.

As the first lift is attempted, I'm sure Andrea's startled shriek can be heard in the hallway. There she is, airborne, curled up in a ball with her head between her knees. That's because she and that gorgeous East Room crystal chandelier just had a close encounter. Uncle Fred to the rescue. He simply restages those "lifts" just to the *right* of center stage.

On a five-minute break, I saunter, ever-so-casually, over to one of those velvet-draped windows to take a peek outside. I need to print in my brain forever the view from *inside* the East Room. It's the dead of winter. No garden. No flowers. That's okay. Still quite the view. I hear a click behind me and know that Mike has memorialized this moment.

Ah, that little click I've had to train myself to ignore. That's the funny thing. In real life, a tiny noise close by might make you stop and turn around. But when somebody is "documenting your day" (I love the sound of that), you have to learn to ignore the little camera click. Otherwise, you ruin the moment. That's why, in the beginning of our experience together, the six words I hear most from Mike are, "Just keep going. Just keep going."

Swan Lake "spacing" rehearsal, done. It's the actual performance. I'm standing in my vertical line of Swans during the *Pas de Deux*, when I hear one camera click almost in my ear. I'm such a good girl. I don't blink an eye. Not easy.

I'm also noticing that this "performance" has less "zing" for me. It almost feels like just another run-through rehearsal. Maybe because "no Jackie?" Plus, I'm still grieving.

When the article comes out, I can see that Mike has memorialized that moment in *Swan Lake*.[27] There I am, from the waist up, clear as a bell. The chandelier has been relegated to a dramatic, albeit blurry, image in the background.

Photo of dancing "onstage" in the East Room. Photo of me peeking out its velvet-draped window. These could qualify as best ever. Agreed? Not even close. Hard to believe that something else tops the East Room of the White House.

Well, believe it. But this photo doesn't make it into the article.

You see, while I was soaking up George Balanchine's choreographic greatness and desperately trying to make those small-but-essential adjustments that suddenly make every move cry out, "Now, *that's* Balanchine!," Mike had been clicking away the whole time. Throughout my days in the studio with Mr. B, for hours on end. Still clicking away as he readied us to present our brand new, polished-to-a-shine, Balanchine Program. In all the excitement, I might've forgotten these photos were ever taken. Until…

Fast forward to 2003. I'm now the Artistic Associate for Ballet San Jose. One day, our Stage Manager, Craig Margolis, approaches me on a ten-minute rehearsal break. He tells me a guy called the office today, says he knows me from the past (hmm…), and needs to send me something? Says he had no clue where I was until thumbing through an old *Dance Magazine* and stumbling upon a tiny picture of me captioned, "…now with Ballet San Jose." I okay giving this guy the ballet company's address.

Sure enough, about one week later, Craig brings me my "something." I gingerly open the large manila envelope. And nearly burst into tears.

Staring back at me is a black & white photograph of Mr. Balanchine rehearsing me in "Choleric" from *The Four Temperaments*, 39 years ago.

I'm aghast. Craig is about to fall over. I have never even seen this rehearsal photo, captured so expressively by that young Mike Mitchell I'm hearing from now. This one never made it into the article in *The Star*.

Here's the interesting part. Mr. Balanchine is standing to my right. In this

"Mr. B" coaching me in the role of "Choleric" in his ballet *The Four Temperaments* at the National Ballet in February of 1964 (Photo by Mike Mitchell).

blink-of-an-eye moment, you don't see him facing left, watching me in real life. That's what would usually happen, yes? Instead, Mr. B is gazing intently into the studio mirror in front of him. Checking to see if I have that "Balanchine look." His intent gaze is fixed upon me *in the mirror.* You get why Mike's photograph captures that wonderfully pensive, almost portrait-like, expression on Mr. Balanchine's face. Mr. B is assessing my reflection.

I, on the other hand, am *not* looking at myself in the mirror. Instead, my eyes are cast gently downward. I clearly remember that moment. I'm determined to "feel" this decidedly different posture Mr. B has placed me in. I'm trying to "print it in." Exactly how it "feels." No mirror on stage, Roni. You'll have to "feel" that you're doing it right. Standing behind me, his left arm is wrapped around the top of my rib cage to steady me. His right hand, on my lower back, is urging my hips diagonally forward.

Mr. B is trying to get these hips to understand a position that is completely alien to me. That Famous Balanchine Forward Pelvic Thrust. Gently coaxing. Ever-so-gently coaxing. Trying to mold my body into that specific shape he's determined to achieve.

In this instant, I'm his proverbial unmolded clay. There's something so reassuring about that. Knowing that I'm not in charge here. For one exhilarating moment, no pressure. Just compliance. Acquiescence.[28]

When my heart stops racing, I finally look at the enclosed note. It reads, "Please accept [this picture] as a gift of gratitude for exemplifying such passion for and commitment to your art. You were probably the first person I'd ever met from whom I learned that when you know you've got it inside you to do something, nothing can stop you if you commit to the work it takes to overcome whatever obstacles are in the way."

The indelible photo hangs on both of our walls to this day.

National Ballet on Tour

Eventually, the National Ballet goes on tour. So, it's back on the bus for me. But, after two years with the Ballet Russe de Monte Carlo, I'm no longer a rookie. You're talking to a veteran now. Once again, so many one-night stands. So many cities. So many theaters. They can all seem to blur together, but some manage to stand out.

* * *

One such city is Melbourne, Florida, because of its theater. A brand-new performing arts facility. A source, no doubt, of tremendous civic pride. It's the early 60s. Performing Arts venues with the word "civic" in their titles, are springing up everywhere. The National Ballet's one-night appearance in Melbourne is in just such a place. This spanking-new theater is playing host to its first performance *ever.* The National Ballet is feeling lucky to be the "opening act."

Or, are we? I enter the bright, new, and extremely clean dressing room. I drop my theater case somewhere on the floor, because it's really heavy. I plop my purse and tote bag on my dressing table, because they're really heavy. I pull out my dressing table chair, so I can flop down and take a load off.

Not so fast. Apparently, my chair isn't "my" chair. It's "our" chair. Unfathomably true. The dressing room chair situation in this cutting edge theater is actually a "twofer." I'm not kidding. Two uniquely-designed chairs forever connected by a piece of wood underneath. That's right. When I push back to go to the bathroom, my seatmate's lipstick goes all over her face.

But, wait. There's more. Fast forward to the "onstage" call. The program is opening with *Les Sylphides*. Three fully-costumed Sylphs are primed and ready to go to the stage. Once again, not so fast. None of us can manage to open the door. Repeated top-of-the-lungs yells of "help" finally summon the cavalry. No. There's no "lock" button on this door, mistakenly pressed. This is your plain old generic stuck door.

Five minutes, two stagehands, and one platitude later ("The show must go on," right?), this door is finally pried open. Three somewhat-rattled Sylphs finally make it to the stage. The delayed curtain finally gets to go up. And, yes. The show (finally) gets to go on.

* * *

Denton, Texas. What a wonderful performance. And in front of such an appreciative audience. The local Ladies' Auxiliary is entertaining us with late-night, picnic style, fried chicken suppers. We're all guests in one of their gracious homes. Including dancer, James Thurston, who happens to be Black. Just one big happy family, eating and laughing until almost two o'clock in the morning.

Don't look so surprised. The curtain of our 8:30 show doesn't come down until close to 11:00. We dancers are exhausted. But, happy. Off comes the makeup. A quick shower. Be sure to grab the dirty performance tights you have to wash tonight. Don't forget the dirty practice clothes that also need washing.

It's close to midnight when we're piling onto the Company bus. Somebody's going to feed us. Yay. Nothing's open this late. Much better than that flip-top can or two of fruit salad which is "supper" on other nights. Who's worried about the lateness of the hour tonight? Not me.

In fact, my roommate, Helen Heineman, and I don't plop down on our motel beds until 2:00 a.m. I lie on my back with both legs up in the air, until all the blood drains. Anticipating that nice "buzz" to them when I quickly stand up again.

Then it's a quick letter to Mom. This, so she doesn't have you paged in the theater again. Letter finished. Wow. It's four o'clock already. Did I forget to tell you that this is another one of those "illegal" 7:00 a.m. bus departures? Tomorrow's 2:00 p.m. matinee is so far away that the driver will need the extra hour to get us there on time. Yes, we voted to "waive" the no-departure-before-8:00-a.m. regulation and start at that ungodly hour. What's a girl to do?

So everything's backed up an hour. I now have to be at breakfast at 6:00 instead of 7:00, according to the trusty system I developed on that first Ballet Russe tour.

"Well," I declare out loud, "I'm not going to sleep for two hours. I'll just stay up and get to six o'clock breakfast. Easy-peasy." I tell Helen that I'm going for a walk in the cool night air. It will feel good on my face.

I'm enjoying my 4:00 a.m. Denton, Texas, stroll, until I begin to feel like I'm being followed. By a patrol car, no less. I turn the corner. It turns the corner. I stop. It stops. I'm scared to death.

The cop peppers me with questions. Everything I answer sounds fishy:

1. "Where do you live?" I'm staying at the motel.
2. "Why are you in Denton?" I'm a dancer and we had a show.
3. "Can I see your identification?" (Thank goodness I have my license.)

Then, the words that still make me shudder today: "What's a nice little white girl like you doin' out on the streets like that at night?"

In that instance, I know that if my skin was a different color, if I was James, I'd be in jail. That feeling of guilt because I'm white. Quite an education for this sheltered child of the liberal Northeast.

(In the '70s, I am invited to perform as a guest artist in New Orleans. The elderly matron in charge of contracts says I can, of course, appear with a partner of my own choosing. The next week, I telephone to tell her how thrilled I am that Paul Russell, Principal Dancer of Dance Theater of Harlem, is available to perform with me. Her response: "Oh, honey. Why would a nice little white girl like you want to dance with that colored boy?" I don't sign the contract.)

* * *

A real feather in the cap of any young ballet company is a chance to perform at the storied Brooklyn Academy of Music. Which is, by the way, considered "performing in New York City." Even if it's not Manhattan.

So, a New York performance. The National Ballet has definitely "arrived." Ah, yes. But only to find a stage that is pretty slippery. Fear not. The stagehands will eventually sprinkle Ajax, then spray Coca-Cola. After which, the stage will be decidedly more "danceable." That is, except for the "apron." The apron extends the stage downstage, closer to the orchestra pit. It's the part where the edge of the stage is gently curved. Like all aprons, this one lies *in front of* the closed curtain.

Back to those stagehands. They "doctor" the floor at half-hour, right after closing that curtain. Your guess is correct. Stage, manageable. Apron, very slippery. We open with *Les Sylphides*. The Brooklyn Academy stage is not that deep. During the Finale, the entire cast is eventually onstage all at once. Only the apron is left "dancer-free."

And that's where this Waltz Girl has to do her jumping *temps levé arabesque/pas couru/saut de chat* entrance. A fancy way of saying a hop, a run, and a leap. This sequence repeats to the right, then the left, then the right again. My *temps levé* (hop) on my right is fine. My *failli* (slide across in front) on my left, into parallel *pas couru en avant* (running forward on pointe), is also fine. It's that next *failli* on my left, to "plant" for the carefree *saut de chat* (leap) … Whooooosh.

Down I go. Nothing hurt. Bounce right up into a seamless *contretemps* (quick change of direction). And, without missing a beat, I repeat the same sequence left and right again. To thunderous applause, merely because I got up after I fell. It's a fact: if you fall on stage and continue to dance, audiences will gasp first and then clap a lot.

This evening's performance is especially memorable because my dad is in the audience. He's told my mom that he can stay "for three cigars." (My father's "clock" is often dictated by how many cigars are in his inner jacket pocket.) Dad can definitely be described as "uninitiated," when it comes to ballet. I've always felt that the opinion of the "uninitiated" is the one that means the most. A sampling of our post-performance conversation:

> ME: "How bad did my fall look?"
> DAD: "Best fadeaway slide into second [base] I ever saw."
> ME: "Did you like Mr. Franklin's ballet, *Tribute*?"
> DAD: "Yes. There was a part where you and the taller girl met in the center. You both got there at the same time, but her feet were moving faster."

"Out of the mouths of babes…." The quintessential traveling *bourrée* correction, that the feet should move as quickly as possible, delivered by my "uninitiated" Dad. Noted for next show.

* * *

One of the first lessons I learn, after a season is finally over, is this: You can't stay in tip-top shape forever. Your body has spent time "pushing" on your behalf, even when there was very little in the tank. Now it's time for your faithful body to take it all back.

You sleep a lot for four days. You take a week or two off. You go back to class. Here's the kicker. Okay. So, two to three classes a day, six days a week, and you're finally back in "class shape." But not "rehearsal shape." When you go back to rehearsing three to four hours in a row, your "rehearsal legs" are nowhere to be found. "Rehearsal legs?" Yes, the legs that allow you to stay standing for four straight hours before a break. You see, ballet classes are never more than an hour and a half long. There's an hour between most classes, thirty minutes between some. On the other hand, rehearsal runs straight through, with maybe a 5–10 minute break tops.

What does "no rehearsal legs" feel like? For me, it's aching pains in the bottoms of both heels that kick in during the third consecutive hour. They last about a week. Let's say this is a four-week rehearsal period. What else do I feel during, let's say, the first two weeks of rehearsal? Something I refer to as the "first bruising." It comes from repeating new choreography, or even familiar choreography, over and over and over again. Whether learning or reacquainting. Doesn't matter. That first bruising is giving me significant discomfort.

Just as it subsides, the daily routine is amped up to accommodate complete run-throughs of all the ballets. Hello, "second bruising." This luckily coincides with the end of rehearsals. I now feel like "woven steel." So strong that you can poke me at 3:00 a.m., demand a passage of choreography, and I can deliver. Easy peasy.

This woven steel is my constant companion throughout, let's say, the rest of the season. When that is over, hello, fickle body. No sooner do you take time off to give your body back it's due, than you're back to square one. Out of shape again. I learn to welcome out-of-shape as the friend it is. Maybe a really *good* friend, at that. After all, if you stay in shape constantly, you'll burn-out for sure.

Mitch Miller and Me

When folks hear the name Bob McGrath, who can blame them for thinking *Sesame Street*? After all, he was a cast member for almost fifty years. But I don't think

Sesame Street. When I think of Bob McGrath, I think *Sing Along with Mitch*. What on earth is *Sing Along with Mitch*? It was an NBC weekly television show that ran from 1961 to 1964.[29]

Okay, but what does Bob McGrath have to do with me? Well, I dance on *Sing Along with Mitch* three times, between August '63 and February '64. I don't know if he remembers me, but I can never forget him. To this very nervous 21-year-old, he feels like mentor and guardian angel, rolled into one.

As a seasoned, professional ballet dancer, what do I have to be nervous about? Well, it's like the title of that song, "Stranger in a Strange Land." In the ballet world, you do everything only once. Starting from the beginning and finishing at the end. In the land of Taped Television, things can happen out of sequence. At the ballet, the audience stays put. In Taped TV Land, you have to watch for the little red light so you know which way to face. This camera, here. That camera, there. A quiet, and timely, hint from Bob always seems to smooth the way.[30]

When I arrive to do my first show in August of '63, NBC has just switched *Sing Along with Mitch* from black-and-white to color. Associate Producer and Choreographer James "Jimmy" Starbuck is brimming with ideas. The early '50s found Jimmy producing segments for Sid Caesar and Imogene Coca's *Your Show of Shows*. In 1961, he starts doing the same for *Sing Along with Mitch*.[31] Then, two years later, all in color.

Wait, Jimmy Starbuck? Yes, the same Jimmy Starbuck who was among the group of illustrious former Ballet Russe dancers who adjudicated my scholarship audition when I was 14. Later on, in 1961, Jimmy apparently remembers me when he's invited to choreograph a new ballet for the Ballet Russe. *The Comedians* is a delightfully humorous romp to the Dmitry Kabalevsky score of the same name and goes on to become a real audience-pleaser.[32] (Not surprising. Think of the comic genius of Jimmy's Imogene Coca ballet spoofs.)

By the time 1963's color opportunity rolls around, Jimmy wants to go beyond the ballet-as-comedy days of Imogene Coca. He wants to bring *bona fide* classical ballet into every living room in America. And sell it as "American as apple pie." No "sylph" or "waif" will do here. This calls for a rosy-cheeked ballerina who looks like your girl next door. Guess who pops into Jimmy's head? And, doubly-lucky me. My annual seven-month contract with the National Ballet doesn't start for another four weeks.

* * *

Jimmy's vignette casts me as a ballerina who has just finished rehearsing. Draped in a shawl to keep myself warm, I hear beautiful music. I stop to enjoy watching teenage twin sisters, who are rehearsing the "Arensky Waltz" (from his *Suites for Two Pianos*). I'm hopelessly engrossed. Suddenly, the power of the music compels me to throw off that shawl in true Hollywood style. I burst into swirling choreography until the music ends. The twins and I hear, "It's a wrap," just like in the movies.

Soon, it's time to view the "rushes." We all huddle in front of the control-room monitor. I'm not at all prepared for what comes next. Just your usual end-of-day stuff for everyone else. For me, a painful reckoning. A first time for everything. Ouch. Is that what I look like when I'm dancing? They pay me to do this? Well, nobody's fired me yet. Audiences haven't exactly been asking for their money back. Hard to keep smiling, while everyone is ooh-ing and ahh-ing and loving it. (Dancers I'm telling this story to today can't imagine a world where they're not seeing themselves dancing, constantly. And, correcting themselves.)

Not all rushes are painful. At the end of every show, everyone gets to "sing along" with the Mitch Miller Singers. There's a hymn and a final popular song. To this day, I know the words to "He Walks with Me." But, wait. There's more.

During this singalong, the camera pans around for headshots of the featured performers. You heard right. I get a close up of me, singing! (Ten years later, who gets the last laugh now, you Junior High Talent Show judges?) But, wait. There's even more than that. Every end-of-show singalong also features a mystery "cameo" showbiz personality, who wasn't in the show. Someone whose face is so familiar, they need no introduction. This time, it's vaudeville star and Broadway singer Pearl Bailey, as we're all singing "Bill Bailey, Won't You Please Come Home." Forget those dumb rushes. This is fun.

* * *

I guess Jimmy's classical ballet experiment was a success. I am hired back for two more shows. In December 1963, I'm *pirouetting* to Nat King Cole's mellifluous tones urging me to "Dance, Ballerina, Dance."

For this episode, Jimmy portrays a ballet master, putting me through my paces. First, the barre exercises. Then, the center combinations. The fun comes when I have to spin forward in a straight line toward the camera. This calls for what is known in ballet as *chaînés pirouettes,* a series of consecutive turns. A "chain" of turns, if you will. Then we break. I change into a tutu. (Thank you, National Ballet.) Now, dressed as a ballerina performing onstage, I duplicate the same *chaînés pirouettes,* once again spinning directly toward the camera.

This time, I go on to complete the rest of the choreography and take my bow. When we view the rushes, we are looking at two identical segments: one in practice clothes, and the other in a tutu. I have to wait until the show airs to see the impact of the amazing edit. The camera catches me starting to spin forward in the practice clothes. Then, presto! I'm suddenly spinning the rest of the way in that tutu. Impressive. All in all, a pretty special gig for this 21-year-old fledgling ballerina.

If changing costumes while spinning toward the camera isn't enough magic for you, I give you my show with Leslie Uggams. At the ripe old age of twenty, Leslie is a regular on *Sing Along with Mitch*. Most likely because she's just one year younger than me, I am completely mesmerized by her. Her wonderful singing voice is as expressive as her face. And her smile actually lights up the room. (A former child actress, Leslie is just four years away from the starring role of Georgina in the Broadway musical, *Hallelujah, Baby!*[33])

When I run into scheduling shenanigans, it's because of Leslie's schedule. Currently appearing in two shows nightly at the iconic Rainbow Room (Rockefeller Center, 65th floor), she is burning the candle at both ends. Finishing her second show of the evening close to midnight. Then taping her songs for the TV show the next morning.

On the morning in question, trouper that she is, Leslie shows up for her scheduled taping. Spur of the moment, Mitch decides to give her vocal cords a rest. She will not have to sing until the afternoon. Suddenly, yours truly has ten minutes' notice to "shoot my number" … at nine o'clock in the morning.

Here's the thing. In the ballet world, you learn to calculate how much time you have before you "go on." If you're "on" as the curtain goes up, it's easy. The stage manager calls half-hour, fifteen, ten, on stage (at the five), places (at the two), curtain up. For the rest of us, the ongoing choreography tells you how much time you have, to get ready to be at your peak.

When you're taping, though, anything goes. Once, they filmed the end of my "number" before I even danced it. Now, out of the blue, I've just been given my "ten-minute call." Yikes. I warm up as quickly as possible, and keep my leg warmers on until the last minute. Mitch glances over and quips, "What are those? Your 'one-ones'?" They're now my "one-ones," forever more.

My second show is memorable for another reason. The most-unforgettable-Sing Along-mystery-cameo-guest, ever. And that would be … piano-conductor-composer Skitch Henderson. Conductor of NBC's *The Tonight Show*. Why is Skitch so unforgettable? Allow me to set the scene.

It is Saturday. A light snow is falling in Brooklyn, the site of the famous NBC taping studios. I finished all my dancing this morning. The not-to-be-missed Sing Along is being taped in the afternoon. Thing is, I am cast to dance the Act III "Dawn" solo in the evening performance of *Coppélia*. Back in Washington, D.C. With the National Ballet. I may not exactly be burning the candle at both ends, but it sure feels like playing with matches.

I already know it's going to be a tight squeeze. Naturally, I've calculated how much time I'll need to be peak-performance ready for my Act III solo, from the moment I am seated at my theater place, until I *piqué arabesque* onto the stage.

Tonight, my plan will be significantly altered. Makeup, hair, headpiece, pointe shoes, as usual. But tonight I will put on my costume immediately. Yes, before warming up backstage, so I can *keep* warming up until the last possible moment. This required Special Dispensation from Wardrobe Mistress May Ishimoto. Rules specify that costumes are donned as close to going onstage as possible. (And out-of-costume must occur as soon as possible after curtain down.)

But back in Brooklyn, the snow is now falling a little heavier. I make a tragic (albeit, necessary) decision. I tell Mitch I'll have to skip the Sing Along because I have to find a taxi to LaGuardia to make my flight.

That's when I hear, "No, no, no, no, no. Take my limousine. I'll find a cab." Ladies and Gentlemen, I give you my savior, Skitch Henderson. Immediately after the taping, Skitch personally introduces me to his driver, puts me in his limo, and changes the destination to LaGuardia.

Off I go, with necks craning at every red light. (Which celebrity is sitting inside?) On-time take off. On-time landing. Readily available cab to the theater. "Peak performance" calculations spot on. Lots of moving parts. A Universe smiling down. Mission accomplished.

* * *

My last Mitch Miller show is unforgettable for a bunch of reasons. First, I get scrolling screen credit at the end of the show. I'm also mentioned in the *TV Guide*, with a Guest Artist listing alongside Leslie Uggams. (Knock me over with a feather.)

The great thing about working with Jimmy Starbuck is the way he dreams up these amazing ideas. This time I'm a Gypsy Dancer, performing to the musical stylings of the famous 101 Strings orchestra, named for their roster of 100+ musicians. And what else would Jimmy have them playing? "Golden Earrings," an all-time favorite. That melody, so haunting. Their rendition, so poignant. It makes it easy to pull off the heart-wrenching choreography. This time, Jimmy's imagination has me dancing and weaving in and among all those wonderful (seated) musicians. Amongst those 101 players, I can almost feel the music's vibrations inside me. Being so close to their instruments is transformative for me. I wonder if they feel the same?

I even come away with a remarkable souvenir. The show's hairdresser finds a 24-inch, real-hair "fall" (hair piece) that matches my color exactly. Ah. The illusion of long, *non-frizzy* hair. Like any other self-respecting Gypsy, yes?

After "the wrap," the hairdresser tells me this fall is mine to keep. This is not just a gift. This is a lifesaver. I've been blessed (cursed?) with naturally curly hair. Because I'm a hopeless scalp-sweater, after every performance I look like someone plugged me into a light socket. Not anymore. Now I look like a real ballerina with long, smooth, flowing tresses.

My February '64 show is my last. As a matter of fact, 1964 is the last year for any new *Sing Along with Mitch* shows. Two years of reruns follow. It is also the year the Beatles cross the Atlantic. The music scene is never the same.

I began this story with Bob McGrath, so he gets my closing thought. Of course, Bob turns out to be great with kids on *Sesame Street*. He was great with this kid, so many years ago.

Albert and Me

I often ask my ballet students which famous person said, "Imagination is more important than knowledge." The answer I often get is "Walt Disney." Thoughtful response. Incorrect. Albert Einstein is the speaker of those indelible words. Their glow has defined my life for many, many years. For as long as I can remember, my imagination has been my constant companion. Everybody has one, even if they're not readily in touch with it.

I'm in touch with mine, thank goodness. It's the Spring of 1964. I'm 22, and have been dealing with right-ankle pain. Apparently, an inflamed cyst on a nearby tendon. A wonderful "dancers's doctor" has been keeping it under control with ultrasound treatments. However my authoritarian father ("osteopaths aren't real doctors") drags me to the orthopedic surgeon who's just given him a spinal fusion.

Seeing this orthopedic surgeon? Like using plastic surgery to remove a mosquito bite. Before I know it, three vials of serum are being emptied into my poor captive cyst. Right ankle getting puffier and puffier with each vial. Result: one immovable ankle. The doctor says to "stay off your feet for a week or two." When I finally try to walk again, it's like my Achilles is stuck in its own sheath. It can't slide up. It can't slide down. It is just stuck. How long is this going to last?

When I return to Washington in the Fall for the '64-'65 season, it's time to come clean to Uncle Fred. His optimism is encouraging. We have two months before we open. Just rehearse everything carefully, without dancing "full-out." It might improve.

On October 10 (who can forget?), Uncle Fred asks the dreaded question. My dreaded answer escapes my lips.

    Me: "You'd better replace me."
    Uncle Fred: "It happens. This, too, shall pass."

What a difference eighteen months can make. Back in March of 1963, I was flying high on the wings of my first review ever. Now, in October of 1964, I'm missing the entire Fall Season. Hopelessly adrift in The Sea of Will-I-Ever-Dance-Again?

Suddenly, a life preserver from an unexpected source. Mrs. Riddell. Jean Riddell, granddaughter of the founder of PET Evaporated Milk, is the founding President and Treasurer of the National Ballet.[34] Now on October 10, this hopelessly-adrift and injured puppy somehow finds herself in Mrs. Riddell's office. In tears.

Mrs. Riddell just lets me cry and cry. And then she tells me about a toy she had as a little girl. With a weighted bottom. Righting itself whenever she tried to tip it over. I name her childhood toy "Up-Up." There is Jean Riddell explaining to me how she decided to be just like her toy. Urging me to believe in Up-Up, now.

Up-Up and I hatch a plan. My dad's "civilian" doctor immobilized me. I need a "sports" doctor who can relate to ballet's athletic intensity. Hallelujah! I get an appointment with the orthopedic surgeon of the (then) Washington Redskins.

Dr. Eugene Lipow's plan of action is brilliant. Fifteen minutes, three times a week. Exhaust the calf with electric-current "cramping" therapy. The calf goes limp from "exhaustion," eventually relaxing its grip on my "frozen" Achilles. But *can* my Achilles then free itself from those meddlesome adhesions sticking it to its own sheath?

With Mrs. Riddell's help, I telephone Violette Verdy, New York City Ballet's inimitable, French-born ballerina. According to the ballet world grapevine, Violette suffered a similar injury fourteen months earlier. Delighted to hear from me, Violette immediately makes an appointment for me with her doctor in New York City. When I consult with her Orthopedic surgeon, William Hamilton, he concurs with Dr. Lipow's proposed treatment. Thank you, Violette. A much-relieved Roni flies back to Washington.

I finally see the source of Dr. Lipow's "passive exercise" for my calf. Let's just call it the "cramping machine." It's two electrode pads strategically taped to my right calf. And this process is far from passive. His nurse keeps turning up the knobs when she thinks I can take more cramping.

Here's where Albert Einstein saves me. I come up with a game. I'm being interviewed on live television from the waist up. Under the table, the cramping machine is sizzling away. No grimacing. No wincing. Calm voice. Calm face. All, while answering questions. "Yes, I have a dog. No, she doesn't like asparagus."

Strangely enough, it helps. Imagination wins. All hail Albert Einstein.

Who hasn't seen Albert Einstein's iconic photograph, sticking out his tongue? What better way to "honor my friend!"

* * *

Bottom Line: Although successful, the road to recovery is not smooth. No Fall Season for me. But out of the blue, something good. A chance to understudy the Female Lead in *Othello,* a new dramatic ballet from choreographer Juan Corelli. *From the waist up.* No steps. Just acting.

On Mr. Corelli's last day, my run-through is a chance to move around the studio and tell the story with my arms, upper body, head. What a gift. A transporting experience. Straight to Cloud Nine. The visit is short-lived.

Back home, my Achilles is purple and throbbing so badly that I can almost hear it. Maybe all that running around was too much? A long, painful night. Lying on my bed, my feet as perpendicular as possible up on the wall.

It's morning. Assessment time. Achilles: now, a faint pink. Throbbing: now MIA. Adhesions: who knows? Tendon: shakily, but freely, sliding up and down in its sheath again. Recipe: months of electric-current therapy. One risky run-through. Stir vigorously until throbbing and purple. Let stand overnight. Success. And I don't even cook.

I'll spare you the rehab. Eventually, everything seems to be working just fine. Except that the pointe shoe ribbons that cross around my Achilles are killing me. *Serenade* will be the first ballet I dance during our Winter Season, and rehearsing it is torture. So much running. Pointe shoe ribbons digging deeper and deeper into that poor Achilles tendon.

I call Violette in tears. She had the same problem when returning from her Achilles injury. She's figured out how to cushion the Achilles from those "digging" ribbons. She sews an elastic strip insert into each pointe shoe ribbon, strategically measured to cover the Achilles on the first go-round. In what is surely an hour-long phone conversation, Violette patiently explains every detail of the measuring and sewing process. *Et voilà*. Problem solved.

A little Einstein "insurance?" I reimagine my Achilles tendon as One Big Nostril that just keeps breathing and breathing as I'm running and running. Dear Albert Einstein: If I were wearing a cap, I would doff it to you.

(In a Pointe Class video I make in the '90s, I demonstrate this elastic insert innovation and talk all about Violette. Dance merchants now sell ribbons with pre-inserted elastic strips. They should call them, "Violettes." Then, every girl who dons her first pair of pointe shoes can learn of Mme. Verdy. This extraordinary ballerina whose enormous heart was immediately felt by all who saw her light up a stage.)

* * *

After Albert and I battle our way back from injury and dancer oblivion, I rejoin the National Ballet's '65-'66 season with a renewed sense of appreciation. And also, a new title. Despite my injury, I've been promoted to the rank of Principal Dancer. I'm pleased, but it doesn't change much for me. But why? Wasn't I over-the-moon about my promotion to Soloist just a few years ago? Well, that was because of my dad's two-year clause. Once I managed to "bust out of the *corps*," I was free. The shackles came off and I knew I could live in this challenging but magical world of ballet forever. All the rest, including reaching the rank of Principal Dancer at the National Ballet, is just icing on the cake.

Over the course of my time at the National Ballet, I have wonderful male partners. Roderick ("Rocky") Drew's "Thief" to my "Captain of the Amazons," in Lew Christensen's *Con Amore*. Daniel Franck's "Cavalier" to my "Snow Queen" in Franklin's *The Nutcracker*.

But by far, my most memorable is the inimitable Ivan Nagy, "Franz" to my "Swanilda" (Franklin's *Coppélia*). "The Prince" to my "Persian Princess" (Jimmy Starbuck's, *The Legend of the Pearl*). "Tancred" to my "Clorinda" (William Dollar's, *Le Combat* or *The Duel*).

In 1965, Ivan wins a Silver Medal at the International Ballet Competition in Varna, Bulgaria. Artistic Director Frederic Franklin invites him to appear with the company faster than you can say, "National Ballet."[35] Just like that, 21-year-old Ivan Nagy is heading to Washington, D.C. A native of Budapest, the only thing he knows about English is from *Voice of America* radio broadcasts. ("*Dah-ball-yoo Ay … Bee … See.*")

I'm a 22-year-old National Ballet Principal who adores languages. Ballerinas know pantomime. Pointing to me first, and then him: "I … you … English." Pointing to him first, and then me: "You … me … Hungarian." It's settled.

We forge ahead. I start with the basics: Numbers 1 to 10, the days of the week, "please," "thank you," "hello," "goodbye," "God bless you," "bathroom." While Ivan is a quick study, this Wannabe Magyar is struggling. I do learn that all Hungarian words accent the first syllable. At least what I manage to remember is pronounced well. Another fact: The Hungarian language does not have common roots with any of the romance languages. Not French. Not Spanish. Not Italian. But it does relate to Finnish. (Not helpful.)

One rehearsal afternoon, Uncle Fred is teaching Ivan and me a *pas de deux*. Ivan and I are struggling with a *promenade en attitude*. Facing each other, we are holding right hands as I am standing *en pointe* on one leg. (My other leg is raised behind me, bent at the knee.) I must keep my balance while revolving to the right, as Ivan slowly walks in a circle. I keep falling off pointe because I can't make my body keep up with him in that circle.

After watching two failed attempts, Uncle Fred springs up from his bench like a jack-in-the-box and says, "Ivan. Ivan." Replacing him as my partner, Uncle Fred shows Ivan how to keep his shoulders and hips facing mine completely, even as he is walking. Ivan and I try the *promenade* again. Done.

About five minutes later, we keep missing this pirouette called a "finger" or "whip" turn. Once again, Uncle Fred springs up. Now taking my part, he shows me how to coordinate "pushing off" Ivan's left hand with my left hand. Ivan and I try the pirouette again. Perfect.

Ivan to Roni: "*Wahn.... Wahn.*" (That's Ivan's Hungarian accent saying, "One.... One.") So the kid has a sense of humor?

(Fast-forward two years. I'm living my post–National Ballet life, and Ivan and I have lost touch. Then my son, Erik, is born in April of 1968. I send a birth announcement to Ivan and his lovely Australian ballerina wife, Marilyn Burr. Months go by. One day, a birth announcement arrives from Ivan and Marilyn, introducing their daughter, Aniko. I dial the phone.

[**Hungarian accent**]: "*Hahlo....*"
ME [**re: our new arrivals**]: "*Wahn.... Wahn....*"
IVAN: "*R-a-a-w-n-i!!!*"

Yup. He remembers the rehearsal.)

A month or two later, that humor pops up again. This time, on tour. Naturally, Ivan and I are seatmates on the bus. Our language addiction takes no timeouts. Since it's a bus tour, I must be saying the word "bus" a lot. Each time, Ivan chuckles.

Finally he mutters, "Hungarian...." Then, it's pantomime to the rescue. He quietly slams his left palm three times against his right fist. (International language?) That day, I teach Ivan the word "slang."

I soon have evidence that Ivan is picking up some vocabulary on his own. Remember when I mentioned playing Clorinda to Ivan's Tancred, in William Dollar's *Le Combat/The Duel*? Let's set the scene: It all takes place during the First Crusade.

The ballet's plot: Tancred, Prince of Galilee, has fallen in love with Clorinda, who is disguised as a male Saracen warrior. Tancred soon mortally wounds an opponent in combat. He is inconsolable to learn that the dying soldier is none other than his beloved Clorinda, whose hair was obscured by her helmet. The ghastly truth is revealed when she tears off her helmet just before dying, and Tancred cradles the beautiful Clorinda in agonizing grief.[36]

I want my hair to appear as a cascade of gently flowing tresses in that final love scene. It has been set in huge rollers all day, trying to tame my natural curl. You can be sure I'm keeping those big fat rollers in until the very last moment, when I have to put on my helmet. Did I mention that I'm a head perspirer?

My Herculean efforts are no match for sweating profusely under a helmet until the very end of the ballet. All those hours spent in curlers? Out the window. I've been attacked by the frizzies. When the curtain finally comes down, Ivan turns to me and quips, "*Look like somebody plug you in.*" Limited vocabulary? Perhaps. Still able to make his point.

Ivan is certainly picking up English much faster than I am learning Hungarian. I do remember how to count from 1–10. And it is easy to remember "God bless you." Like the English "achoo," it too sounds like a sneeze. My best transliteration: *eh-geh-SHEH-geh-drah*. Most of all, I remember how to sing *Frère Jacques* in Hungarian. *Jànos Bàcsi, Jànos Bàcsi….* Most likely because there is music involved.

* * *

After Albert Einstein gets me through my Achilles injury, I'm forever turning to him whenever my imagination has to come to my rescue. As is the case one very cold February day in 1966. While dancing in a very cold Detroit. Performing our very, very charming production of *Coppélia*, staged by Uncle Fred himself.

Since its premiere, I've always done the "Dawn" solo (*L'Aurore*), in Act III. Now, I've finally been given my first crack at the principal role of Swanhilda. (Our heroine's name is more often spelled without the "h." But this is the spelling Uncle Fred has chosen to use.) In all the *Coppélia* rehearsals, I feel like I'm living a fairytale. As if one happily-ever-after isn't enough, guess who is my Dr. Coppélius? My Uncle Fred.

Coppélia is a three-act comedic ballet that tells the story of Franz, a village youth, who is under the influence of an infatuation based on a huge misconception. Poor boy. He thinks the beautiful, life-sized doll, reading a book on toymaker Dr. Coppélius' balcony, is a real girl. In Act II, a very jealous Swanhilda, his *fiancée*, sneaks into the toy shop to confront her competition. She discovers that those limbs are flesh-colored wood, and the beautiful eyes are only painted enamel. The ensuing chaos finally gets sorted out. Act III finds wedding bells chiming for Swanhilda and Franz.

The first production of *Coppélia* was in Paris, in 1870. Performed at Le Théâtre Impérial de l'Opéra, it was based on the darker E.T.A. Hoffmann short story, *Der Sandmann*. In the late 19th century, Marius Petipa revived *Coppélia* in St. Petersburg as a lighter comedy which is still widely performed today.[37]

The first time I get to perform Swanhilda is on a Friday night in Detroit. My mother has flown in for the weekend. She bunks in with me at the hotel. This means she can also see my 10:00 a.m. Student Performance the next morning. It will be followed by a second Student Performance at 1:00 that afternoon, danced by the usual Swanhilda, Andrea Vodehnal. Both of these abbreviated shows will eliminate Act III, to accommodate the schedules of the attending schools. A full house is expected for each show. Unloading that many students from buses, and then reloading them onto those buses, requires a strict Busing Procedure, as follows:

1. Nothing happens until all buses have arrived.
2. All buses unload in a predetermined order.

3. Sequentially and in single-file, all students enter the theater. Their pre-arranged seats are in blocks from front to back.

4. To exit the theater, this process is replicated *exactly in reverse*. It's the *only* way.

On that Friday of my first Swanhilda, my mom learns that I eat a full "dinner" no later than 3:00 in the afternoon. I am one of those "early arrivers," choosing to be in the theater no later than 5:00 p.m. This way, I have plenty of time for what a student of mine would one day describe as my "transmogrification from driftwood into spun glass."[38]

What I remember from my Swanhilda debut is the fun of being so utterly wrapped up in the story. Besides, what can go wrong when your first entrance is a buoyant and playful solo, danced to a buoyant and playful waltz?

For our regular performances, the curtain goes up at 8:30 p.m. and comes down around 11:00 p.m. Given my post-performance "high," it's a while before Mom and I finally leave the theater.

Now comes the leisurely third meal of the day. No surprise that we arrive back at the hotel around 2:00 a.m. In bed by 3:00 a.m.? Asleep, who knows when? Breakfast at 6:00 a.m. Back in the theater by 7:00 a.m., three hours before the student show, with a 10:00 a.m. curtain. Since I'm moving sort of slowly this morning, I'm giving myself extra time. Warming up is certain to be a challenge. Is running on fumes as good as running on adrenaline? We'll soon find out.

Let the 10:00 a.m. show begin. Here's where it gets interesting. Act I is nearly complete. All that remains is the two "break-ins" inflicted upon poor Dr. Coppélius's Toy Shop. The first, by Swanhilda and her Friends, then quickly followed by Franz.

Let's start with Swanhilda. I am determined to have a peek inside that Toy Shop. I've seen my fiancé, Franz, blowing kisses to a somewhat-attractive girl sitting on the balcony. I've also seen where Dr. Coppélius hides the front door key, when he locks up his Toy Shop from the outside. Now I sneak onstage from the upstage right wings. I stop center stage and beckon my Friends to silently join me. Facing squarely to the audience, I'm supposed to clearly pantomime, "I … saw … the key…. Wait here." I never do the pantomime.

The entire balcony is filling with smoke. Someone has already opened the side fire doors for air. Orchestra members, smelling the smoke, have stopped playing and are staring up at the balcony. A puzzled Maestro Ottavio de Rosa stops pretending to conduct. He is also turning around to look at the smoke-filled balcony. There is no music. Just the ever-louder sound of worried audience mutterings. I look into the wings. There is Dr. Coppélius … I mean, Uncle Fred … standing next to the Stage Manager's console. He is desperately gesturing at me to continue. I can read his lips and pantomiming hands. "Go on…. Go on…. Go on!"

I'm terrified. I want to run out of this burning theater as fast as I can. But my Lord and Master is in the wings, commanding me to continue with the performance. Even though the orchestra has stopped playing. What's a girl to do?

Wait. Albert Einstein to the rescue. In my imagination, I am suddenly a soldier on the battlefield, heeding my Sergeant's commands, though peril be nigh. Aye aye,

Sir. I dutifully and bravely deliver my pantomime, albeit to no music. "I … saw … the key…. Wait here."

I run stage left to the Toy Shop. My back is to the audience, while I am reaching on my tippy toes high above the door for the hidden key. I suddenly hear one instrument, then another. The orchestra is beginning to play again.

Miraculously, after that long pause, Maestro de Rosa has managed to pick up the music in exactly the right place. Of course, he has. "Otty" really pays attention to the stage. He doesn't "coddle" us. He just keeps track of us.[39]

Right now, his timely musical reentry infuses me with courage. I continue to ignore the smoke-filled theater. Followed by my faithful Friends, I creep into the Toy Shop.

That's it. I'm done. I'm offstage at last. In my imagination, I hear my Sergeant: "Well done, soldier. At ease." Once again, I doff my imaginary cap in gratitude to my imaginary friend, Albert Einstein.

Now it is Franz's turn. Carrying a tall ladder, he tiptoes from the upstage right wing onto a now-empty stage and looks adoringly toward the Toy Shop balcony. Unaware that Swanhilda is already inside, he places his ladder against the balcony rail and begins his climb. From the second rung, he blows her a kiss. As he continues to climb, the Act I curtain comes down.

Suddenly, there is an announcement to evacuate the theater immediately. All the students begin exiting, willy-nilly. Not an organized single-file in sight. Did I mention that a light, wet snow has begun to fall? Backstage, we are told to leave everything behind, dress warmly, and get outside as quickly as possible. My independent-minded mother has a different idea. She's determined to get me completely packed. She wants to take everything, because it is not clear that we will return. In what seems like no more than two minutes, mission accomplished.

I can see it as clearly as if it were yesterday. Me, standing in my pointe shoes in the lightly falling snow. My royal blue wool winter coat, sticking out wide over my short, stiff Swanhilda tutu. A hastily packed and bulging theater case, safely wedged between my mother and me. Mom and I each clutching an overloaded shopping bag. And, of course, each clutching an overloaded purse.

Fortunately, after only about ten minutes, the all-clear is sounded. It's safe for everyone to go back inside. The culprit has been identified as an electrical fire in the balcony lighting booth. It's instantly obvious that there will be no time for Act II. Getting all these students back onto their assigned buses is going to take a lot of time. But why, you ask? They are already outside. They can simply go straight to their buses. Not so, say The Bus Gods. There is only one way to account for every student. They must all first return (single file) to their theater seats. Only then can each busload, row by row, exit the theater (single file) to begin boarding. Ah, yes. That Confounded Bus Procedure, exactly in reverse.

You haven't forgotten about the one o'clock Student Performance, have you? No sooner do the reloaded ten o'clock buses clear out, than the one o'clock buses arrive to duplicate the entire process. Those students are luckier. They get to see the magic of Act II. I have to be content with Act I.

Weeks later, I am still trying to organize my theater paraphernalia after all that hasty packing. I find a missing false eyelash inside a pointe shoe.

Looking back, the most significant takeaway from the whole adventure is my Uncle Fred. So cool and collected under fire. Pun intended. He never wavered. He knew the Act should finish, to avoid mass hysteria. He trusted that, if I kept going, the orchestra would start up again. And I trusted him. All I had to do was keep doing the steps.

I'm in awe of how his equanimity led me through that harrowing escapade. It brings to mind another time ten years earlier. That day, the tiniest nod of his head corrected my errant *promenade en attitude* and earned me a full scholarship. He was already my Dr. Coppélius, even way back then.

With a trusted "Sergeant" at the helm and new roles on the horizon, the National Ballet is truly feeling like home to this young Principal dancer. But even though I didn't know it then, my days with the National Ballet were swiftly coming to an end.

Second Intermission
The Kennedys

A Definite Perk

Flashback to the early '60s in D.C. There I am. Decked out to the nines in my high school prom dress. A tiara on my head. A faux bunny-fur stole. Short white gloves clutching my small purse. Frozen in the middle of a very wide intersection, while President Kennedy's limousine politely swerves around me to make its turn. A deer in the headlights is an amateur compared to this. Now, JFK is looking right at me with the broadest grin, as the limousine passes slowly by. My grin is splitting my head in two.

But also, yikes. If he gets there before we do, they won't let us in. Gets where before we do? Won't let us in to what? Hang on. Let's start from the beginning....

Roderick "Rocky" Drew is an insanely handsome Principal Dancer with the (then) brand-new National Ballet of Washington. We all arrived after Labor Day, to begin four months of rehearsal before our January opening. Rocky comes a little bit later, to honor a previously-signed contract. He is temporarily staying in the home of noted D.C. arts philanthropist Gerson Nordlinger, Jr.

Mr. Nordlinger is a dear friend of Marjorie Merriweather Post May. Yours truly is a dear friend of Rocky Drew. When the Bolshoi is coming to town, Mrs. May plans to be at her home in Palm Beach. She gives her tickets to Mr. Nordlinger. Mr. Nordlinger is eventually persuaded by Mrs. May to join her in Palm Beach. Mr. Nordlinger gives his tickets to Rocky Drew. And that is how Rocky and Roni end up attending the Bolshoi Ballet's Opening Night in November of 1962.

As the day draws closer, it is a miracle that we manage to rehearse at all. Every spare minute seems taken up with finding things for me to wear to the Bolshoi Opening Night. I feel like Cinderella, when all the little forest creatures are helping her dress for the ball. Thankfully, when leaving home to join the Company, I had packed the dress and low satin heels worn to my senior prom three years ago. How I wish I could remember who lends me that perfect white faux bunny-fur stole. And how I wish I could remember who contributes the *pièce de résistance*, a rhinestone tiara to nestle into the curls above my forehead. Two tiny diamond stud earrings. One ruby ring. One small clutch purse. Two white gloves. Done.

The Bolshoi's full-length *Swan Lake* will be performed at the Loew's Capitol

Theatre on 14th and F Streets. The Four Georges Restaurant is not too far away. It is most likely why Mr. Nordlinger suggests that Rocky make a dinner reservation there. Nordlinger's treat. Of the four dining rooms, George III is the swankiest. The antique furniture. The china. The silverware. The goblets. This 20-year-old feels like she has stepped back in time.

Lest we get too carried away, there is one very real fact to keep us grounded. The newspaper has said that, because President and Mrs. Kennedy will be in attendance, F Street will be closed to all vehicular traffic at exactly 7:45 p.m. The curtain goes up at 8:00 p.m. sharp. Rocky tells the waiter that we must be out the door by 7:30. The waiter promises to notify us at 7:25. This way, we can be in a taxi on time.

The dinner is divine. The waiter forgets his promise. "So sorry. It's 7:40." Mad dash. Cab right outside. We soon find ourselves on 16th Street, passing the White House; 16th Street dead-ends at F Street. All cars will have to turn left. As our taxi approaches that left turn, there is one car ahead of us. The policeman motions it to stop, but the car turns left, anyway. We, however, are out of luck.

I jump out first. Rocky is paying. My memory is of lots and lots of pavement. 16th Street must be very wide. F Street must be very wide. I turn back for Rocky and see, instead, a big black limousine with lots of flags. It is heading directly toward me. I am, after all, standing in the middle of the street.

It is as if the pavement concrete has dried around my ankles. The big black limousine has to avoid me to make its turn. President Kennedy is grinning broadly at me through the window, as he rolls slowly by. It suddenly dawns on Rocky and me that we have to beat that limousine to the theater, or we will be out of luck again. It is two short blocks. Nick of time. The usher takes our tickets and begins leading us to our seats.

Allow me to paint this very deliberate picture. In every theater, there is the obligatory horseshoe-shaped ring of box seats directly above the orchestra. Tonight, each box has four chairs. Two in front. Two directly behind.

Let us begin with the first box on the right end of the horseshoe. In the first two chairs sit President Kennedy and First Lady Jackie. Still in the first box, in the two chairs behind, sit former United Nations Ambassador Henry Cabot Lodge, Jr. and his wife. As protocol dictates, in the first box on the left end of the horseshoe, the first two chairs are unoccupied. Soviet Union Premier Khrushchev and wife Nina are *not* in attendance. In the two chairs behind the empty ones sit the Soviet Ambassador to the United States, Anatoly Dobrynin, and his wife.

In the second box, the one behind Dobrynin, in the first two seats sit Roderick Drew and Roni Mahler. In the two seats behind them sit Secretary of the Interior Stewart Udall and his wife. Polly Guggenheim Logan is sitting in box three, *behind us*.

The gentlemanly Rocky gives me the seat closest to the orchestra. When I gaze down, everyone seems to be whispering to one another and then looking up at us. As I stroll the halls in the first intermission, women gasp audibly as they pass by, eying my rhinestone tiara.

JFK leaves after Act III. Jackie stays for Act IV. Maya Plisetskaya breaks hearts as the unearthly Odette in Acts II and IV. She utterly dazzles as Odile in Act III. I will never forget how she reenters, downstage left, after the Black Swan *Pas de Deux*. Striding triumphantly across the front of the stage … heels first!

November 22, 1963

It is one o'clock on Friday afternoon. What should I call myself? Lucky puppy? Happy camper? I have a full hour of private rehearsal in the large studio. National Ballet Artistic Director Frederic Franklin is going to watch me dance some of my upcoming solos. Tweaking will be involved. We have just finished running my Soloist variation from Mr. Balanchine's *Pas de Dix*. This is one of my favorite ballets. I confess to Uncle Fred my dream of one day performing the exotic Female Principal solo. His response: "Let's have a go, shall we?"

But then…. the National Ballet President, Jean Riddell, is suddenly standing in the studio doorway. Are those tears in her eyes?

"Kennedy's been shot."

Racing up three flights. Staring at a small black-and-white office TV. The wait is agony. Has it only been thirty minutes? Walter Cronkite, struggling to speak the unspeakable words.

I remember feeling like there is nowhere to go to be comforted. Everyone is stricken. Born three months after Pearl Harbor, I was too young to experience the world wars. Now, at 21, I am floundering in universal grief for the first time.

I walk the neighborhood for hours. Walking. Walking. Walking. Sometimes, I notice that I'm actually standing still. Putting one foot in front of the other isn't automatic, today.

I look up. I can't believe I'm standing at the front door of the National Ballet. Maybe the Sylphs and Wilis brought me here? Maybe I didn't even go anywhere? I can't remember.

It's a little before 6:00 p.m. I throw myself into Pointe Class. Why not? At least it's familiar. What else to do?

I can barely go through the motions. He is gone. He is gone. Will this class never end? The sound of my own clapping snaps me back from somewhere. Applause. Class must be over. For an instant, I have to actually remember. The class took over at some point. No idea when. Or, for how long. Scary, that class can do that to me. I must remember this. Safe place? Denial? Is there a difference?

Glued to my television. Live coverage. Nonstop. Jack Ruby, murdering Lee Harvey Oswald in real time. Real life. Not a movie. Horror, on top of grief. I am reeling. Procession. Funeral. They blur together. How long before I realize there are no commercials? Jackie is like a black ghost behind that veil covering her face. At times, her blank stare seems barely human.

On Wednesday, I pull myself together and go to Arlington National Cemetery. I'm guessing it will feel like visiting the Tomb of the Unknown Soldier, when I was ten. I am so wrong. I didn't know the Unknown Soldier. This is not that.

One lonely flame. Such a thick carpet of flowers surrounding it. Departing dignitaries had paid their respects. It's been raining. The ground is muddy. No fence. No ropes. No guard. No crowds, yet. I'm standing as close to that flame as the flowers allow. I have no idea how long I stare. Its flickering is hypnotic, just like they say. His words. His smile. His wit. They replay in my mind. Over and over. I do not remember going home.

The feeling of helplessness is overwhelming. Then, Jackie is promising to answer every condolence letter. No matter how long it takes. Who knows how many there are? (Later, in her first public statement post-assassination, Jackie puts the number at nearly 800,000.)[1] Jackie's secretaries are setting up a committee. There is a number to call. I must have dialed.

I'm standing in a cluttered room with overhead fluorescent lights. I don't remember where. I only know that this is a long way from Camelot. That's what Jackie is calling JFK's brief White House years. American Camelot. We're seated at long, picnic-style tables. I pore over interminable names and addresses on lists that never end. Our job is to write these names and addresses on envelopes. Place note cards in envelopes. Seal envelopes. Sometimes, I feel like a robot. Just what the doctor ordered. Busywork.

Jackie's expression of gratitude, and her signature, are on these unadorned, ivory notecards. The ones that open from bottom to top, not sideways. My memory is that only her full name appears in lovely script on the front. No mention of First Lady. Like a note from a friend.

We dub ourselves the "condolence committee." Four months later, I've become sort of organizer-in-chief. One day, Jackie drops by to personally thank us all. I'm thinking, "No, Jackie. Thank you. You gave me something to do." That night, I cannot remember what she said. All I can remember is fighting back tears.

Time passes. I am feeling some "camaraderie" and, at the same time, a sense of being "alone." Camaraderie, in a shared grief. Alone, because no one can comfort me. I think back to when I was little. I fell and my knee was bleeding. My worried question: "Mommy, will it leave a scar?" Who can help me live with this scar, now?

Art Buchwald? Ben Bradlee? That's it. Humor. My ticket out. A Buchwald column reminiscing about the President has me in stitches. And disbelief. Disbelief that I'm actually laughing. About *him*. And Bradlee's unforgettable memory: Coming upon his good friend, stalled on the side of the road in Hyannis Port. Hood up. Peering inside. Screaming, "The f-----g f----rs won't f—k."

JFK was my first funny President. That is what I can do. I can remember him funny.

Act Two

American Ballet Theatre

It's 1968. Two years have passed, and I'm back at the barre with Madame Swoboda. A familiar setting, yes, but just about everything else in my life has changed. I left the National Ballet and my beloved Uncle Fred. I moved to New York to marry someone I thought I'd be spending the rest of my life with. And most importantly, I gave birth to my son, Erik.

The Scandinavians think I spell his name with a "k" to honor Erik the Red. The ballet world thinks I spell his name with a "k" to honor the great Danish ballet dancer, Erik Bruhn. The truth? My son, Erik, is named after a cigar. Yes, in the late 60s, there's an ultra-slim cigar masquerading as a cigarette. Its name: ERIK. Its slogan: "Erik is here!"

That's never more true than on April 1, 1968. The day Erik Mahler Stone is born. Erik's father is Art Stone, owner of the dance supply firm, Art Stone Theatrical. I get a great price on leotards. Short-lived. We divorce six years later.

When I choose a hospital to give birth, Arthur and I are still living in the city, in a one-bedroom on 19th and Third. Beth Israel is on 16th and First. So close. So perfect. By the time I go into labor on Monday, April 1, we're living in a two-bedroom in Bayside, Queens. Not so perfect.

I'll make this short. Awakened by contractions at 2:00 a.m. Examined at Beth Israel around 9:00 a.m. Contractions too far apart. Come back when they're closer. Back to Beth Israel at 6:30 p.m. I'm sure it's the real deal this time. Into an examination room. Into a hospital gown. Arthur and I are waiting. A doctor I don't recognize pops his head in.

SCENE:
"Hi. I'm Dr. Greifinger, the Resident. Dr. Berk will be here shortly. I'll be giving you your internal examination."

Arthur steps out. Examination, complete. The resident leaves. Arthur comes back in. I try to tell him something, but the resident reappears in a flash. All I have time for is a quick, "Watch this."

"Dr. Greifinger, is your first name Martin?"
"Yes."
"Did you go to New Rochelle High School?"
"Yes."

"Well. When you were a Junior and I was a Sophomore, you took me to the Junior Prom."

END SCENE.

Happy April Fool's Day, anyone?

ABT on Tour

So now, I'm back studying with Madame Swoboda. She's teaching at American Ballet Theatre's School of Ballet, on 57th Street between Broadway and Eighth.

Two-year-old Erik in a *penché arabesque* at a playground in Bayside, Queens. Maybe his mother is a ballerina?

I'm not really sure how I get into ABT. There's certainly no audition. But let's examine some clues. Fact: Famous choreographer Agnes de Mille is working in the small studio, on some ideas for a new ballet. Fact: Agnes invites me to work with her. Does ABT co-founder Lucia Chase suggest me for that? Does Agnes subsequently tell Lucia I am a good fit for "dramatic" ballets? Those that tell a story?

Fact: Ellen Everett, one of Lucia's favorite soloists, has just left the Company. I remember whispers that I "remind Lucia of Ellen." Fact: Ellen's specialty? The ballets that "tell a story." Conjecture. Conjecture. Who knows?

I have a vague recollection of Lucia and ABT Ballerina, Toni Lander, watching class one day. Next thing I know, I'm signing a soloist contract.

But, here's the indisputable fact. I'm suddenly a bona fide member of the iconic American Ballet Theatre. Holy mackerel. The same storied ballet company that enchanted me when I was four years old? Universe, you're working overtime. Thank you, thank you…

Into the Lake

It's now the second week of February, in 1969. I've just finished about a month of intensive rehearsals, learning a ton of new choreography. I forget exactly how many ballets. All I know is that the full-length *Swan Lake* stands out in my mind above all else.

With a live-in nanny securely in place, this new mom is about to embark on her first ABT tour. Mind you, it's not at all that easy. A horrible nor'easter manages to hit smack dab in the middle of the tri-state area (NY, NJ, CT). Our first stop, a Tuesday, is supposed to be Red Bank, New Jersey. Impossible to get there. Performance canceled.

Leaving the swirling snowflakes behind, the Company manages to "open" on Wednesday at the next stop, Baltimore. Continuing southward, it's over the Mason-Dixon line toward less belligerent weather. Thursday finds everyone in Greensboro, North Carolina.

The Company is opening tonight with former Royal Ballet principal David Blair's staging of *Swan Lake*. And we're performing it for the next five shows in a row. That's one way to get the kinks out of a spanking-new, scenery-laden, full-length production.

In ballet, a "full-length production" can be two acts (such as *Giselle*), three acts (such as *Coppélia*), or four acts (such as *Swan Lake*). Okay. *Swan Lake*. Here goes:

Act I: In the Palace Gardens, Queen Mother tells her Prince son he must choose a bride.

Act II: By a Lake in the forest, the Prince pledges eternal love to Odette, the Queen of the Swans. She's really a Princess trapped inside a Swan's body by an Evil Sorcerer, because she wouldn't marry him.

Act III: That evening in the Palace Ballroom, the Evil Sorcerer's daughter, Odile, tricks the Prince into thinking *she's* his beloved Odette, only now dressed in black instead of white. (Odette and Odile are performed by the same ballerina.) He falls for the scam and declares his eternal love for the wrong girl, dooming Odette to "Swandom" forever.

Act IV: Back at the lake, the Prince finds his devastated Odette. Trapped in their shared grief, they plunge, one after the other, to their deaths, finally free to celebrate eternal love in the hereafter. The Evil Sorcerer's spell is broken at last, and all Odette's friends turn back from Swans into Princesses again.[1]

In the "swan acts," I'm one of two Lead Swan attendants to Swan Queen Odette. Rosanna Seravalli is the other. In Act III, Rosanna and I perform the Spanish Dance with Marcos Paredes and Robert Gladstein.

(Rosanna and I end up being paired together often at ABT. Example: As Gypsies, with Marcos Paredes as Drunken Merchant, in *Petrouchka*. To this day, we occasionally run into one another in the faculty dressing room at Julia Dubno's gem of a ballet school in New York City, Ballet Academy East.

> **RONI:** "I think I was the Red Gypsy. Do you remember being the Yellow Gypsy?"
> **ROSANNA:** "No. I think *I* was the Red Gypsy."

And so it goes. Every time. We're still not sure.)

Thursday, February 13, 1969. My *Swan Lake* debut with ABT. Rosanna and I perform our "Big Swans" duet, after those cute little Cygnets. We get through the quick and intricate footwork of our Spanish Dance, in Act III. Most miraculously of all, I think, we pull off leading the *corps de ballet* through what feels like myriad patterns in the last act, back at the lake in the forest.

I'm on cloud nine. And lucky for me, my casting stays the same for the *next two nights*. There's comfort in knowing that I get to repeat the same choreography both Friday and Saturday evenings. Three performances in a row is certain to engrave this *Swan Lake* role into my body and mind. One down. Two to go.

* * *

After Thursday night's hitchless performance, Friday is moving along nicely. Company class onstage at noon. The rehearsal that follows is for ballets that haven't been performed yet. First up, *Concerto* with choreography by (soon-to-be) Royal Ballet Artistic Director Kenneth MacMillan. I get to rehearse my Third Movement solo.

Next, current soloist Dennis Nahat is rehearsing the dancers in his new ballet, *Momentum*. Current principal Michael Smuin to follow, rehearsing his *Pulcinella Variations*.

At the end of Dennis's hour, he glances at the off-stage clock. Time to cede the stage to Michael.

DENNIS: "Mike. Can I just run the Finale one more time?"
MIKE: "Sure."

My life is never the same.

Dennis begins running the Finale again. Principal Cynthia Gregory sprains her ankle. It's a chaotic scene. Three things are happening simultaneously: Mike's rehearsing his dancers. Dennis is in a corner upstage right, desperately massaging Cynthia's rapidly-swelling ankle. The ABT powers-that-be are realizing the extent of their sudden casting problem.

Tonight's Odette/Odile is Toni Lander, but then she's leaving the tour for a few days. Tomorrow's matinee is scheduled with Eleanor D'Antuono in the role. But what if Cynthia's ankle stops her from dancing her own *Swan Lake* tomorrow night? The more Dennis massages, the more her ankle balloons. Who can jump in to perform Odette/Odile? No available Swan Queens as far as the eye can see.

Eureka! Ballet Master Enrique Martinez remembers that yours truly has just finished guest performances with Carolyn Clark's New Jersey Ballet. What role was I dancing? Odette in *Swan Lake, Act II*. (This act is famously included as a standalone option on many a mixed bill.) Inserting me into ABT's Act II will not take too much time.

Act IV? That's another story. Is the remaining rehearsal hour enough to push Roni through the complicated Act IV choreography? It better be. But, wait. There's certainly no time to rehearse me in Act III's Black Swan *Pas de Deux*. Not even in overtime. And I've still got to get ready to dance Big Swans in *tonight's* show.

Enter Ballerina Eleanor D'Antuono, the original Energizer Bunny. Eleanor generously offers to perform the Black Swan *Pas de Deux*, in my place, in Act III of Saturday night's show. This way, I'll only have to dance Acts II and IV. But, won't she have just completed her own full-length Odette/Odile that afternoon? Not called Energizer Bunny for nothin'.

(Eleanor's generous offer doesn't *exactly* fly in the face of history. True, the Moscow [1877] and St. Petersburg [1895] *Swan Lake* premieres *did* feature one ballerina in both roles.[2] But, floating in the ether is also a vague reference to *different* ballerinas dancing Odette and Odile in the same performance.)

No rehearsals allowed on a matinee/evening day like tomorrow. So, the impossible. Roni learns the entire Act IV in an hour. Two new *Pas de Deux*, yes. But what about dodging all those crossing and swirling Swans in The Storm? And all that running in circles? And tons and tons of strategically-timed pantomime? Yes. All of that, too.

And topping it all off, Odette has to plunge off a roughly six-foot cliff to her watery death. That is, if she wants to be reunited with the love-of-her-life, Prince Siegfried, in the hereafter.

About that plunge. The sensible way to cushion Odette's fall off that cliff? Maybe a huge mattress? With a stagehand or two, at the ready for a wayward bounce? Not in ABT's 1969 version. The "mattress" is only the locked forearms of the four newest men in the Company. And, mind you. That's regardless of dissimilar height, weight, and strength. So why the newest, you ask? That's because none of the men in the Company need to stay in the theater after Act III. Except the Catchers. So we have the seniority monster, rearing its ugly head once more.

Odette's final onstage moments are filled with 16 slow counts of Tchaikovsky's famous, and ominous, "theme." First, my heartbreaking pantomime of, "I … here … will die…" (1 … 2 … 3 …); next, running all the way to the back of the stage (4 … 5 … 6 … 7 …); then, pulling my staggering self up the six-ish steps to the plunging platform (8 … 1 … 2 … 3 …); Finally, left hand clutching my broken heart and right arm reaching out to my beloved Prince (4 … 5 … 6 … 7 …).

Now, arching gracefully sideways, my right arm overhead (8 …), I plunge (on the new musical phrase) into the waiting "forearm basket" of The Catchers.

I really, really have to stay exactly on my musical counts. I can't get behind even the tiniest bit. The Prince has been patiently waiting throughout my pantomime. My running, staggering, and plunging. Sixteen counts. Then he has to repeat, albeit quicker, my same pantomime, running, staggering, and plunging. *Off that same cliff.* So, I have to really skedaddle out of that forearm basket. It needs to be empty for his plunge, *and in half the time.*

But how on earth am I going to get to practice this daring feat before tomorrow night? I've just made it through my second *Swan Lake* with ABT. And, my second Act IV Big Swans. But tonight's Act IV has been decidedly different from opening night. Because, tonight, I've had my eyes glued to Toni Lander's every move as Swan Queen Odette.

Finally, the curtain is down. The Stagehands and Wardrobe obligingly look the other way. Many union rules are about to be broken. For starters, my four Catchers and I are still in costume. (Dancers must change immediately.) So are the several Swans still hanging around to sing the music.

It's now or never. Practice that plunge, or forever hold… You know. With thumping heart and no time for jitters, I manage two practice run-and-plunges. I swear, for a minute after each one, I cannot feel my legs. And, my Four Catchers. So helpful. So supportive. But also? So mismatched. I clearly remember two out of the four. They're like Mutt and Jeff, separated in height by at least a half a foot. Either somebody's up on his tiptoes, or somebody's really bending his knees. I try not to think about it.

I can never say enough about my Prince Siegfried. His name is Gayle Young. Gayle always partners Cynthia in her *Swan Lakes*. That makes me incredibly lucky when I "inherit" him. Gayle's instincts as a partner are infallible. It's why I call him Mr. Million-Dollar Hands.

When you're with Gayle, you're always "on your leg." There is no errant move on my part that he cannot save, with a practically-invisible, minor adjustment of those million-dollar hands. Of course, he wins the coveted Ventriloquist Award for his "inaudibles." He can remind me, without moving his lips, of exactly what steps are coming next. Lucky, lucky me, because I have to learn those two Act IV *Pas de Deux* in a New York minute.

Picture this. The whole time I'm learning Act IV, complete with Gayle's inaudibles, Cynthia is still nestled in that same upstage right corner, where she was carried after rolling her ankle. Dennis is still feverishly, and maybe even painfully, massaging that poor ankle. Yet, Cynthia is still managing to dictate a meticulous Act IV play-by-play for me, as I scribble furiously on the tiniest of note paper.

How meticulous? She's telling me where I run each minute I'm on the stage. For instance, how I interact with groups of Swans, right before my Prince desperately bursts into the forest searching for me. Not to mention how to navigate the "The Storm." Avoiding vertical lines of Swans which are frantically crossing each other on very specific counts of music. And at breakneck speed. While all of us are trying to look distressed and frightened.

Cynthia continues dictating and dictating, while grimacing from Dennis's messaging. And I'm scribbling and scribbling. "Run to stage right and cry. Run to stage left and cry."

(I still have those little pieces of paper. Scribbled in pencil, on one of those notepads that sports three perforated blank sections on each page. Eighteen years later, Cynthia is a permanent guest artist with Cleveland Ballet. Dennis Nahat is the Artistic Director, and I'm his Artistic Associate. He's choreographing his own full-length *Swan Lake*. On a rehearsal break, I surprise Cynthia with my scribbled notes. We both tear up.)

* * *

Saturday morning finds me eating breakfast alone at a table for two in the hotel coffee shop. It's pretty obvious that I am reviewing choreography, because my arms are waving all over the place. A voice interrupts. "May I join you?"

A young male dancer in the Company is standing by the chair facing me. Startled, I blurt out, "Sure." It is the last thing I need. After he settles in and orders, the next unbelievable words out of his mouth are, "Do you really think you can pull this off?"

To this day, I still cannot believe that I answer in a civil tone. With my guardian angel perched protectively on my shoulder, I simply look up and say, "Of course I can. In my mind, I am not dancing *Swan Lake* tonight. I am doing this step, then that step, followed by the next step, and the next, and the next ... until the ballet is over." Turns out, I'm actually thankful for that off-the-cuff comment at breakfast. It forces me to crystallize my "plan of action."[3]

Understandably, I'm in a haze. Not an unfocused haze. No, I'm very focused. Everything just feels very unreal. I'm sure that I get to my dressing room extra early, so I can do my hair and makeup and put on my feathers. I'm sure that I warm up in the wings, so Gayle and I can meet as planned, to go through all of Act IV before the "onstage" call. Thankfully, Gayle's Prince Siegfried doesn't enter immediately at the top of Act I. My Odette, even more thankfully, doesn't come on until Act II.

As we review Act IV in sequence, I remember thinking that even my memory lapses are instructional. They show me exactly what I am still unsure of. That way, tonight, my brain can blink a yellow caution light to warn me of uncertainty ahead.

Back to the haze. I must have changed into my performance pointe shoes. I must've stood still while my dresser applied body makeup to my back, neck, chest, and arms. She must have then hooked me into my tutu.

All I know is that suddenly I am standing in the upstage left wing. Those three ascending phrases of vibrating violins are heralding the eight repetitive, drama-building chords. The chords that thrust me forward onto the stage … in that explosive *grand jeté*. One solitary *piqué arabesque* later, and this Odette is now free to quietly preen in my own private world.

Until … wait. Who's that disturbing my private world? Odette's Act II entrance might be the very best "first entrance" in all of Ballet. So explosive, followed by total serenity, followed by abrupt panic.

Are you wondering if I remember anything at all about this storybook performance? Yes, but I can count on one hand the five treasured moments seared into my consciousness:

1. Upstage Left in the Act II *Pas de Deux*: the urgency of my plea to Von Rothbart, then floating my arms behind me, in a deep, succumbing backbend.
2. During the same *Pas de Deux*: no longer frightened by the Prince, I find myself melting in his caring embraces.
3. In my Act II solo variation: hitting a long balance in that first *relevé arabesque*, following those two forward-traveling *sissonnes*. I remember hearing a happy gasp from my pals in the wings. The same step immediately repeats twice more, and the magic of that initial balance is nowhere to be found. It rarely is, after "hitting" the first one.
4. Both Act IV *Pas de Deux*: Ventriloquist Gayle "muttering" me through all that hastily-learned sequencing.
5. And, yes. I remember The Plunge.

Strangely enough, I *do* remember every tiny little thing about the bows. (No more pressure?) Gayle's left arm around my waist in the upstage right wing. My left hand in his left palm. That wonderful walk together down a center aisle, left for us by the entire cast. Applause. So much applause.

The bouquet, brought to me from stage right, by someone I *don't* remember. The single rose with a little bow tied around it, indicating which one has been loosened, ready for me to give to my partner. Gayle kissing my hand after accepting it. Then leading me a step forward and immediately backing off … so I have to take a solo bow. Lots more applause.

Feeling Gayle's gentle touch around my waist again, easing me backwards now, behind the closing curtain. Then, easing over a little to stage right. (He's done this before.) Stagehands "paging" the left side of the curtain, pulling it back from the right one. Gayle, taking the first "paged" bow in front of the curtain. Our stage manager gently pushing me out to replace Gayle. Even more applause.

Gayle joining me in front of the curtain, for one last bow together. Gayle gently turning me and chivalrously leading me back behind the "still-paged" curtain. Watching the two stagehands release the left side of the curtain to its rightful place overlapping the other one. Listening with a touch of sadness, as the applause dies down. Because it's over.

So, I guess I pulled it off. I danced Swan Queen Odette in my third performance *ever* with ABT. Everyone says I did great. I wouldn't know. I just did this step, then that step....

Cynthia's Ankle and Me

I have Cynthia Gregory's sprained ankle to thank for my knights in shining armor during that first ABT tour.... Knights? Plural, Roni? Really? Usually, there's only one, if you're lucky. Ah, but you see I'm talking about my ABT male principal dancers. My rescuers. The ones who get me through every last-minute role after last-minute role after last-minute role. I'm talking about Gayle Young. Bruce Marks. Ted Kivitt. Saviors, all.

Turns out, getting through *Swan Lake* is just the beginning of how Cynthia's ankle changes my very first tour with ABT. Before the ankle, I'd been learning the Third Movement soloist role in Kenneth MacMillan's *Concerto*. After the ankle, forget that Third Movement solo. I'm now learning Cynthia's Second Movement role. Goodbye solo dancing. Now I have a partner. And it's none other than Mr. Ventriloquist himself, Gayle Young. Good thing, too. Because the entire Second Movement is one gorgeous, very, very long *pas de deux*. I'm guessing the powers-that-be figure Gayle can talk me through yet another one.

I'm immediately thrown into Second Movement rehearsals with Gayle. All two hours of them. All I can say is, "God bless the ventriloquist." That, and his million-dollar hands get me through performance after performance of this divinely serene choreography. At least, "divine" and "serene" is the way it makes me feel.

My next rescue involves Antony Tudor's *Gala Performance*. Tudor choreographed to a young Prokofiev's first symphonic endeavor, his *Classical Symphony*. Composed along Mozartian lines, the *Classical's* impish sense of humor and charming melodies match Tudor's satirical take on classical ballet.[4]

Original casting: Roni, understudy to the Russian Ballerina. Cynthia, Italian Ballerina. Is the ankle ready? No, it's not. Jenny-Jump-In (my new nickname), reporting for duty. All those hours learning the garishly-outgoing Russian Ballerina get put on hold. Pompous, reserved Italian Ballerina beckons, instead. Never mind that I haven't been understudying *her*.

Bruce Marks, ABT principal dancer and partner extraordinaire, is the Italian Ballerina's Cavalier. And he's quite the challenge. Not because of his partnering. No. His partnering is impeccable. Bruce, with his dry humor, is just too funny. He has me constantly chuckling, as we attempt to rehearse this *pas de deux*. And chuckling doesn't exactly broadcast "pompous." Nor, "reserved." The master of *sotto voce*, Bruce can make me laugh at the most inconvenient moments, while never breaking character, himself. Beyond impish. The Italian Ballerina would never approve.

Getting to perform with Bruce is a special icing on my ABT cake, because of our personal connection. He is married to Company ballerina Toni Lander. The Parenthood Pixies had been toying with us. Back in 1968, Toni and I were both expecting our "firsts" on March 31. Toni's is early. March 11. Mine, late. April 1.

Performing as "The Italian Ballerina" (center) in Antony Tudor's *Gala Performance* with ABT, alongside Sallie Wilson (left, "Russian Ballerina") and Eleanor D'Antuono (right, "French Ballerina") in 1969. (Photographer unidentified [Louis Peres?]. Courtesy of American Ballet Theatre; Jerome Robbins Dance Division, New York Public Library for the Performing Arts).

Absolutely coincidentally, we both name our baby boys Erik. Within two years, both little Eriks are wearing glasses. Who can forget Erik Stone scrambling up the slide in his bedroom to say hello to Erik Marks? Glasses bump. Two startled toddlers, frozen in time.

But Jenny-Jump-In's not done yet. George Balanchine's *Grand Pas Glazunov* (known as *Pas de Dix*) from *Raymonda*, is about to be performed for the first time on this tour. I'm one of four soloists. My usual soloist spot is the First Variation.

Erik ... and Erik!

Cynthia's *Pas de Dix* role? Of course, the principal couple. With apologies to *The Red Shoes*, Cynthia's ankle will not be dancing "tonight, or any other night."

No, her ankle is not nearly ready. Yes, I'll be performing for her in the principal couple spot, with Ted Kivitt as my partner. This time, the process is not quite so terrifying. I've recently danced this principal role as a guest ballerina with the Westchester Ballet. Tonight, *Pas de Dix* is up first. (Pardon the baseball lingo.) The entire cast is milling about onstage, behind the closed curtain. We're on time. We're ready to go. Not so fast…

There's a woman on a microphone out front, talking on and on about a fundraising drive? She seems determined to thank everyone who may have ever contributed. Over the ages. Two minutes turn into five. Then seven. I need to stay warmed up.

How about repetitive ballet jumps in place? Nope. My pointe shoes make too much noise. What's a girl to do? Luckily for me, Ted has a gift for entertaining banter. All while coaxing me through endless (and, thankfully, silent) "partnered" *pirouettes* and *promenades*.

Banter away, Mrs. Congeniality. Who has time for stress when you're fielding Ted's one-liners? When the curtain finally goes up, I am comparatively warm … and surprisingly relaxed.

Summing it all up, it's been quite a first ABT tour for me. Five weeks. Five Jenny-Jump-In performances. Three different partners. Whirlwind? Dizzying? Cinderella, going to the ball. Again. And again. The clichés abound.

There is one small downer amidst all my success. It's March 1, 1969, and Mickey Mantle announces that he's retiring from baseball. This time we're definitely *not connected*. My career is taking off, and his is ending.

Thank goodness there's a silver lining for The Mick. The Yankees immediately celebrate his remarkable career, by retiring his No. 7 on Mickey Mantle Day in 1969. This is actually his third one.

* * *

The year 1969 is also when Ivan Nagy and I are dancing together again in the same Company. You remember my dear, sweet Hungarian buddy Ivan from my National Ballet days? My former English student is bursting to show me how much he's learned:

IVAN: "My English is *'proving.*"
RONI: "O-k-a-a-a-y."
IVAN: "Last night, I was almost *'rested*, because I didn't have any *'dentification.*"
RONI: "O-k-a-a-a-y."

It breaks my heart to tell him that he's missing all those first syllables. I explain that it's really not his fault. He's been learning by listening, and who among us ever fully pronounces those first syllables?

All kidding aside, Ivan has succeeded mightily. His English really *has* improved. And there's still that irrepressible sense of humor. For instance, telling me that his favorite author is now one "Anna Neemus," after encountering so many attributions to "Anonymous."

He then has me in stitches, recalling his adventures in English during ABT's recent tour to Japan. Like the time he blurted out "sauce and cupcer." Or, when he greeted his breakfast server with a heartfelt "Massa*chu*setts," rather than "Ohio," which Americans are told sounds like "good morning" in Japanese.

I'm in total awe of his progress. You plop yourself down in another country. You don't speak the native tongue. Or anything even close. It takes undistilled guts to keep forging ahead.

Still, after working your head off to become reasonably fluent, you can be heartlessly blindsided. It happens to Ivan after a performance one night in Chicago, while on tour in the winter of 1970. ABT is appearing at the recently refurbished Auditorium Theatre, that shining example of Art Nouveau architecture. On the program is Dennis Nahat's *Brahms Quintet*, to be accompanied by Chicago's own Fine Arts Quartet, led by Leonard Sorkin.

After the show, Leonard and his fellow musicians host Dennis and his *Brahms Quintet* dancers for a lovely *soirée* in his home. Understudies, most welcome. Thank goodness. Because that's all I am. Can you guess for whom? Seven letters. Begins with a C….

After the premiere of Dennis Nahat's *Brahms Quintet* at Brooklyn Academy of Music, December 10, 1969. (From left to right: Antony Tudor, Eleanor D'Antuono, Dennis Nahat and mother Linda Nahat, Gayle Young, Cynthia Gregory, Terry Orr, me, and Martha Hill).

Lots of food. Lots of animated conversation, mostly about music. Ivan sits by, quietly. He seems sad. His eyes look like they're far, far away.

The next day, I question my friend. In a voice that's barely audible, he tells me how much he loves to talk about music.

Back home in Hungary, he'd studied music history, music theory. Alas. He hasn't yet learned the words in English to talk about that. There was so much he wanted to ask last night. And contribute. But he couldn't. You don't wake up one morning and say, "I think I'll learn music vocabulary today." Suddenly, you need it, and it's too late.

The isolation of it all hits me like a punch in the gut. I marvel anew at the intestinal fortitude it takes to do what he and so many others have done. Plop yourself down in a strange land and learn English on the fly. In *my* eyes, that's real bravery. I hug my friend.

The Queen and the Duchess

We begin rehearsals for our Lincoln Center 1970 summer season, my second with the company, at The Met (Metropolitan Opera House). The repertoire is posted on the call board. Yessss! *Giselle* is scheduled for two successive Saturday evenings. Although ABT lists me as a Soloist, in Act II I'm performing the *principal* role of Myrta, Queen of the Wilis (pronounced "Willies"). And my family will get to see me dance it. The best thing about home field advantage is dancing in front of people who actually know you.

Myrta and Me

Queen of the Wilis is quite the adventure. "Daunting" and "incredibly challenging" come to mind. It's a female role requiring male jumping ability. After all, male ballet dancers are famous for jumping really high. So many *grands jetés*. And often, the exchanging of your legs front and back in the air before landing, or "beats" (*batterie*). I work so hard on my *batterie*, but mostly on my *grands jetés*.

The game I play? After thrusting my leg forward while becoming airborne, in my imagination I then "jump over and beyond" my foot. People watching tell me it's as if I'm suspended in the air for a split second. Did I mention that some of the guys in the Company are in the wings, watching, whenever I'm dancing Myrta? Maybe my little game is paying off?

Wait a minute. I've just put the cart before the horse. Before your legs can be put through the "jumping test," they must first become completely pulverized by the "*bourrée* test." Yes, those signature *bourrées* covering the entire stage from wing to wing.

Bourrées are a traveling step with your feet in 5th position, one slightly over-crossed behind the other. You travel by moving your feet up and down and up and down, over and over again. Like the up-and-down of a sewing machine. Only a sewing machine stays in one place, while the fabric moves. In this case, *you're* doing the traveling. And sideways, while your feet stay seemingly forever slightly crossed. The secret is the back foot. Your over-crossed back foot keeps inching sideways, as the front foot plays catch-up while never being allowed to lead the way.

Mind you, there's no time to think of all this when you're out there in front of an audience. By then, you're just deep into your role. It's called performing. You're dancing with whatever technique you've already got, thanks to all the endless hours you've already put in, during class and rehearsals. They've become part of your "Ballet DNA." Now, you just dance. And, of course, it's back to the studio tomorrow, for more endless hours. But, perfection is never the goal. I've heard that Mr. Balanchine says performing is about taking a risk. He says the audience will be bored, if you don't.

So, Myrta, Queen of the Wilis. What on earth *is* a Wili? According to European folklore, *Wilis* are betrothed maidens who die before their wedding day and become spirits.[5] Doomed to roam the forest after midnight, they are forever searching for any man foolish enough to enter their domain. Angry about dying before their wedding day, Wilis will ensnare a hapless male and make him dance until he dies. Ever hear someone say, "It gives me the Wilis?"

Myrta, the Queen of the Wilis, is their heartless leader. Although steeped in athleticism, your role is essentially a dramatic one. Every step, every gesture, has to be executed while maintaining a cold-as-steel demeanor. Because you're of the hereafter. You're a *Wili*. You can never appear perturbed. Steely detachment, your only option. And, your strongest weapon.

The first time Myrta is seen by the audience is hopefully a bit chilling. She's wearing a long white tutu, and her head is covered, front and back to the waist, by a white wedding veil. And, yes, she is doing lots and lots of *bourrées*. She must use these *bourrées* to glide smoothly across the stage, like the other-worldly spirit that she is.

Her first entrance is a diagonal from upstage left across the entire stage, exiting stage right. She reappears, eerily quickly, from the closest upstage right wing she can get to, and immediately crosses the stage once again with *bourrées* before disappearing off stage left.

The third entrance finds Queen Myrta (without the veil) reappearing yet again. This time, from the most downstage left wing. Still more *bourrées*. But now she's here to stay, making a circle that lands her smack dab in the middle of the stage. Hello, legs. Still with me? Because now comes the nerve-racking part. A short *adagio* of slow, controlled movements, while balancing on one leg.

The choreography has you stepping into an *arabesque* on your right leg. That means standing on one leg with the other extended straight behind you. You then revolve once around in place on that leg (*promenade en arabesque*). Still on the same leg, you now have to bend forward toward the floor as your leg in back goes higher and higher (*penché*). Then you must come up again, all without losing your balance.

Finally, you get to switch legs as you do a quick little backbend and come up. The important word is "quick," because everything I just described happens within only eight counts of music. And, in case you got through it well enough on your right leg, don't rejoice yet. You have to repeat the whole sequence to the left.

So many fast *bourrées*. So much standing still and balancing. And *now* you're expected to begin jumping like a man? Complete with the beating *entrechat cinq* and *entrechat six*? Feats that require jumping up and crossing your legs front and back several times in the air before landing? Good grief.

But, to be honest, I'm in heaven. It feels like this tomboy has been preparing to dance Myrta, Queen of the Wilis, her whole life. Since childhood, I've been addicted to sailing through space. Say hello to the 5th-grade Hop-Skip-And-Jump Champion at the Roosevelt Elementary School Field Day. I simply love to jump. Wheeeee! Doesn't every tomboy?

Legs, don't fail me now. You're in the wings with one more "jumping solo" to go. But how about "breath endurance?" Have you been able to get that one breath that takes you "over the top?" The one that normalizes your breathing again, which I've nicknamed my "Myrta breath?"

My most crucial "Myrta breath" comes after my next-to-last sequence of jumping choreography. I'm in the wings, breathing heavily, while the *corps de ballet* is busy onstage for a mere 16 counts of music. This is not a lot of time to find your "Myrta breath."

The *corps de ballet's* choreography? Those infamous forward-hopping *arabesques* in alternating crossing lines. Eight forward-hopping *arabesques* in one direction. Eight immediately back again, in the other.

Okay. Here I go. My last, climactic "jumping" entrance. My favorite. (After that, just pantomime.) And what an entrance it is. The Wilis are posing in a ¾ circle around the edge of the stage as I literally burst out of the upstage left wing in an exultant *grand jeté*. One of three flying leaps toward downstage right. Followed by three more in an upstage half-circle, as if inspecting my obediently-posed Wili troops along the way.

Arriving downstage left once again, I continue with another full, clockwise circle of alternating *grands jetés enterlacés* (leaps that make a half-turn in the air) and *pique en dehors développé pirouettes* (turning on one leg, while raising the other in a high arc in front of you). Count this thrilling-to-perform sequence of two moves as "one," and repeat the sequence three more times in that second clockwise circle. So exhilarating. Okay, one more clockwise circle, while running. This time, calling my troops into action.

So much jumping and turning and jumping and turning and jumping and turning. These three circles are definitely the prelude to a frenzy. Building to a tumultuous climax. This General, closely guarded by her faithful Lieutenants, Moyna and Zulma, is finally leading her troops in a high-energy *grand allegro* with those 16 Wilis of hopping fame now in multiple horizontal lines behind me.

Finally, the impossible. Stopping on a dime. *En pointe*. Then, remaining completely motionless and on balance. With both feet glued together in what ballet calls a *sous-sus*. For what seems like a really, really long time. Because the audience is applauding. And applauding. And Maestro's theatrical sense has paused the music, until the clapping dies down.

***

Stay motionless, Roni. Hide your heavy breathing. The footlights are starting to feel too close. I'm sure there's a hole in one of my lungs. My skin is starting to feel too small for my face. What if it bursts and everything splatters everywhere? Funny, what you think about when you're trying not to fall into the orchestra pit. In Denver's thin air.

Dancing the Queen of the Wilis is never easy. But at a high-altitude of 5,280 feet above sea level? Yikes! Funny, how some roles definitely influence the way you approach and perform others. Even funnier, how some roles actually impact the way you *live your life*. I compare every day-to-day challenge I face to dancing Myrta, Queen of the Wilis, *in Denver*. The Mile-High City. If it is not as hard as dancing Queen Myrta in Denver… it's easy.

In my early 50s, I once scampered up a 1,000 foot high mountain, arriving ahead of everyone else in unbelievable time. When questioned about how this is possible, my uncomplicated reply: "It's easier than dancing Queen of the Wilis in Denver."

How *does* one build the leg and lung endurance to survive just about anything? Madame Swoboda's method is diabolically simple. She "simply" makes me do all my choreography three times in a row, from beginning to end. My lips may be turning blue during the third go-round. Never mind. When I only have to run it once in performance, I'm Wonder Woman. Coach Swoboda? Only thing missing is her whistle.

* * *

It's impossible to talk about *Giselle* without mentioning the storied partnership of Carla Fracci and Erik Bruhn. The quintessential Giselle and Albrecht. Needless to say, performing Myrta with them is … heaven on earth? A dream come true? A gift from the Universe? Take your pick. None suffice. What's more, Carla's theater-director husband Beppe Menegatti gives me "Myrta" coaching tips that practically transform my dramatic interpretation of the role. For starters, he reminds me that my power comes from the earth below the forest floor.

Back to Erik Bruhn. Fate has quite the surprise in store for him. Performing *Giselle* with Carla Fracci is not to be his only storied partnership at American Ballet Theatre. In September of 1970, Natalia ("Natasha") Makarova defects to the West, while performing with the Kirov Ballet in London.[6] Soon after, she joins American Ballet Theatre. Giselle was her signature role with the Kirov, and America can't wait to see her perform it here.

And with none other than Erik Bruhn. In Act I, a feckless nobleman-turned-peasant with a refined charm impossible to resist. Then he breaks your heart in Act II with his legendary Romantic, almost-poetic presence.

Ideally, this iconic performance should take place on the spacious stage of "The Met." But, ABT's Met season doesn't happen till summer. Its upcoming December season is at New York City's City Center. Never mind that the City Center stage is narrower and less "deep."

Our scenery pieces will just have to fit. The choreography will just have to fit.

Director Lucia Chase's delight at presenting a Makarova/Bruhn *Giselle* on Opening Night is short-lived. Poor health scratches Erik from his role as Albrecht. Incredibly, my buddy Ivan Nagy is tapped to replace Erik as Albrecht to Natasha's Giselle.

Lucia naturally wants a star-studded cast for this historic performance, so she *naturally* approaches Cynthia Gregory to dance the Queen of the Wilis. Cynthia has danced it many times. Beautifully, of course. But, in her own words, jumping has just never been her favorite thing. She's a natural turner and a natural balancer.

> **Lucia:** "Dear, I want you to be Natasha's Myrta."
> **Cynthia:** "Thank you, Lucia, but I think you should give it to Roni. You've seen how she jumps in the role. She's a natural jumper, and I'm not."

Now, *that's* a good friend. And that's how I get to share this momentous event with Ivan. And how soon-to-be-a-star Ivan Nagy gets to partner soon-to-be-a-star-in-America Natalia Makarova. This turns out to be a very "beshert" (Yiddish for "meant to be") pairing of two dancers whose styles really, really mesh. And, as Natasha's Myrta, I receive more press than I ever have, in my whole life. Of course, my mother is saving e-v-e-r-y-t-h-i-n-g.

Three months later, our Winter Tour lands us on the West Coast for a string of *Giselles*. First up, Carla in Los Angeles. (Rave reviews.) Now it's Natasha's turn in San Francisco. With Erik Bruhn. At last. This Kirov Ballet defector has become the darling of American audiences, for her touching and ethereal portrayal of that star-crossed peasant girl.

Erik has bravely committed himself to tonight's performance of *Giselle* with Makarova, no matter what. He's determined to give the performance he didn't get to do last December. The "no matter what?" No matter that he's just gotten out of the hospital, after suffering a bleeding ulcer.

Once again, I'm dancing Myrta, Queen of the Wilis. My "preparation ritual" for this role in Act II? I am one of those dancers who needs to sweat in her costume before the curtain goes up. A personal imperative. So, I'm always waiting in the wings, in full costume, when the curtain rings down on Act I. Waiting, that is, for the stagehands to give me the "all clear," that the Act II scenery is sufficiently in place for me to begin "marking" all of my choreography. This intermission is my best friend. I cover the stage from end to end. Getting that blood flowing. Working up the aforementioned perspiration.

My only competition for the space is, of course, whoever is dancing Albrecht that night. Except for a few easy steps, poor Albrecht's Act I contribution has mostly been pantomime. This intermission is his only chance to warm up for some really hard dancing. While he's working on his demanding Act II solo, I confine myself to whatever part of the stage he's not using. When he gets to the part where he's practicing his double *tours en l'air* (jumping up and turning around twice in the air), I'm careful not to be moving in his peripheral vision.

That may be true of other Albrechts, but not Erik Bruhn. Even in good health, I've seen Erik pare down his warm-up for Albrecht's Act II solo to simply this—Eight exceedingly slow, and fastidiously-executed, *petits assemblés*:

1. Jumping off one leg, while brushing the other leg out to the side.
2. "Assembling" both legs together in the air.
3. Returning to the same 5th position he began in, but now with the other foot front. In that all-important *demi-plié* (knees bent).
4. Straightening both knees. Bending them again.

5. Repeating everything with the other leg. As slowly as a drum beat playing a dirge at a funeral march.
6. Then, the entire sequence, six more fastidious times.

When he's done, Erik walks into the wings. The first time I see *his* "preparation ritual," he and I are the only ones onstage. I stop dead in my tracks. Soaking up what I'm seeing. So perfect:

- The heel of the foot that's about to propel him up into the air off one leg. It doesn't budge even a sixteenth of an inch, before leaving the floor.
- The two airborne legs, so perfectly placed, one in front of the other. With the straightest knees and the most pointed toes possible.
- The impeccable 5th position landing in *demi-plié*.

I simply can't take my eyes off any of it. I'm recording it in my mind. Detail for detail. For always and forever.

But tonight's performance will be like no other. Remember, Erik is fresh out of the hospital. Once again, we're onstage alone at the intermission. Out of the corner of my eye, I can tell that Erik's warm-up ritual is very, very limited. Conserving energy, no doubt. Then, the most unexpected conversation.

ERIK: "I may not be able to get through my whole variation. If I need to come to you early, you'll have to do something."
RONI: "Of course. I'll figure it out. Don't worry."

Okay. *Giselle.* Overture, finished. Curtain, up. Act I, over. Middle of Act II. Myrta's command post, after all that frenzied choreography described earlier, is downstage left. There I stand, facing the audience. Motionless and unfeeling. As Giselle, Natasha is now heading in a diagonal from upstage right, embracing an armful of lilies. She'll allow them to spill downward from her embrace, when she reaches me. Lilies at my feet. Quite the attempt to buy leniency. To spare her beloved Albrecht from the fate of being danced to death.

Mind you, these are not the silken lilies from our Prop Department. Those can land silently on the stage behind me, as I'm facing the audience. These are plastic lilies. The ones Natasha has bought herself, and wants to use. Something about the way it was in Russia? Let's just say, in performance, those plastic lilies don't exactly land soundlessly on the stage behind me. Can't react. Not even an eyelash moves.

The time has come for Albrecht's variation. I am still at my downstage left command post. Only I'm no longer facing the audience. Having heartlessly commanded Albrecht to keep on dancing, I'm now facing stage right. Erik's dancing is looking more labored than usual. Thinking to myself, "Thank goodness, at this point in his solo, every Albrecht is supposed to look exhausted. After all, my Wilis have been trying to make him dance until he dies."

Sure enough, after getting through only his first sequence of steps, Erik "falters" downstage right. Is he playacting? Is he for real? I don't have to wait long for my answer. Here he comes. Straight towards me. True, his lunging, "exhausted" steps along the footlights are definitely theatrically enhanced. But the emotion in his eyes, when kneeling in front of me, pleading to let him stop dancing? That's *not* pretending. One look says it all. This is the moment he predicted would come.

Need to fill the music. Need to fill the music. In my life, never so slowly have I delivered the pantomime gestures that mean, "You ... here ... must ... die." Now I'm suddenly commanding him to stand. Now, even more suddenly, my index finger is pointing fiercely toward upstage right. He appropriately "staggers" backwards.

Is this really happening? Is Roni Mahler using strong, unyielding, methodical steps to force an off-balance Erik Bruhn backwards, practically all the way into the upstage right corner of the stage? But, here's the best part. My strong, unyielding, methodical steps are scrunching and crushing those plastic lilies underfoot. Now, *that's* a sound to remember.

The final measures of Albrecht's solo are finally, thankfully upon us. With Erik safely ensconced upstage right, I quickly about-face and hightail it back to the safety of my downstage left command post. Leaving Erik free to pull off Albrecht's classic "collapse," smack dab in the middle of the stage.

The audience erupts. Wild applause. Lots of bravos. At the exotic restaurant where we all dine afterwards, I vaguely remember doing vodka shots for the first (and last) time.

Channeling Francisco de Goya

One of the greatest gifts a ballet company can give its dancers is a rich and varied repertoire. The chance for artistic growth through diverse roles of varying texture and psychological motivation. American Ballet Theatre bestows just such a gift upon me. During a single season, I get to morph from the impassive and steely resolve of a dead Wili into a character so different, it strains credulity. How about a hot-blooded, fearless, and haughty woman? All this is made possible by life's tiny little twists and turns, without which some really huge things might never have happened.

In 1950, a Broadway dancer, Herbert Ross, is recuperating from a broken ankle. He goes to a museum and is inspired by the most important artist of the Spanish Enlightenment, Francisco de Goya, whose paintings include "The Black Duchess" and "La maja desnuda." Ross is thoroughly captivated by a series of Goya satirical etchings, entitled *Los Caprichos* ("The Caprices").[7] Francisco de Goya seems to have expertly captured the extremes of human emotion. Ross is moved to choreograph in a workshop setting. He calls his resulting effort, *Caprichos*.

American Ballet Theatre is impressed. They include *Caprichos* in the Company's 1950 10th Anniversary season. Now, almost twenty years later, ABT is reviving *Caprichos*. And I get to perform one of my most stirring, albeit brief, roles ever.

One of Goya's sketches depicts a lonely woman wearing a Spanish shawl and a very high hair comb. The Duchess of Alba. In *Caprichos*, this haughty creature ventures out alone, late at night. Decked out in her recognizable accessories, and intentionally courting a danger she fully believes she can control. What begins as the teasing of two men on the street quickly spirals into a violent rape. She is last seen fleeing, almost strangling herself with her once-majestic shawl.

Now, here I am in a studio with "Herbie." I've been learning the role of the haughty Duchess of Alba. When a woman shows up to coach, you could knock me over with a feather—ABT ballerina Nora Kaye. Herbie's wife of ten years, and an icon in her own right.

Nora's dramatic interpretations are legendary. "Hagar" in Antony Tudor's *Pillar of Fire* (1942) makes her a star. Another memorable role: "The Accused" in *Fall River Legend*, Agnes de Mille's depiction of the Lizzie Borden murders. Nora can also pull off classical ballet roles. She receives kudos for her portrayals of Odile, when performing the *Black Swan Pas de Deux* as an excerpt from the full-length ballet.[8]

Is this ballet luminary actually going to *coach me* today? Yes. Nora Kaye is watching now, as I go through the *Caprichos* choreography she herself once danced. Pinch me. It's the second time I'm being coached by the originator of a role.

The first time was also at ABT, by Eugenia Delarova, Léonide Massine's second wife. And the very first Flower Girl in his *Gaîté Parisienne*. Mme. Delarova teaches me the importance of being at the "other end of the spectrum" from the "elegant" Glove Seller. After all, this feisty Flower Girl chug-a-lugs beer while joking around with the Waiters before the café doors open.

And now, it's Nora Kaye who's sharing her priceless nuances and even some practical suggestions about securing that very tall comb of a headpiece. She's

Performing "Flower Girl" in Léonide Massine's *Gaîté Parisienne* with ABT in 1970, alongside "Waiters" (from left to right) James Zynda, Robert Gladstein, and David Coll (Photo by Martha Swope. Courtesy of American Ballet Theatre; Jerome Robbins Dance Division, New York Public Library for the Performing Arts).

especially helpful with the subtleties of what I call my "gradual transition." Evolving from haughty enticer into fearful stalkee. Thank you, thank you, Nora Kaye.

The power of this role is almost overwhelming. But it's the exit that's especially emblazoned in my psyche: Circling the stage, while madly wrapping that shawl three times around my neck. Jerking my chin back with my upward-thrusting arm. Fleeing into the wings in a frenzy of pain. I end up performing those three turbulent minutes of choreography a total of 11 times on the Winter Tour.

Now, here's the kicker. The dynamics needed for this portrayal of the Duchess seem to add another dimension to every other role I'm performing on tour. Even the happy ones. Just like Valerie Bettis's Tomboy did for me, not quite ten years ago in the National Ballet. That Tomboy in *Early Voyagers* is the only other time I can remember being asked to portray such raw emotion onstage. Such an ephemeral sensation. Like watching yourself evolve.

* * *

The Winter '71 tour is in the rear-view mirror. It feels like we've been rehearsing forever for this upcoming summer season at The Met. My third. Leg endurance and breath endurance are more than ready. We know which ballets will be performed, and how many times for each. My beloved *Caprichos* has one performance. Great. I've been writing home from tour about this role. Now, "home" can finally see what I've been writing about.

Nothing can prepare me for what happens next. Rehearsals are posted 48 hours in advance. (Union rules.) The cast to be on the floor, for each ballet being rehearsed, must be listed. Role by role. Understudies for each role are in parentheses next to each name.

You always check The Board at night, when leaving the studios. You do it without thinking. I see *Caprichos*. What I see next almost knocks me over:

DUCHESS: *Serrano (Mahler)*

Lupe Serrano is dancing the only *Caprichos*? After all my hard work? Not possible. Don't get me wrong. Lupe Serrano, an ABT principal dancer for years, is a glorious ballerina. Strong technique that never stops. A fiery personality that never fails to ignite the audience's passion. Lupe is one of several former stars making guest appearances during the season. Well-known fact: Lucia Chase worships her stars.

I cry for days. Inconsolably. My friends say I must talk to Lucia. Lucia Chase? The one and only? A native of Waterbury, Connecticut, Lucia is whispered to be tied to the Chase Brass fortune. More importantly, she is also a co-founding director (with Richard Pleasant) of American Ballet Theatre.

Yes, Lucia does all the casting. But why bother talking to her? Her mind is already made up, and Lucia never changes her mind. My friends persist. They say I need to tell her how I feel. She has to know, and I will feel better. I doubt it. Still, my feet finally wend their way to Lucia's dressing room.

> **ME:** "Lucia. I can't believe you are taking me out of *Caprichos*. I worked myself to the bone for that ballet. I danced it eleven times. And I got good reviews." (Lucia always reads the reviews.)

> LUCIA: "Well, dear. You see, Lupe is one of our Guest Artists for this season. Our Guest Artists have to appear at least once in each week. And *Caprichos* is the only thing Lupe can do in the second week."
> ME: "When was the last time she danced it?"
> LUCIA: "Ten years ago, on television. I'm sure you can help her, dear."
> ME (through tears): "Lucia. I'm begging you. New York is my hometown. My chance to dance in front of my family. My friends. Please."
> LUCIA: "Just a minute, dear. I'll give you an extra Queen of the Wilis. You can dance Myrta in the matinee next Saturday. It is Mimi's [Paul] first *Giselle*. You see, I am putting it in right now. (Erasing and rewriting.) See?"
> ME: "But Lucia. I am already dancing Myrta that same evening."
> LUCIA: "Yes, dear. You can rest between shows."

I leave her dressing room in stunned disbelief. Can anyone even get through a matinee and evening of Myrta? Heaven help me. As for the *Caprichos* rehearsals, I hatch a plan. Hang back. Watch Lupe's every move. Learn. Admire. Be invisible.

How quickly my plan dissolves. Invisible will not work. Lupe is pretty lost. I jump in to help. And help. And help. Finally, she turns to me:

> LUPE: "You performed this a lot?"
> ME: "Eleven times, on this past tour."
> LUPE: "This is ridiculous. I'll talk to Lucia."

Surprise, surprise. Lucia is undeterred. The great thing about the rest of our rehearsals is getting to know Lupe. Is it possible that she's the nicest person on the planet? Warm. Gracious. Funny. We have a ball. She even has some hot tips on getting through my Double Myrta.

In the end, the World-According-To-Lucia unfolds just as she planned it. Fact: The Earth does not fall off its axis. Fact: My legs do not fall off after a Double Myrta. Fact: When the sun rises, it is always tomorrow. Imagine that.

Apparently, *New York Times* Dance Critic, Clive Barnes, reviews *both* performances of *Giselle* that day.

On Monday June 29, 1970, he writes:

> *A final word for the fine performances given by Roni Mahler as Queen of the Wilis.*[9]

Plural. Hmmm. Clive Barnes says I pulled it off.

The Casting Pixies and Me

Sometimes "casting pixie" mischief occurs because of injuries. As in the case of Cynthia's ankle. At other times, it can be Lucia Chase's whims. At still other times, the mischief of these casting pixies can be traced directly to the inscrutable nature of one very specific nemesis. This is the story of how I lose three roles. All because of the enigmatic antics of just such a nemesis.

The ballets change. The choreographers change. My nemesis never changes. She-Who-Will-Not-Share-Her-Roles is an overpowering constant throughout my ABT career. Jerome Robbins succumbs once. Agnes de Mille, twice.

Act Two

* * *

Let's begin on the Winter Tour in 1970. *Fall River Legend* is de Mille's wrenching take on the alleged ax murderer Lizzie Borden. Lucia wants me to have a crack at second cast of "The Accused." First cast is none other than She-Who-Will-Not-Share-Her-Roles.

We are performing in Houston. The show that evening is a mixed bill of repertoire. No matter. There's an afternoon rehearsal of *Fall River Legend,* a completely different ballet. Principal roles, only. Apparently, Agnes will be popping in to see a rehearsal of *Fall River* when we get to Chicago. It's Lucia's plan to have me dance the run-through then. If Agnes approves, I can keep working on the role for a future performance.

Today's rehearsal involves a twenty-minute Company bus ride to Houston Ballet's studios. Maybe they're on tour? Anyway, we have the run of the place. We make ourselves at home in their large main studio. We're concentrating on the flashback sequence. Lizzie, in blood-spattered clothing, encountering her deceased Mother.

The first cast has the floor. We of the second cast are learning by copying. In the very, very, very back. You could say I'm uncomfortable. Openly having to emulate Miss Nemesis. Her every move. Her every gesture, glance. Nevertheless, I forge ahead. Lucia and her watchful gaze are seated in front, in the corner on the other side of the door.

On the hour, stage manager Ralph McWilliams calls the five-minute break. I remain shakily ensconced at the back of the studio. Suddenly, Miss Nemesis is slowly headed toward the One-Who-Has-Been-Shadowing-Her. The studio doesn't feel large enough. Her measured pace never falters.

Still walking, she intones, "Are you learning me?" Without pausing. My stammering, "yes," almost addresses her back, as she continues walking back to the front of the studio. I turn away, trying to erase her from the room.

When I'm facing front again, Lucia's index finger is silently beckoning me to come to her. Clear across the studio. She stands and takes my hand in both of hers.

"Dear. There's been a mistake. I'm sorry, but you must go now." It takes a moment or two for me to realize that she's pressing something into the palm of my hand. As I walk away, I open my clenched fingers. A twenty-dollar bill? Cab fare back to the hotel.

* * *

The tour has ended. Soon, we're in Spring rehearsals for our 1970 summer season at The Met. My second. Here we go again. If this story starts to sound familiar, it is. Just replace "Agnes" with "Jerry."

As in, Jerome Robbins. You see, Director Lucia Chase has told "Jerry" that she wants to bring back his triumphant production of *Les Noces*, which he choreographed five years earlier, for ABT's 25th Anniversary Gala.

In Lucia's words back then: "No 25th Anniversary of ABT would be complete or conceivable without a new ballet by Jerry Robbins." Jerry decides to tackle *Les Noces*, composed by Stravinsky and staged by Bronislava Nijinska for Diaghilev's Ballets Russes in Paris in 1923.[10]

The first scene depicts the ritualistic preparation of the Bride's long tresses, led by the Female Matchmaker. The second scene takes place in the House of the

Bridegroom. In the third scene (ending Part One), the Bride journeys to the Groom. Part Two is the Wedding Feast.

Ahead of the 1965 Gala Premiere, Jerry lays it on the line to Lucia:

1. Four hours of rehearsal a day.
2. "Full" first cast present at all rehearsals.
3. He can "pull" *Les Noces* at the last minute, if his vision feels unrealized.

Conditions met. *Les Noces* premieres to accolades galore.

Now, five years later, Jerry isn't making it any easier:

1. He will view a run-through, after his stellar assistant, James "Jimmy" Moore, sets the entire ballet.
2. If Jerry doesn't think our run-through is up to snuff, we can't perform *Les Noces* at The Met this summer.

"But Jerry," pleads Lucia. "There won't be time to ready another ballet in its place." Not his problem.

Our Day of Reckoning is finally here. So is Jerry, and he's not a happy man. Maybe it has something to do with that cast on his broken leg? Lucia has given me Mother of the Groom in the second scene. I would be second cast, of course. Never mind that the first cast is my nemesis, the Notorious-Non-Sharer-Of-Her-Roles. Since Jerry has already seen her perform the role at the premiere back in 1965, I'll be the one dancing at the pivotal run-through. No pressure, right?

Still, this tomboy is over the moon. Anyone who's ever seen *West Side Story* or *Fiddler on the Roof* knows Robbins is at his zenith when choreographing for men *en masse*. This time, Jerry gets to see *me* vibrating within his male force of controlled frenzy. A female holding her own on a stage brimming with testosterone.

I've just spent four weeks bruising every inch of my body. Now I'm about to throw every bruised inch into a portrayal I hope will win Jerry's approval. Pounding. Stomping to throbbing percussion. Aching. Unrelenting vocals propelling me forward. Exhilaration. When I finish, all eyes turn to him. "Fine. She can do Female Matchmaker."

Just like Jerry to pull a switch like that. "Reward" me with an entirely different role. It jolts me like an earthquake. Two weeks. Only two weeks to master the opposite of everything I've just learned. But, hey. I did get to dance for Jerry. And he *did* put me in his ballet.

I guess I'll never know what *really* happened. My Rasputin mind comes up with this: Perhaps, Nemesis told Lucia, early on, that she didn't want me to *perform* her Mother-of-the-Bridegroom role, even as second cast? And when Jerry arrived to watch our run-through, Lucia let him know that I can never actually perform Mother-of-the-Groom, but I could be "reassigned" if he likes me?

I wonder again. Why *does* Nemesis hold such sway over Lucia? Impossible to understand.

* * *

So, after the Houston "episode" during our '70 Winter Tour, there goes Lizzie for Agnes in Chicago. Fast forward a year. It's the spring of '71, following *that* year's

Winter Tour. Once again, we're rehearsing in those studios at City Center. Agnes is in the early stages of a possible new work, *A Rose for Miss Emily*. In her words, the "experimenting" stages of the choreography process.

It's a low-key Sunday morning in one of the smaller studios on the fifth floor. A glance at the Call Board. I don't have to tell you who's first cast for the role of Emily. Nemesis. *My* name, of course, is the one in parentheses. During our first five-minute break, I retreat to the comforting confines of the adjacent dressing room.

Right on cue, in walks Agnes. "I'm so sorry, Roni. For some reason, she says she cannot learn with you in the room. I'm going to have to ask you to leave." No cab fare necessary. The subway's on the corner. I'm in tears well before the train doors open.

So, that's all she wrote with Agnes. But there are some glimmers of hope. On the just-completed ABT Winter Tour, I *did* get the chance to perform (as second cast) a coveted principal role. You guessed it. First cast: Ms. Nemesis. The powers-that-be were apparently pleased enough and I'm rewarded with another performance during the summer season at The Met.

After the bows, I'm still reeling from the thrill of it all. At The Met, you ride the elevator, still in costume, to your dressing room. My elevator makes an unexpected stop. In walks Lucia.

"It was lovely, dear. A pity you'll never dance it again. It is, after all, Sallie's role." No more tears left.

Rest in peace, Nemesis.

José and Me

The word is out. Toni Lander is, indeed, pregnant with her second child. Why does this matter? In June of 1970, American Ballet Theatre premiered its production of *The Moor's Pavane*, José Limón's iconic take on Shakespeare's *Othello*. The cast is stunning: Bruce Marks as The Moor, Toni Lander as Desdemona, Royes Fernandez as Iago, Sallie Wilson as Emilia.[11]

The Moor's Pavane is a hit. Toni is being hailed for her touching portrayal of Desdemona. And *Pavane* will be scheduled for both the '71 Winter tour and the '71 Summer season at The Met.

Job One. Rehearsing a new Desdemona ... *right now*. In the Fall of 1970. But who? Cynthia Gregory, of course. Her lyricism and dramatic impact are perfect for this tragic role. Fact is, so much of Desdemona's choreography also involves Emilia. Decision made. Train a new Emilia right along with her. Ta Da!

* * *

Cynthia and I are placed in the capable and talented hands of Jennifer Muller. Jennifer has recently appeared with the Louis Falco Dance Company at New York City Center and is currently teaching at Sarah Lawrence College. ABT is rehearsing at New York City Center studios. Company Class, 9:30 a.m. Rehearsals, between 11:00 a.m. and 8:00 p.m. We can only be scheduled for any six of those nine hours.

Jennifer's Sarah Lawrence schedule leaves her free for only the 6:00–8:00 p.m.

rehearsal slot. Cynthia and I are practically guaranteed the previous hour for a much-needed break. Easy decision. Out the stage door. Across 55th Street. A booth at Francine's Luncheonette. Our home away from home.

"Two root beer floats, please." The magic words that will be fueling us through these early evening hours of rehearsal. When it comes to paying the check, Francine's owner, Gregory, is a hoot:

> **Owner Gregory:** "35 cents each."
> **One of Us:** "Yesterday it was only 30."
> **Owner Gregory:** "Okay."

Cynthia and I have always insisted that the basis for our enduring friendship is food. If there's an hour off, someone is asking, "Anyone up for Francine's?"

"I am," chime two voices in unison. We're always ready to eat.

Jennifer's magic is actually all the fuel we need for these *Pavane* rehearsals. Aware that Cynthia and I know nothing about Limón technique, she wisely begins with a 15–20 minute "Limón" warm-up. I adore this new way of moving. It's all about the concepts of weight, of arc, of flow. Limón turns my technique world upside down.

It's those three words: weight, arc, and flow. Everything is so "rounded" now. You're not only "connected" to the floor, you seem to be drawn right *through* it. Ballet dancers defy gravity? Modern dancers use it. I've spent my dancing life trying to appear "light and effortless," in order to look "graceful." In *this* world, swooping in a *downward* arc is graceful.

Something else I'm not prepared for. Portraying a somewhat-layered friendship onstage, with someone who's actually a good friend. Desdemona and Emilia are close-knit. So are Cynthia and Roni. Once, when Limón's expressive choreography has me tending to Desdemona's hair, I almost tear up. It happens again, when things get complicated later on.

"Give *of* yourself, but *not* yourself." Did anyone ever say that? Well, they should have. I guess it's my way of saying, "Roni. It's okay to draw on your feelings. But, not to the point where you're in so deep that you lose your focus."

I'm so glad Bruce Marks is still The Moor. I think he and Cynthia make a very powerful couple. My pal Ivan is tapped for Iago, to my Emilia. Iago and Emilia dance that tension-filled "handkerchief" duet. I can't wait.

While Cynthia and I are having our dinner-hour sessions with Jennifer, the men begin working with Daniel Lewis during the day. Danny has been performing with the Limón Company since 1962. You could say José is in his threads. When the full cast finally begins rehearsing in the daytime, he takes the helm.

I'm fascinated by Danny. He's one of the most Zen-like people I've ever run into. Calm. Focused. Patient, to a fault. Sometimes, an almost other-worldly look in his eyes. Get this. In 32-degree weather, his winter coat is a quilted vest. If it dips below 15, he adds a wool scarf. Something about preserving the body's natural self-warming mechanisms?

Costumes are ordinarily worn only for the "tech" rehearsal on stage. The lighting designer needs everyone in costume then, to tweak his "plot" (lighting plan).

But, Emilia's gorgeous (and heavy) plush orange velvet dress brings with it about four feet of gorgeous (and heavy) plush orange velvet train. It's going to take more than one rehearsal to get comfortable maneuvering it. *This* costume definitely has its own choreography. And cries out for extra rehearsals.

Wardrobe has agreed. I'm able to wear the velvet costume in the last two studio rehearsals before the tour. Tips from the other Emilia? Not forthcoming. Never mind. I still get better and better, handling that train. And you have to agree. Wearing the costume always infuses you with the "spirit" of a role. These two studio rehearsals definitely help me find the essence of Emilia.

* * *

Goodbye, studio rehearsals. Hello, Winter Tour '71. Beginning with two whole weeks at the Dorothy Chandler Pavilion in Los Angeles. And *The Moor's Pavane* is on the program in the second week. The moment I've been waiting for. My first performance of Emilia.

It's now the Monday of our second week. The Company is having its "free day." I've come to the theater anyway. I need to try making sense of my dressing room theater place, before the new week begins. A little housekeeping is definitely in order.

I've been dancing multiple ballets each night. Eight performances in six days. Double shows, Saturday and Sunday. This can definitely contribute to Dressing Table Disarray. Your makeup and hair paraphernalia are all over the place. I'm sorting the hairpins. Normal... Tiny... Extra thick. Each has a different job. Pancake, rouge, eyeshadow, mascara. All back in the makeup box. Oh-so-carefully peeling caked liquid adhesive off false eyelashes. Otherwise, not even a lash curler keeps them from sitting too "flat" on my eyelids. Finally, order restored.

This is a good time to meet Jennifer ("Jenny") Scanlon: Limón Company dancer since 1963; dancer of principal roles; eventually, José's associate artistic director. Jenny has popped into LA to help Danny put *Pavane* on the stage at tomorrow's Tech rehearsal. Definitely, a two-person job.

Tech rehearsals are so important, not only for the lighting designer. This is also when Danny and Jenny place all of *Pavane's* choreography exactly where it's supposed to happen on the stage. Upstage, away from the audience? Downstage, toward the audience? Stage right? Stage left? Diagonally downstage right...? You get the picture. Danny and Jenny also tell you precisely which wing to use for each entrance and exit. No collisions.

Now that my theater place is sufficiently organized, I find myself staring down at it, totally lost in thought. Staring at what? Why, the beautiful hairpiece Jenny has so graciously handed down to me, for my Emilias. The exact one she always wore. I can't believe she's given it to me. The brown curls, beautifully entwined with gold brocade ribbon. Evoking the gold brocade trim of my cherished orange velvet costume. Jenny's gift makes me feel so "connected" to the rich Limón history. To its mystique. Can you tell I adore this ballet? This costume? I can't practice in it today, though. The Union says a Wardrobe person would have to be present.

Instead, I'll practice attaching Jenny's hairpiece a couple of times. For the performance, I'll be making a quick change from dancing the ballet right before. So a little repetition couldn't hurt. Besides, I need to "audition" my assorted hairpins. Now, so neatly organized by size and strength.

It's like learning another piece of choreography. The art of securely attaching a new hairpiece to the back of my head. A familiar challenge, since my short hair doesn't leave much to pin into. Will this work? Or, as I like to say, "Will it dance?" Tomorrow's tech rehearsal will tell the tale.

So, here I am. Sitting at my theater place two flights down from Stage Level at the Dorothy Chandler. Concentrating madly in my own little world. Hair pins in my teeth and more hair pins in my hands. A loud voice over the PA system shatters my concentration: "Mahler on stage. Mahler on stage."

Did I forget a rehearsal? Am I late? Holding hair pins everywhere, I dash up the two flights of stairs, two steps at a time. I am too rattled to remember that it's my free day.

As I run into the wings on Stage Right, I stop short just in time to see the Los Angeles Philharmonic seated on stage. Their Maestro is tapping his conductor's stand for attention. One or two musicians cast a puzzled glance my way, but quickly look back to their scores.

They are, of course, about to rehearse the "Mahler selection." Good one, Roni.

So, how did my *Pavane* debut go? When people ask me that, I always want to say, "Don't ask me. Ask the audience." But, how did it *feel*? I was in heaven, and I think it went off without a hitch. Lots of positive feedback.

* * *

It's now August of 1971. I'm in the middle of ABT's summer season at The Met. My third. I have one performance of *Pavane*, and it's coming up soon. Then we hear the almost unbelievable. The Man, himself, will be arriving. José Limón, in the flesh.

José is still mourning the passing last month of his wife of thirty years, Pauline Lawrence. The Limón Company's costume designer since the late '40s, and José's other half. Still, Limón will rehearse with us for two days. I know he's going to be working section-by-section, because I'm scheduled for two hours with him. Unmolded clay in the hands of the Master Sculptor. Don't wake me up from this dream.

The first hour is "The Duet," with Ivan. José is watching me and wants *more*. It's the moment when I've managed to get my hands on Desdemona's lace-bordered handkerchief. My husband, Iago, is demanding that I hand it over. I'm holding back, out of loyalty to my friend.

José concentrates on that intense moment when I can no longer resist my husband's "stroking." Sexual desire proves stronger than loyalty. I succumb to the will of my conniving husband, and my body must express that total submission. A word here and there from José, and I even amaze myself.

The next day, it's just Mr. Limón and I. In that rehearsal room for a whole hour. Pinch me. He's working on Emilia's "Handkerchief Solo," which precedes "The Duet." Emilia is wrestling with her guilt, after having spirited said handkerchief away from dear friend, Desdemona.

José speaks so quietly, so gently, through his grief. It's breaking my heart. He urges me here. Challenges me there. I'm transfixed by those large, expressive hands.

Spellbound by the authority emanating from the back of his neck. All this, burned into memory, for what turns out to be only one more performance.

A mere sixteen months later, El Maestro loses his battle with cancer. He's with Pauline, now.

As "Dawn" in Coppélia with American Ballet Theatre in Winter 1970 (Photo by Martha Swope. ©Billy Rose Theatre Division, The New York Public Library for the Performing Arts. Courtesy of American Ballet Theatre).

Third Intermission
Looking Back

The Critics and Me

I guess I'll spend a little time talking about my "reviews." Meaning, what Dance Critics have written about my performances over the years. These are tricky waters. Any discussion of dance critics is fraught. The choices are:

1. Like the critics who give you good reviews? (Nah.)
2. Dislike the critics who don't? (Nah.)
3. Hop off the roller-coaster and decide to believe neither the good ones, nor the not-so-good ones? (Good idea.)
4. Maintain that even the worst review contains a speck of truth? (Emotional stability and maturity, required.)

Some dancers claim never to read reviews at all. Not me. I'll mention five.

You already know about my first review ever, which incidentally turns out to be my best review ever. When Uncle Fred came running down the street, waving a newspaper. How can I ever forget P.W. Manchester writing, "All the soloists were excellent, but Roni Mahler stood out by taking the stage as if by divine right, that touch that marks the special ones"?

Moving right along. Let's go a little bit out of order. I want to get the other good reviews out of the way now. Because, then the fun begins. We're jumping from the National Ballet of Washington to American Ballet Theatre.

It's ABT's summer 1970 season at Lincoln Center's Metropolitan Opera House. Two *New York Times* dance critics are commenting on my same performance as Queen of the Wilis.

Don McDonagh: "In the second act, Roni Mahler was icily precise as Myrta, the implacable head of the revengeful Wilis."[1]

Clive Barnes, referring to my *grands jetés*: "Roni Mahler is as high-flying as ever as Myrta."[2]

I'm especially grateful for Mr. Barnes's "high-flying" label. He had called me "the punchy Roni Mahler" the year before, at the Brooklyn Academy of Music. When Cynthia Gregory, Ted Kivitt, and I appeared in *Divertissement D'Auber*.

I actually get to humorously broach the subject with the Man Himself, at a post-performance gathering a few months after "punchy" makes it into the *New York Times*.

Roni: "Mr. Barnes. You called me punchy."
Mr. Barnes: "In England, 'punchy' means feisty."
Roni: "In America, it means drunk."

Okay. Three reviews down, two to go. Let's hop backward to the National Ballet, again. And switch gears to Jean Battey, Dance Critic of the *Washington Post*.

She happens to attend a Sunday matinée, circa 1964. I happen to be dancing the Waltz in *Les Sylphides*. I also happen to have awakened with a completely stiff neck. Can't turn to the right. Can't turn to the left. But the show must go on.

I end up clipping and saving what Ms. Battey pens that day:

"Roni Mahler seemed a bit tentative in the Waltz." One of my all-time favorites.

Saving the best for last? Courtesy of Jean Battey again. I return to the National Ballet for some guest performances, following marriage and the birth of my wonderful son, Erik.

The Ballet: Anton Dolin's staging of *Pas de Quatre*, depicting four of the 19th century's most illustrious ballerinas. Marie Taglioni, Carlotta Grisi, Fanny Cerrito, and Lucile Grahn.[3]

My role: Ballerina Lucile Grahn, the lone Dane among three Italians. Trained from a young age by famous ballet teacher August Bournonville, she is known for her excellent jumps and glittering "*batterie.*" That's the art of alternately crossing one's legs in the air while "beating" them together, before landing.

Lucile Grahn's solo famously ends with 32 *entrechats quatres*. One *entrechat quatre* requires jumping in the air, "beating" once with the other leg in front, and then landing with the original leg in front again. That repeats 31 more times. So, 32 jumps in a row.

Childbirth is known to have some residual effects. Notably, in the area of bladder control. 32 jumps in a row is still as easy for me now, as before. The issue isn't muscle or cardio endurance. It's repetition. As in, 32 jumps in a row. What's a girl to do? Not too much, aside from adding some significant padding.

Ms. Battey's review: "Roni Mahler executed her 32 *entrechats quatres* with a faint smile on her face." I don't doubt it for a minute.

Okay. I lied. There's a sixth review. I almost forgot about this one, because it occurs so much later. In 2006, when I'm 64 and only dancing character roles.

This time, I'm portraying Giselle's Mother in Dennis Nahat's Ballet San Jose production of *Giselle*. Janice Berman prefaces her mention of me in the *San Francisco Chronicle* with the words, "The legendary Roni Mahler...."[4]

I guess that's what happens when you're around forever.

Lucia's Roles and Me

American Ballet Theatre's storied director, Lucia Chase, hails from Waterbury, Connecticut. As a young girl, she actually dreamed of an acting career. In 1933, after the untimely death of her husband Tom Ewing, the 36-year-old grieving widow throws herself into studying ballet with Mikhail Mordkin. Four years later, she dances as a soloist with his Mordkin Ballet, the artistic outlet for talented ballet students in his School.⁵ Lucia co-funds that performance. Her father was president of Waterbury Clock Company. Her uncle founded Chase Brass and Copper.

In 1938, the Mordkin Ballet adds many new soloists. Lucia is still performing as one of them. By 1939, the nascent Ballet Theatre (ABT's predecessor) launches as an outgrowth of the Mordkin Ballet.⁶ It is co-directed by Lucia Chase and Richard Pleasant, and Lucia is still a soloist. Her eye-popping stage presence more than compensates for her late start in classical ballet training. And critics praise her character performances.

Why am I talking about Lucia's performing career? Because, when I'm in ABT, Lucia is always casting me in roles she used to dance. Do I, in some way, remind her of herself? Hopefully, it's my presence onstage.

Exhibit 1: I dance the Waltz in *Les Sylphides*. Lucia used to dance the Waltz in *Les Sylphides*. Noted ABT dancer and choreographer Antony Tudor has a doozie of a story about Lucia in *Les Sylphides*. It's about how she created added momentum for her *bourrée* reentry from downstage left, in the opening *Nocturne*.

Every performance, Tudor watches Lucia prepare in that downstage left wing. Ahead of time, she perches up *en pointe*, with both feet in 5th position. On her entry music, she gamely "pushes sideways off" a backstage pole. How swift are those *bourrées*, as she glides sideways onto the stage!

Exhibit 2: I dance the Eldest Sister in Tudor's *Pillar of Fire*. Lucia was the original Eldest Sister in *Pillar of Fire*. In 1942, when choreographing *Pillar*, Tudor creates the role of Hagar's Eldest Sister especially for Lucia.⁷ Aware that her pointe technique has its limitations, he's extremely accommodating.

He knows she can easily manage to *relevé* on two feet. Starting with both heels on the floor, knees bent in *demi-plié*, she can then simply push up onto pointe, as both knees straighten.

But, the art of *piqué*? That takes a different strength. To *piqué* onto one foot with the requisite straight knee, you have to push off from your other leg, in *demi-plié*. Lucia can't do that. The only way *she* can *piqué* up to pointe on one leg is to first bend her knee, "planting" her pointe shoe like a stake in the ground. *Then* she can straighten her knee. Voilà.

Mr. Tudor brilliantly decides to choreograph exactly what Lucia *can* do. On her very first entrance from the downstage left wing, her 4th position *relevé* is, safely, on *two feet*. The bare mechanics of her subsequent *piqué* onto *only one foot*? That takes three moves. Tudor has her:

1. First, cross the foot wishing to get up onto pointe in front of the other foot, with a bent knee, so she can....
2. Then, plant that pointe shoe of the now-bent leg securely and squarely on its toes, so she can....
3. Finally, push up onto pointe as the knee of her crossed leg straightens.

Tudor now has two steps that work for Lucia. The two-foot *relevé* and the one-foot, bent leg *piqué*. He masterfully creates an unusual choreographic sequence for Lucia's first entrance from downstage left. And repeats it three times, emblazoning it in your memory. I once heard a balletomane comment on Lucia's entrance: "So innovative. He was years before his time."

Exhibit 3: I dance the Fourth Song in Tudor's *Dark Elegies*. Lucia danced the Fourth Song in Tudor's *Dark Elegies* in 1940. Tailor-made for her dramatic abilities. She even gives me coaching tips for one of the most moving gestures.

I've decided to take this similar casting as a compliment. Lucia was known for her acting skills on the ballet stage. She was a powerful presence. Does she see a bit of that in me? I hope so. After all, I really do prefer roles that are not just a string of pretty steps. Instead, something I can sink my teeth into. *Dark Elegies* and *Pillar of Fire* definitely give me that.

Act Three
Onward and Upward

It's the summer of 1971. Erik is now three, and the tug-of-war is killing me. To the point of feeling almost unbearable. As a soloist with ABT, I'm dancing up a storm. Roles of a lifetime. Total exhilaration. But, all the while, so inconveniently shackled to an inflexible touring schedule.

Inconvenient, because, as a mother, I face a more crucial mission. Guiding Erik's path through a maze of learning challenges so often encountered in the preschool years. Excruciating. Is it too much of a cliché to say I feel like I'm being torn from limb to limb? With a jolt that feels like an earthquake, I depart ABT. And appease myself with performing now and then. A guest gig here. A guest gig there.

The brutal truth is that this is a pretty traumatic time. There are moments when I feel really fragile. Like I've almost disappeared. I've lost such a major "label." Soloist with American Ballet Theatre. A divorce is beginning to feel inevitable. Soon, I may be saying goodbye to yet another label. Wife.

There *is* that one recurring label. But, only now and then. Guest Artist. But … only now and then.

It's in between those "now-and-thens" that I'm struggling. Forget no labels. Nobody expects me to *be* anywhere. No one misses me if I don't show up. I try calling friends, but they're always at work. My only "job" is that crucial, all-important one. Helping Erik find his best way forward through early learning disabilities.

Don't get me wrong. I wholeheartedly embrace this job. And, it turns out, I'm pretty good at finding people who know people who know people who can really help.

But, still, all those unfilled chasms of empty hours. Too much time to feel like I'm nowhere. I end up washing my hair only when I can't stand the smell on my pillow case. I wear the same clothes every day. Who's to know? Brushing my teeth? A really good day. Oh, how I'm longing for "onward and upward." The very words with which dear Uncle Fred signed an autographed picture to me years ago. But, right now, I can barely figure out which way is up.

(Looking back now, Erik is my crowning achievement. Early challenges, completely overcome. A University of Toledo graduate. Marketing and Sales for radio station KRSL in Russell, Kansas. On-Air Personality. And play-by-play announcer for every high school football, basketball, baseball, and softball game within reach. Heaven for him. Beyond words, for me.)

The Land Down Under

Then suddenly, a lifeline (albeit temporary), from my doldrums. It's late August of 1972. Meeting Georgina Parkinson while performing in Sydney is the single biggest takeaway from my Australian adventure. That's saying a lot, but I'm still going to say it. "George's" wit. Her wisdom. Her cooking. All of them get me through. Get me through what, you may ask?

For starters, picture a moderately-insane 37-year-old who has always dreamed of being the artistic director of his own ballet company. Presto! I give you the Sydney Festival Ballet, instantly created by using the ballet students in his School.

It seems that this 37-year-old wannabe fancies himself a real Sol Hurok. Not only has he asked the husband-and-wife ballet luminaries, Ivan Nagy (American Ballet Theatre) and Marilyn Burr (a Sydney native), to perform with his "instant" ballet company, but also he has tasked them with inviting three more ballet couples to perform with the Sydney Festival Ballet. The plan is to "star" all four couples in *pas de deux* of their own choosing.

Thus begins this "Sol Hurok's" relentless use of the phrase, "international stars." So when dear friends Marilyn and Ivan telephone to invite me to perform in Sydney (with a partner of my choice), I instantly become an "international star." Nifty.

This neophyte impresario's plan is simple: Open each show with *Swan Lake, Act II*. The students will perform as the *corps de ballet*. We "international star couples" will rotate as Swan Queen Odette and her beloved Prince Siegfried.

Also in this rotating fashion will be two classical ballet *pas de deux* a night. These will be selected from a mix that would delight any balletomane. Royal Ballet artistic director Kenneth MacMillan offers the iconic Balcony Scene from his *Romeo and Juliet*.

Featured, as well: the *Coppélia Act III Wedding Pas de Deux*, and the two *Pas de Deux* so often extrapolated from both *Paquita* and *Don Quixote*.

The latter are two of the most high-energy, *tour de force*, audience-pleasers in all of ballet repertoire.

Five-year-old Erik in our Riverdale apartment, imitating me as "Queen of the Wilis."

The Sydney audiences are warm and enthusiastic. They adore their native daughter, Marilyn Burr. They adore the ever-gallant Ivan Nagy. And they're absolutely wild about the two of them in everything they perform. Especially the *Don Quixote Pas de Deux*.

In MacMillan's Balcony Scene *pas de deux* from his full-length *Romeo and Juliet*, Royal Ballet ballerina Georgina Parkinson is reprising her role as Juliet. Her Romeo is Ross Stretton, a rising young star of the Australian Ballet.

I'm performing the *Coppélia Wedding Pas de Deux* and the *Paquita Pas de Deux*. First, Ivan gets me this "starring" gig. Then, Marilyn makes both my tiaras. Nothing like friends in high places.

I've asked Peter Malek to be my partner. Easy choice. We just finished performing as a guest couple in New Jersey. Everything seems on track. What could go wrong?

Turns out, Peter has never been vaccinated. No, never. Years ago in his native Austria, his physician father decides to conduct an experiment. As in, "Let's see if these vaccinations really make a difference." The first-born daughter gets the whole treatment, while Dad blithely ignores the science with his son. Fast forward to the present.

On this sunny, mid–August afternoon in 1972, Australian Customs is not amused. Like a stray cow being captured for branding, the Austrian is unceremoniously hauled off to be vaccinated. Fully, and all at once. Otherwise, no visa stamp for you, buddy. Predictably, every possible physical reaction occurs. Fully, and all at once.

I am reduced to rehearsing alone for two days, as I "search for my legs" after those grueling 21-hours on the airplane. I'm walking through the opening *adagio* section by myself, to the music of course, desperately trying to retain the phrasing and the partnering details. Is he lightly guiding me by my waist during this pirouette? Or is this the one where I grasp his finger over my head to start? And what is the preparation for that overhead lift?

I'm also doggedly running through my solo variation and solo coda choreography. Have to keep up that stamina. The third day finds us together in the rehearsal studio, at last. Madly scrambling to put our two *Coppélia* and *Paquita pas de deux* back into performance shape.

I'm delighted to report that, despite obstacles, all ends well. The performances are a huge success. Audiences are showering us with their appreciation. It takes about ten days to realize that our work environment is a bit bizarre.

You see, the weekly "free" day has disappeared. The necessary day off for the body to "recover," just like an athlete. In its place, hours of extra rehearsal. The Svengali side of our personal "Sol Hurok" has decided on a whim to switch partners on his ballerinas. What? And jettison months of painstaking efforts to fix this supported pirouette? That overhead lift? What about the hours spent synchronizing arm and head angles? Does he enjoy watching us struggle to become comfortable with someone new? He should know better. He supposedly once partnered Dame Margot Fonteyn. (Can you spell "sadistic"?)

Our objections are many. What about synchronized timing? What about adjusting to the different height and weight of your new partner? Our pleadings fall on deaf ears. Svengali cannot be dissuaded. We even think of quitting, until we remember the unthinkable. Under the pretext of some return-flight issues, The Snake has separated each and every one of us from our tickets and passports.

What our begging fails to do, the London flu accomplishes. "The wog" has made its way to Australia. Suddenly, whimsical casting changes must take a back seat to replacing ill dancers. Or so one would think. But Svengali has advertised that his international stars will appear at every performance and, by golly, we're going to be on that stage.

Fever, or not, Ross Stretton succumbs to Svengali's pressure. He gamely performs his *Romeo and Juliet Pas de Deux* with Georgina. Yours truly refuses. My fever is a little over 101. I just can't pull it off. I make that clear to Svengali, when he telephones me in my hotel room.

What happens next can't be real. I'm thinking *The Red Shoes*. Victoria Page, being terrorized yet again, by her artistic director, Boris Lermontov.

SCENE: My hotel room, where I'm curled up under as many blankets as I can find.

ACTION: A knock at the door. Am I actually pushing a table up under the door knob, as I hear, "Roni, dear?" The dresser is just in time. The knocking is getting louder.

"Open up, Roni dear. I have the doctor with me. You're just a little depressed. He's going to give you a shot that will make you feel much better."

I'm completely on my own here. Georgina is already at the theater. Not a peep, girl. You and your 101 fever mustn't say a word. If they get no response, they'll go away? She convinces herself, blanket-clad, cowering in the bathroom. They eventually do.

Back from the performance, Georgina shifts into crisis gear. Luckily, she knows everyone. That includes Australian-born Deborah MacMillan, artist in her own right and wife of Kenneth. Deborah and Georgina are friends. Deborah and Kenneth are in town to watch "George" dance.

The rest is easy to picture. George calls Deborah. Deborah and a man rush over. In my feverish haze, I'm guessing it's maybe Kenneth. I do remember Deborah's soothing voice, as she nestles feverish me into their station wagon. Away from the asylum. On to the MacMillan Haven, wherever that is. Time-honored chicken soup and bed rest. Soon, I'm recovered and back onstage. Feeling much better. *Without* Dr. Feelgood.

Congratulations, Roni. You have emerged the winner in the head-to-head battle with your very own "down under" Boris Lermontov. You have vanquished this moderately insane 37-year-old who always answers his phone, "William J. Gill here. Your artistic director."

Rest in Peace.

The thing about performing in faraway places is that you never really get to experience the faraway place. Rehearse. Perform. Eat. Sleep. Rehearse. Perform. Eat. Sleep. Theater. Hotel. Theater. Hotel. Squeezing in one short sightseeing adventure? Quite the bonus.

Like our jaunt over to Canberra, about three hours from Sydney. This Australian capital city is home to the National Zoo and Aquarium. We never make it to the fish, but the kangaroos and koalas are more than enough. Photos don't do them justice. Seared in my mind, the sight of a baby kangaroo with a heightened sense of adventure. Having dived head first into its Mama's pouch, its upside down legs are all I can see. Kicking and kicking and kicking.

* * *

It's 1973. My phone rings on a New York winter morning. It's my long-time dance-teacher friend, Patsy Swayze. Over the years, I've been a guest teacher at her Houston studio. And also for her excitingly innovative Houston Jazz Ballet Company.

"Roni, Buddy's in trouble." Buddy is her son's family nickname. Patsy goes on to explain that she's choreographing in Europe, and Buddy is in the hospital. A staph infection has found its way to his oft-injured left knee. They're worried he might lose his leg. How quickly can I get to his bedside?

In a flash, I'm peeking into his hospital room. A sheepish Buddy confesses, "I forgot to go to the dentist." Staph infection, contained. Leg stays. This 21-year-old has learned his lesson. After discharge from the hospital, he's eying an upcoming scholarship audition at the Harkness Ballet School, where he's been studying. Alas, now completely out of shape.

"They can't see me like this at Harkness. Can you give me private lessons?"

A few lessons in, Buddy is looking sheepish again. Uh-oh. He's gotten himself into an uncomfortable apartment situation—$200 can set him free. Too embarrassed to ask his Mom, he promises to pay me back. Buddy gets the scholarship. We lose touch. Patsy hears about the $200. Every time she sees me, "Did Buddy pay you back yet?" Never happens. No biggie. A favor to my friend, Patsy.

It's July of 1993. Patsy's now living in California. She invites me to guest-teach for a few days at her School in Simi Valley. Guess who drops by to watch the Pointe class? Buddy and his beautiful wife of almost twenty years, Lisa Niemi. Of course. They were always palling around with each other at Patsy's studio.

Buddy, known to the world as Patrick, is now a star. As in, Patrick Swayze. Thank you, *Dirty Dancing* and *Ghost*. Lisa, an actress in her own right, is asking if I have time to give her a private lesson *en pointe*. She needs to brush up to replace Marla Maples in the role of Florenz Ziegfeld's "Favorite" in *The Will Rogers Follies* on Broadway.[1]

The next afternoon, Buddy picks me up from Patsy's. A short drive to the beautiful ranch they call home. Lisa is so talented. *And* she's blessed with the gorgeous legs and feet that are born to dance *en pointe*. I leave her with a lesson plan. She's a natural for the role.

The fun begins. Obligatory swim in the pool. Delicious outdoor barbecue. Buddy says he recently finished filming *Point Break*, that they taught him how to skydive. Back now to the house. Without a word, he throws a video cassette into the VCR.

I'm looking at the twelve lessons that got him to that terrifying freefall scene. Lesson #1 is a "tandem" jump. Completely strapped to your instructor. There's Buddy. Completely strapped to the incomparable Jim Wallace, skydiving teacher to the rich (a Mercedes-Benz commercial) and famous (Patrick Swayze).

"Buddy" and me at the barbecue.

I *cannot* believe what I'm watching. Tandem jump. Who knew? My heart starts pounding. I *could* leave the plane, if someone else is in charge. I'm telling Buddy I want to do this. Buddy's telling me, "Promise me you only go up with Jim." He's handing me Jim's business card, as he's repeating, "Promise me." I promise.

As I'm tucking Jim Wallace's card in my purse, Buddy's asking if I want to see his horses. Off to the stables. The horses *are* beautiful. He proudly shows off the recording studio he's built. Where he co-wrote and sang "She's Like the Wind" for *Dirty Dancing*.

Now, we're in his office. He's opening his middle desk drawer. Without a word, he pulls out a checkbook and starts writing. I remind him that Lisa's private lesson is "on the house." He keeps writing. Then I hear him murmur, "The interest." The check is for $800. I am guessing Patsy asked him if he'd paid me that $200 back yet.

The evening is winding down. On the drive back to Patsy's, Buddy realizes his tank is low. We stop for gas. He reaches into his back pocket for his wallet. There's that sheepish look again. "Could you lend me $2.00? I promise I'll pay you back." I fork it over on one condition. He must never pay me back. I've gotten used to the feeling that he owes me. I like it.

Six months later, I have a video cassette of my own. On screen, there I am, strapped to Jim, free-falling 13,000 feet out of the sky. All set to the soundtrack of "Forever Young." The videographer's choice. What the camera doesn't capture is the tense moment when I'm frantically searching for the elusive cord that will deploy my parachute at just the right moment, for a safe descent. Before panic sets in, trusty Jim pulls it for me.

Mom and Erik are both furious with me, when they receive their videos out of the blue. Not a good way to break the news?

> **ERIK:** "Why didn't you tell me? You should've told me."
> **ME:** "You would've said no. I would've done it anyway. This way, I wasn't going behind your back."

The conversation with my mother is strikingly similar. I don't regret keeping them in the dark. I do regret not pulling my own cord.

* * *

It's April 1974. My divorce is finally "final." I've been meandering in and out of that "disappeared" feeling for a couple of years now, and feel a growing need to start looking for my "next act."

Tandem skydiving over Lake Elsinore, CA in 1994 (courtesy Joshua Hall).

The previous fall, my younger sister Lyn, now Dr. Lyn Mahler Shelton, began teaching at Kansas State University in Manhattan, Kansas. Lyn has a PhD in Theater, with an extensive background in dance. She and her husband, Dr. Lewis Shelton (also a Theater PhD), were hired by Dr. Norma Bunton, KSU's Head of the Speech Department.

At the same time, Dr. Charles ("Chuck") Corbin, Head of HPER (Health, Physical Education, and Recreation) at KSU, wants to bring back dance classes on his watch. Dr. Bunton suggests Lyn as his answer. Dr. Corbin immediately creates two sections of "Ballet 1" for her, in the Fall of '73.

I visit Lyn that December, and am drawn to the stability of a life in academia. I instinctively sense that Erik will thrive in the small-town feel of Manhattan, Kansas.

The success of Lyn's classes lead to plans for some interdepartmental cooperation. A new dance "concentration" for both Theater and HPER students. And now, the need for a full-time ballet teacher to run it. I go back to New York and apply for the job.

Around this same time, life throws me a very welcome curveball. I am introduced to Gestalt Therapy. A form of psychotherapy where rather than looking back, you evaluate your current situations and work on making adjustments to deal with them.

Next thing I know, I'm sitting opposite this soft-spoken mid-thirties male. And I'm very busy telling him that I don't even know the Ronnie (*real* spelling) who's sitting in front of him. It's like I've never even met her before. She goes through

Celebrating with (from left to right) sisters Stephanie and Lyn, that Kansas State University has just offered me an assistant professorship of dance.

these really long stretches when she's so lazy, she can't seem to get anything done. The other Roni (professional spelling) used to have so much discipline. Something needed doing? (I snap my fingers, emphatically.) She *did* it. Done.

> **THERAPIST:** "Which Ronnie do you like better?"
> **ME:** "Excuse me?"
> **THERAPIST:** "The stronger one or the weaker one?"
> **ME (in disbelief):** "Maybe the weaker one? She's nicer?"
> **THERAPIST:** "Well, how about giving weaker Ronnie a hug once in a while. Tell her how much you love her. And maybe she'll get a little stronger?"

POW. Like being struck with a thunderbolt. A good one. Four more weeks of spot-on insights and then it happens. The news that I've been hired by Kansas State. Have I just been reborn? My salvation? A steady job that's going to pay me to stay in one place.

But also… Yikes. Barely three months to prepare Erik and me for an entirely new life. Besides the name, Manhattan, Kansas, and Manhattan, New York, have just about nothing in common. Leaving New York City? My beloved Yankees will just have to understand.

My therapist sends me on my way with two thoughts: Every once in a while, I should pat myself on the back and say, "Yes, Ronnie, you have pushed yourself." And then he tells me his word for me is "valiant."

Kansas State University

Say hello to the new Assistant Professor of Dance at Kansas State University. Those first "baby feathers," way back when I was 19, have finally sprouted into bona fide teaching wings. Smack dab in the middle of the Department of HPER.

And now, I'm sitting in my first faculty meeting at Kansas State, in the Fall of 1974. Unfortunately, skepticism over my lack of college degrees is rampant.

At this meeting, my new colleagues are using the standard "three-school formula" to "tell a little about themselves." When it's my turn, I'm desperate to "fit in." As straight-faced as can be, I announce: "My Bachelor's is from the Ballet Russe de Monte Carlo. I earned my Masters at the National Ballet of Washington. My PhD is from American Ballet Theatre." Skepticism over my lack of college degrees is *still* rampant.

At the end of my first year, vindication. As if on cue, I win the Outstanding Teaching Award for undergraduates. The first time for an HPER faculty member. You think this validates me to Department colleagues? Think again. In academia, the question still remains, "Where did you go to school?" In *my* neck of the woods, it's more apt to be, "With whom did you study?" I fall squarely in the Master/Protégée column.

* * *

You already know that my friend, Albert Einstein, has gotten me through jam after jam with his wise words: "Imagination is more important than knowledge."

Well, he's done it again. But this time it's not a jam. It's a quest. I now give you: "If at first the idea is not absurd, then there is no hope for it."

Don't tell me you've never had a really far-fetched idea that you or your friends are saying will never happen? Don't tell me you've never had a quest?

In 1974, when I arrive at Kansas State University in Manhattan, Kansas, I'm as "green" as green can be. I know everything about ballet and absolutely nothing about University "culture." Protocol? Hierarchy? Nothing. But I'm absolutely ready for my very first Fall semester, ever. I've been hired to teach beginning ballet (Ballet 1) as an Assistant Professor of Dance. I also have a great idea.

This tomboy has been a huge sports fan all her life. First, baseball. Then, football. Watching game after game after game. Noticing similar footwork on the field and in ballet class. The outfielder, throwing to nail the runner at home. The wide receiver or running back, leaping over a would-be tackler to squeeze out a few extra yards. And who hasn't heard that Steeler's wide receiver Lynn Swann credits his Mom's ballet classes when he was nine for his nimble footwork?[2]

My quest? To teach ballet to football players at Kansas State. Everyone thinks I'm crazy. I, on the other hand, think nothing of marching into Head Football Coach Vince Gibson's office to pitch him my idea. Turns out, even Vince Gibson thinks I'm crazy. Not in so many words, but I *am* shown the door pretty quickly.

So, Plan B. Word-of-mouth. At least *one* new Ballet 1 student must know a football player, right? Hello, Mary Kay Zawatzki. She's friends with linebacker Gary Spani. Mary tells Gary. Gary tells tight end pal Paul Coffman. Finally, in walk Spani and Coffman. A steady trickle of athletes into Ballet 1 begins. I even get a soccer player.

Ballet helps Gary stop "rolling" his hypermobile ankles. Ballet stretches Paul's very tight hamstrings and quads. So, less knee pain. Both guys end up in the pros after graduation. Gary's eight great years with the Kansas City Chiefs? Chiefs Hall of Fame in 2003.[3] Paul's seven great years with the Green Bay Packers? Packers Hall of Fame in 1994.[4]

(Guess who, to this day, Paul calls his "favorite college instructor"? Could it be a certain Assistant Professor utterly lacking in college degrees? Imagine that.)

Ballet class makes all students more agile, spry. Lighter on their feet. Fact: athletes wear sneakers to cushion and protect their feet. Fact: you can't get to know your feet while wearing sneakers.

The Arthritis Foundation identifies 26 bones, 30 joints, and more than 100 muscles, tendons, and ligaments in your feet.[5] That's a lot of movable parts. They can propel you forward, sideways, backward. Even up in the air. *Especially* up in the air.

Feet can be easily ignored. Take a boy who's already "hefty" in the fifth grade. Coach says, "Son, you gotta block. You gotta tackle." From that point on, this kid is a means of brute force. He gets older. He gets bigger, heftier. All those movable parts in his feet are still getting so little attention. Bottom line: Long on strength. Short on agility.

Many players arrive in class with feet that operate more like bricks than springboards. I can improve agility by even slightly increasing flexibility in the metatarsal joints. But, you have to lose the sneakers. Leave 'em at the door. That's a huge hurdle, right there.

Teaching Ballet 1 in Ahearn Field House, my very first semester at Kansas State University, fall 1974 (Photo by Fred Wrightman, courtesy of *The Manhattan Mercury*).

And bring a lot of patience while saying hello to your 10 metatarsals. Yes, the 10 bones at the bottom of your 10 toes. You might call them the balls of your feet? Your metatarsals are the key to agility and springing for a jump.

Sneakers aren't the only thing you have to give up. "Looking busy" and "running around" are the others. At least, for now. These exercises are slow. Their focus is narrow. Worried you're not looking "tough?" Not "working really hard?"

Oh, you're working hard, all right. Working hard to make sure you're standing more on your 2nd and 3rd metatarsals, when lifting your heels off the ground. Not easy. Because the "natural" way is to rise up more on those 4th and 5th metatarsals, the "outside" of your foot. And weakening your ankles, to boot. But ballet changes that. Just give me 11 months.

Meet Ballet 1 student Theopilis Bryant. Theopilis is a tough case because he's anything but lithe. The circumference of one of his thighs nearly equals the circumference of *both* of mine. A lot more weight on those metatarsals we're targeting.

Theopilis is a bundle of joy. His smile makes you smile right back. Eager. Attentive. Conscientious. *And* determined. But, feet like two bricks. He could've been that 5th grader being told, "Son. You gotta block. You gotta tackle." Feet: not a priority.

Theopilis is telling me that Coach says he has to move faster. Bingo! Let the 11 months begin. First, the "litmus test": Toes only slightly turned outward. Heel of one foot in front of big toe of the other. (A ballet 5th-ish position?) Now, try jumping high enough off the ground to land with the other foot in front, in the same position. (A ballet *changement*.)

Theopilis can barely leave the floor. His feet almost hit one another, while trying to change places. Two bricks.

Now, the work. Holding on with both hands while facing the barre. Shifting the weight sideways onto one foot, raise the opposite heel while *pressing towards the big toe as much as possible.* Lower the heel, centering the weight. Bend knees to stretch calves and Achilles tendons. Repeat everything to the other side. (In an attempt to increase flexibility, the ankle is also being strengthened.)

Three months later, Theopilis revisits the litmus test. His eyes grow big. His whole face smiles. He's managed the tiniest of bounces, as he changes feet.

A year later, my Uncle Mort, Dr. Mortimer P. Starr, is a guest lecturer in microbiology at Kansas State. We've just finished lunch at Manhattan's Ramada Inn and are in the guest-filled lobby. Through the front door walks Theopilis. Seeing me, he immediately does a *grand jeté* (forward leap), with arms open wide. And, while in the air, exclaims, "She taught me how to f-l-y-y-y through the air!" *In the lobby of the Ramada Inn.*

Word gets out about my work with the K-State football Wildcats. Holy mackerel. I'm invited to give my "Ballet Movement for the Athlete" presentation at the 1977 national convention of AAHPERD (American Alliance for Health, Physical Education, Recreation, and Dance; yes, "dance" has been added!) in Kansas City. The quest continues.

* * *

During my six years of K-State teaching, I also perform on two occasions as the ballerina I once was. Tutu and all. Squired by two talented Guest Artists. In 1975, it's ABT male principal Clark Tippet. We perform the *Grand Pas Classique d'Auber.* In 1976, it's Dance Theatre of Harlem male principal Paul Russell. We perform the *grand pas de deux* from *Le Corsaire.*

Both are fully aware of the unusual task ahead when they accept my invitation to come to Kansas State. Partnering a ballerina who has had to whip herself into "principal dancer" shape in only a month's time. Why only a month? Because all she's been doing up 'til now is teaching, teaching, teaching.

"Principal dancer shape?" Now there's a phrase that begs a definition. It involves having "performance legs." Which is infinitely different from "teaching legs." Even, let's say, 20-classes-a-week "teaching legs."

"Performance legs" is an ephemeral state of fitness easily achieved by consecutive performances onstage, but impossible to achieve by any other means. Mind you, this performing has to be in front of an audience. In costume. With lights. And it has to be part of a string of performances. To be clear, after an extended rehearsal period, the dancer has definitely attained an elevated fitness level. But, performance legs? No. That's another matter altogether.

Performance legs come from "facing the bull," show after show. It's that slight additional tension, in the moment of truth. A moment known to produce

Demonstrating for my Ballet 1 class at Kansas State University, in costume for the *Flower Festival in Genzano* Pas de Deux. (Photo by Fred Wrightman, courtesy of *The Manhattan Mercury*).

performance jitters. No, not loss of nerve. Rather, a heightened sense of anticipation that can "take away your legs."

But, aren't you staying in shape just by teaching? Not in the least. You see, demonstrating ballet steps is so "intermittent," especially ballet steps at the beginning level. There's no cardio or muscle endurance involved. You demonstrate. You watch your students. Start. Stop. Start. Stop.

Well then, can't you just do your own nonstop, personal workout daily? Keep up that cardio and muscle endurance on your own time? Certainly possible, but 304 Ahearn is the only dance studio. And it is booked pretty solid, from 8:00 in the morning on. No time for that nonstop personal workout.

Yikes. Soon I will somehow have to dance like I just stepped off the stage with ABT at The Met. ABT soloist and native Kansan Clark Tippet will be looking just like that, because Clark *has* just stepped off the stage at The Met. By the way, guess who talks Clark into this madcap adventure with a dancer he's never even met? ABT's star ballerina, Cynthia Gregory. Talk about friends in high places.

So how will I *ever* get myself into enough performing shape to match his? By being in first position in 304 Ahearn. At the barre. At 6:30 in the morning. Six days a week. That's how.

Starting out, of course, in soft ballet slippers. First, a rigorous forty minutes of exercises at the barre and in the center of the studio, including small and large jumps. A dancer is never ready to perform without being able to execute all the jumping combinations given in class. Then, it's on with the pointe shoes and ten minutes of warming up and strengthening my *en pointe* technique.

I have thirty minutes left to practice the two pieces of choreography I can do without Clark. My solo *variation* and the *Coda*. First, the solo ... over and over and over again. Repeating and repeating any steps that are giving me trouble. Figuring out *by myself* (without a helpful second pair of eyes) how to make those little problems go away. Yes, this would be so much easier with a coach. Then, it's on to the *Coda*, and drilling those challenging consecutive *fouetté* turns.

Warming up at the barre at Kansas State University, fall of 1974 (Photo by Fred Wrightman, courtesy of *The Manhattan Mercury*).

Unfortunately, that's only about half of the total choreography. The lengthy partnered *adagio* section that opens every classical ballet *pas de deux* will have to wait. I'll be learning it from Clark. As well as the "partnered" choreography of the *Coda*. Pressure. Pressure.

It's 7:50 now. The Physical Education majors are slowly drifting in for their 8:00 a.m. Rhythms for Secondary Education class. What do they see? This supposed hotshot ballerina from The Big Apple, lying spread-eagle on the studio floor. Gasping for breath. A faint smile on her face.

Cardio and muscle endurance sure are elusive. You always have to push beyond what's comfortable. Otherwise, you won't get stronger. Every athlete knows that. It's ten days down and twenty to go, before Clark gets here. The name of the game is perseverance. I'll be back tomorrow morning. At 6:30.

How does it come about that Clark and I are performing this *pas de deux* at the KSU Auditorium? Our University President, Dr. James McCain, is retiring at the end of the Spring 1975 semester. In his honor, the KSU Auditorium is being renamed McCain Auditorium. President McCain's favorite opera, *Die Fledermaus*, is to be performed there in the Spring.

Dr. McCain is also a lifelong fan of the ballet. It's come to his attention that the new ballet teacher, an American Ballet Theatre "alum," recently exited Lincoln Center (in Manhattan, New York) and entered 304 Ahearn (in Manhattan, Kansas). He stops me one day on campus and asks if he's going to get to see me dance before he leaves the University.

Luckily, there is an opera tradition which calls for a "divertissement" opportunity, often in Act II. A sort of timeout for entertainment during a grand ball, perhaps? On just such an occasion, a guest soprano often delights with an aria of her choice. (Yes. An absolute non-sequitur, having nothing to do with the opera being performed.) Or, instead of a "guest aria," a "guest ballet *Pas de Deux*" can be inserted.

And that's how Clark and I end up performing the *Grand Pas Classique* for President McCain at Kansas State University. In the middle of Act II of *Die Fledermaus*. ABT's Wardrobe Director, Robert Hathaway, generously donates the costumes. One condition. Clark must promise to hand-carry them onto his flights.

When we start rehearsing, Clark begins by teaching me the partnered *adagio*. In addition to his clean technique and princely onstage demeanor, he possesses the gift of breaking difficult things down into manageable parts. His patient tutelage brings this ABT alum back up to professional performance level once again. Step by step. Partnering move by partnering move. The operative word here is "patient."

Trust me.

Before every show, I utter the same short prayer: "Please, Dear Lord, don't let me fall down. And, if I do, please let me get up fast."

Our performances are a hit. I actually manage to "pull it off." Thanks to knight-in-shining-armor Clark. Someone who's seen us perform stops me and clasps her hands in mock prayer. "Oooh. When do we see more?"

In that moment, I want to drop down into aforementioned spread-eagle heap on the floor.

The next year, the drill is the same when Paul Russell comes to K-State, courtesy of Dance Theatre of Harlem. This time, I've already been through it once, so it's a bit easier. Paul and I perform *Le Corsaire Pas de Deux* as part of "An Evening of Opera and Dance," brilliantly directed by my sister, Lyn.

Paul is an amazing partner. On our first day of rehearsal,

Clark Tippet and me taking five from rehearsing *Grand Pas Classique D'Auber* at Kansas State University in 1975 (Photo by Fred Wrightman, courtesy of *The Manhattan Mercury*).

Rehearsing the *Pas de Deux* from *Walpurgisnacht Ballet* with Paul Russell (Dance Theatre of Harlem) in a New York Studio, circa 1973.

he announces, "I'm teaching you the (Rudolf) 'Nureyev version' of *Corsaire*." This version of the *pas de deux* is famously filled with very athletic overhead lifts. Paul gets me above his head so effortlessly. And so quickly. Even some light tossing and catching is involved. Throughout it all, Paul makes me feel like the proverbial feather.

In one of the more exciting moments, I'm suddenly over his head and immediately tossed while being flipped around up there, 180 degrees. Then, Paul lets me drop, only to catch me below with a dramatic backward-swooping motion.

It's *not* a non sequitur to mention that on every cheerleading squad, the guys are called yell leaders. And let's face it. These yell leaders are the only ones on campus who toss and catch gals. No surprise that, after seeing the performances of our *pas de deux*, these guys decide to copy that spectacular lift. The K-State Cheerleading Squad performs it at "Nationals." (It catches on like wildfire and becomes known as "the helicopter," in cheerleading circles.)

In the *Pas de Deux,* Paul's entrance to begin the *coda* is tailor-made to show off his "elevation." Translation: He has high leaps (*grands jetés*). Really high.

To increase the visual impact of these *grands jetés*, Paul takes a running start from way back in the wings. He then strategically places his "push-off foot" far enough back in the wing. This way, he's already airborne when the audience gets its first glimpse of him. He then repeats these soaring leaps for almost a complete circle around the stage. The applause is deafening.

I'll never forget one of my male colleagues in Physical Education saying to me, "He takes off in the wings from a mini-trampoline, right?"

This "phys ed" colleague is coming from the only thing he knows: the sports ethos. You want to increase the height of your jump? Use a mini-trampoline.

In the arts, we are less about the numbers, and more about individual artistic achievement. You want to jump higher? Work harder.

* * *

On the same program as *Le Corsaire*, I perform Anna Pavlova's famous solo *The Dying Swan*. A dream come true for me. In 1905, Michel Fokine choreographed this gem for Mme. Pavlova, selecting "The Swan" from Camille Saint-Saëns' *The Carnival of the Animals*.[6] Fokine's brilliant creativity turned initial serenity into ultimate tragedy.

Just like those two *Grand Pas de Deux*, this solo requires a healthy portion of "pulling it off" magic. Talk about getting my performance legs back? This Anna Pavlova specialty is all bourrées, *for four minutes*. Shades of Myrta, Queen of the Wilis?

How do I get to perform my dream solo? As my sister Stephanie would say, I have a cunning plan. I invite Madame Swoboda to Kansas State for a 10-day, guest teaching stint.

"While you're here, could you maybe teach me *The Dying Swan*?" (heh heh.) When Madame danced it in her heyday, a smitten critic once likened her performance to that of Pavlova's.

Learning how to undulate your "swan arms" is a delicious challenge. And quite the triceps exercise. But Madame's coaching shines over all. Guiding me through the physical and emotional journey of portraying a carefree swan, gliding peacefully on calm lake waters. Until a hunter's arrow under the wing plunges her into a hopeless quest to stay alive. Performing the end of this solo almost makes me cry. Every time.

Madame Swoboda coaching me in *The Dying Swan* at Kansas State University in 1976 (Photo by Fred Wrightman, courtesy of *The Manhattan Mercury*).

* * *

It's the summer of 1978. One of the Royal Ballet's principal ballerinas, Georgina Parkinson, has invited my 10-year-old son Erik and me to visit her in her Battersea (south London) home. Yes, the same Georgina of Sydney Festival Ballet fame. She and I have been friends ever since, and "George" is dying to meet Erik. She's equally dying for me to meet her photographer husband Roy Round and their 10-year-old son, Tobias.

George Balanchine also happens to be in London, because The Royal Ballet is preparing to perform Balanchine's *Firebird* this season. I get to watch a tech rehearsal one afternoon at Covent Garden. Pretty exciting.

That evening, someone is watching the kids while Georgina, Roy and I join Mr. Balanchine at a lovely restaurant. Mr. B is in excellent form. He seems to want to be in charge of the evening's menu. It doesn't matter what any of us order from our waiter. There is an immediate polite but firm interruption. Preceded by that cute double-sniff of his.

Mr. B: "*No, No, No. You bring frogs legs, instead.*"

And so it goes, until he has all of us enjoying the exact meal he's choreographed. Finally, just before dessert, Mr. Balanchine shares some exciting news.

Mr. B: "*Today, buy case 1973 red wine. Must wait ten years.*"

Got it. First glass in '83. Exceedingly jovial group toast: "To 1983!"

Ten years fly by. April 30, 1983. It's all over the news. George Balanchine has died. I can't believe it. I can't believe it.

I'm sure I'm not alone in being devastated by this. I just hope he enjoyed the wine he waited so patiently to sample before entering those Pearly Gates.

Something keeps tickling the back of my brain. I'll bet Mr. B purchased that case of immature wine, just to assure himself that he'd live until 1983. Always choreographing.

* * *

The year is 1978. I'm in my fifth year as Assistant Professor of Dance at Kansas State University. But, Kansas State doesn't have a monopoly on the town's higher education. There's Manhattan Christian College. And then there's the intriguing, tuition-free, University for Man.

Intriguing, because of its catalog. These courses are highly unusual. They can be taught by anyone who wants to share a special area of expertise or interest. The "course" can be ongoing throughout a semester or it can be a one-day affair. The venue for those one-day wonders is often someone's home.

Did I mention this is my fifth year in Manhattan, *Kansas*? Five whole years away from my beloved Yankees. At least I brought my two cartons chock-full of Mickey Mantle clippings. I can't stand it any longer. I need an excuse to go through them again. I know. I'll offer a one-day course all about Mickey Mantle. On Friday, October 20, his 47th birthday.

Baseball die-hards are welcome. No matter your team. Come one, come all. Share your stories. Share memorabilia. You see, I've been clipping for years. And years. All the way back to my teenage years at the Ballet Russe School, when a fellow ballet student and Mantle fan, Michael Linda Kelder, bequeathed me her cherished brown spiral notebook of Mickey clippings.

Among my most-prized achievements: a headline for each of Mickey's 52 home runs in 1956, the year he wins the Major League Triple Crown.[7] How about the 565-footer he hits out of the old Griffith Stadium in D.C., in 1953?[8] It's in there.

But I'm no fair-weather friend. I have clippings from the hard times, too. Like the '51 World Series, when Mick suffers a catastrophic knee injury that requires surgery. To make matters far worse, the next morning, when he and his dad, Elvin "Mutt" Mantle, are getting out of a cab at Lenox Hill Hospital, Mutt crumbles to the ground.[9]

The *New York World-Telegram and Sun* runs a picture of the two of them sharing a hospital room, watching the rest of the World Series. (You bet that's in the cherished brown spiral notebook.) Mickey, recovering from repaired torn ligaments in his right knee. Mutt, undergoing test after test after test.[10]

The results of those tests? The doctors tell Mickey the last thing he wants to hear. That his dad is dying of Hodgkin's Disease. There is nothing they can do. Mutt Mantle is only 39 when he passes the following May, just like many of the men in their family, who all died young of Hodgkin's disease. Mickey's guess: He won't live to see 40.

I feel Mickey's pain fiercely and continue to read anything I can about him. Cheering when his knee heels. As he manages to shine in his next two seasons, despite his grief. Clippings. More clippings. Highs and lows. Two pretty heavy cartons worth of evidence of our one-way friendship over the years. One-way, for now…

It's five days before my "course" honoring The Mick and I'm in the home of my dear friends, Karen and Edward Seaton. Edward publishes *The Manhattan Mercury*. At one point, I remind Karen and Edward that they are "enrolled" in my course. Always the journalist, Edward thinks I should try tracking down Mickey and recording a few words to play for everyone on Friday. How hard can it be? I hear him mutter something about "telling Bill to expect my call in the morning." Bill Felber is *The Mercury's* Sports Editor.

I get Bill Felber on the phone. I explain why I'm trying to track down Mickey. Within the next four days, mind you. Bill is pretty matter-of-fact about the whole thing. Says he'll get back to me. Within the hour, he's calling to say he has three numbers, but doesn't know how much help they'll be.

The first rings somewhere in Yankee Stadium. He is not sure where. The second is Mickey's clothing store in Dallas. Here's the best part. He has absolutely no idea what the third number is. If I get nowhere with the first two, I should give it a shot.

The first number never answers. *Steee-rike One*. When I call the clothing store and ask for "Mr. Mantle," they put me on hold for what seems like forever. When someone finally comes back on the line and asks why I want to talk to Mr. Mantle, I panic and hang up. *Steee-rike Two*.

Okay, Mystery Number. You're up. After it rings about four times, I'm just about to give up when an out-of-breath male voice picks up:

"Whaaat?" the voice shouts into the phone.

"Mickey Mantle," I shout back in the lowest voice I've got.

"Not here."

"Gotta reach him," I grunt.

"Roy True. 555–5555."

"Thanks." (Click.)

I'm shaking like a leaf. Hoping the Dallas area code is still 214, I dial away. When I ask to speak to Mickey's agent, Roy True, I'm transferred to his secretary. I tell her how I've been a die-hard fan since Mickey's first year with the Yankees. How I'm getting together with a bunch of folks in my town to share baseball stories on his upcoming birthday. How I would love to record a few words wishing Mr. Mantle a happy birthday, to play for everybody later. Her snippy tone says it all. It's clear that she thinks I am the stupidest thing she's ever heard of.

"I'm sorry. Mr. Mantle will be in Oklahoma City all day Friday, on behalf of the Oklahoma Lung Association." (Click.)

Bingo. I dial the Oklahoma Lung Association. The woman who answers *that* phone thinks I am the cutest thing she's ever heard. She puts me through to the Director, himself. Turns out, he loves my story, too. Even better, he's the one who'll be in charge of Mickey's visit tomorrow. Tomorrow? That's only Wednesday. I've got a shot. He promises to talk to Mickey about me. I tell him to mention that I have that newspaper clipping. The one where he's watching the rest of the '51 Series from the Lenox Hill Hospital room he's sharing with his Dad.

True to his word, Mr. Lung Association calls me back the next day. After hearing about me, first thing Mickey wants to know is, have we ever met? He hears "no." He doesn't get it. Why is this stranger throwing him a birthday party? Mickey thinks I'm nuts. But Mr. Lung Association hits him with, "She knows you and your Dad shared that hospital room in New York." That's another bingo. *Not one* of his Oklahoma buddies knows that tidy little fact. They obviously need to read the *New York World-Telegram and Sun.*

The Mick agrees to tape a short phone call with me. Best news yet. The perfect opportunity will be in two days, on the 20th. His actual birthday. It can happen at a local radio station, where he's already scheduled to tape a 3:30 p.m. public service announcement on behalf of the Oklahoma Lung Association. The Director tells me to have "my people" call the station a little before 3:15. He thinks he can promise to have Mickey on the line. We end our call.

I'm literally trembling with excitement. Wait a minute. Have "my people" call the radio station? Who on God's green earth are "my people?" It turns out, I have "people." My son Erik's third grade teacher, Mrs. Titus, has a husband, Ralph. Ralph happens to be the manager of KSAC, Kansas State University's campus radio station. Can this really be happening? I place a call to Ralph Titus faster than you can say "Commerce Comet." (Another sportswriter's nickname for the speedy Mickey.)

I'm plopping back on my couch, exhausted. What a four days. So much "dumb" luck that allowed things to fall into place. But if you ask me, some coincidences are too much of a coincidence to actually be a coincidence.

I meet Ralph at the KSAC campus radio station at about 2:45 p.m. Even though we've never met before, we greet one another like long-lost friends. Then it's time for Ralph to phone into Oklahoma City. If all goes well, we should have Mickey on the line around 3:15 for a nice chat before his public service taping.

Ralph hands me a headset. Now, I can hear everything anybody is saying. I can't tell you one word of Ralph's "set up" conversation with the KOMA folks. All I hear is my pounding heart. Louder and louder. You'd think I'm about to dance a huge ballet role for the first time.

Then, suddenly, a voice in my headset. "Who are you holding for?" An out-of-breath operator, sounding like she's in a hurry? "I'm holding for Mickey Mantle." Did those words really just tumble out of my mouth? I'm so nervous. My mouth is so dry. No water in sight. What if he doesn't show? What if this is all a bust?

* * *

It's 5:00 in the afternoon on Friday, the day of my "course." Folks begin trickling into my living room. Admission is granted to all *bona fide* baseball fanatics. Doesn't matter whom you root for. The "cover charge" is any item of baseball memorabilia. Or maybe a great baseball story. Or a personal memory. Who's checking?

It seems like townspeople are crawling out of every nook and cranny. Even the Municipal Court Bailiff shows up. Snacks and drinks for all. Baseball is the only language spoken. The next hour or so is spent examining baseball treasures. Listening to baseball stories.

I can't stand it any longer. The anticipation is killing me. I proudly break open my two precious "Mickey Mantle Cartons." Filled to the brim with newspaper clippings, magazine articles, anything and everything Mickey.

Finally, the moment has come. Around 7:00, I announce that I have a special surprise. I "roll tape":

(Author's Note: This conversation should by no means be taken as verbatim recall. It's as close as possible to what I can remember. Plus a few scribbled notes. Amazingly enough, I can still hear his voice. So many of his words still ring in my ears.)

Someone who sounds **exactly** like Mickey Mantle is saying, "Who's this?"

> ME: "I'm a lifelong Yankee fan. I first saw you play at the Stadium in July of '51. I was nine, and you were wearing No. 6 in right field."
>
> MICKEY: "Yeah. They didn't give me '7' till I came back up in August."
>
> ME: "I started keeping a scrapbook about you, and New York had so many newspapers to clip from. That's how come I have this picture of you and your Dad watching the rest of the Series from Lenox Hill Hospital."
>
> MICKEY: "Yeah. Have we met?"
>
> ME: "No. I'm just a fan, but I've always admired the way you played through pain. I was a professional ballet dancer and I always figured if you could do it, so could I. I'll be playing this tape later on for a bunch of folks getting together to celebrate your birthday."
>
> MICKEY: "Well, tell 'em I said thanks."
>
> ME: "So what do you think of the Yanks winning the Series?"
>
> MICKEY: "Well, [George] Steinbrenner says these ['78] Yankees are the best team ever. I don't know about that. I think I played on some pretty great teams in the '50s."
>
> ME (chuckling): "Who do you think are some of the best players on the team today?"
>
> MICKEY: "I'd rather not say."

Awkward lull in the conversation…

> MICKEY: "Did me and you ever … *make it*?"
>
> ME: "No no no no no no no no no no no no no. We never even met. Uh… What was the best moment of your career?"
>
> MICKEY: "Mickey Mantle Day…."
>
> ME (interrupting): "…in 1965, right?"
>
> MICKEY: "Who's telling this, me or you?"
>
> ME: "Sorry."
>
> MICKEY: "In '69. They retired my number. I wish my dad coulda seen it."
>
> ME: "Are there any players in the game today that you really admire?"
>
> MICKEY: "I'd pay to see [Thurman] Munson play."

Totally by accident, he ends up answering the earlier question he avoided.

> MICKEY: "Gotta do a thing for these folks now."
>
> ME: "I know. Thanks so much and Happy Birthday."

And then he's gone.

When it is over, my living room goes from "you can hear a pin drop" to total bedlam. I then entertain the gathering with all the riveting details. When everyone finally goes home, I am dazed and incandescently happy.

But later, thinking back, my heart aches….

"In '69. The day they retired my number. I wish my dad coulda seen it."

I'm sure I'm not alone in thinking that Mickey lost his "compass" the day Mutt Mantle died.

His 21st birthday was still five months away, and now this country boy had to navigate the Big City with only Yankees manager Casey Stengel as a beacon. But that was at the ballpark. Not surprisingly, his alcohol-fueled friendships with Billy Martin and Whitey Ford softened the blow. He wasn't going to make it to forty anyway, remember?

A few days after Mickey dies of liver cancer in 1995 (even after a successful transplant), I'm watching television. I hear this young whipper-snapper of a sports reporter glibly say, "Mickey Mantle, an alcoholic before, during, and after his baseball career…."

I begin screaming at the TV, "How dare you? He hardly ever drank until his Dad died. Do your research, dummy! He was my idol. If you don't know your facts, don't make 'em up. You're too young to even remember Mickey!"

Thank goodness for that April 18, 1994, issue of *Sports Illustrated*. In an article he writes entitled "Time in a Bottle,"[11] Mickey explains that when he began playing for the Yankees at 19, he had hardly ever had a drink. You bet *that* article went into the clippings carton.

Making It

(*This was written on August 13, 1995, after Mickey's passing.*)

An airport TV monitor. Don Mattingly in warm-ups, talking to the press. The question I'm afraid to ask brings a dreaded nod from a stranger. I can't keep back the tears. Who *was* Mickey Mantle to me?

My first game ever was at Yankee Stadium. They were honoring Joe DiMaggio that day, and there was this rookie in right, wearing No. 6, who was supposed to be the next superstar centerfielder in pinstripes. Mickey was 19 and I was nine. He wanted to be a New York Yankee and I wanted to be a ballerina. That memorable afternoon, I sensed a connection. A week or so later, Mickey got sent down to AA and Harry Craft, in Kansas City. Then I took three stitches on the chin from an ill-fated *grand jeté*. Now I knew we were connected. At nine, you know these things.

In summer camp at 12, I pounded my glove and chewed bubblegum in center. I was batting myself third even though I couldn't hit. The Mick and I were battling short tempers. He struck out and kicked water coolers. I missed *pirouettes* and threw pointe shoes. Sometimes my struggle with self-disappointment was almost overwhelming. But when Mickey had a good day at the plate, I could out-leap anyone. He ended up with 18 World Series home runs, and I ended up dancing the world over for 18 years. When my toes hurt in performance, I would "do this one for Mickey." If he could play on those knees, I could dance on these feet.

Now, boarding my late afternoon flight, I am remembering how I used his 47th birthday as an excuse for a party to sift through my Mickey Mantle clippings. Back then, New York City had seven daily newspapers. It was all just as I remembered. Mickey and his Dad sharing a Lenox Hill Hospital room during the '51 Series. A headline for each of his 52 home runs in '56. The priceless photo my dad got Mickey to autograph to me at the '57 Baseball Writers of America dinner, honoring Mickey and Sal "The Barber" Maglie.

At my party, with a little luck and a lot of help, I was able to treat the guests to a telephone conversation I had recorded earlier in the day with The Mick. He was having trouble believing this female adult was trying to reach him simply because of a childhood hero thing. Not too far into the conversation, he suddenly asked, "Did me and you ever make it?" The decisive "no" I delivered into the telephone then, echoes in my head now. As my plane leaves Logan Airport, I drift back 44 years to that July afternoon at Yankee Stadium in 1951. I want another shot at answering Mickey's question. This time I get to tell him, "You bet we did, Mickey. We both made it. And you made it with a capital M!" I feel better now.

Cleveland Ballet

During my six years at Kansas State, the Dance Program flourishes. I achieve tenure. At some point, a "D" (for Dance) is added to HPER.

In 1980, my application for promotion to Associate Professor is nipped in the bud, when it's vetoed by my Dept. of HPERD colleagues. The grounds: lack of academic credentials. Never mind that I'm the first, and only, member of the Department *ever* to win the Outstanding Teaching Award.

I hand in my resignation. Luckily, I have an even better offer waiting in the wings.

* * *

Dennis Nahat and Ian "Ernie" Horvath were both enjoying stellar dance careers, first with The Joffrey Ballet and then with American Ballet Theatre. Yet, both dreamt of directing their own ballet company together in Cleveland.

In the words of George Balanchine, "But first, a school." In 1972, Dennis and Ernie start the Cleveland Dance Center. Since both are still performing with ABT, dear friend Charles Nicoll becomes School Director and its first teacher.

Ernie is a native Clevelander, so his family takes care of everything else. Say hello to Ernie's Dad, Ernest ("Big Ernie"); his Mom, Helen; and his sister, Debby. Big Ernie is unstoppable with a hammer in his hand. He builds the studios. Helen and Debby are dynamite in the Office. Their approach of "welcoming" and "watchful" is a winning combination. The art of saying "no" with a smile.

Ernie leaves ABT in 1974 to join the effort full-time with Charles Nicoll and his family. Although Dennis's last performance with ABT isn't until 1979 (Agnes DeMille's *Three Virgins and a Devil*), he is constantly shuttling back and forth between New York and Cleveland, helping Ernie build the skeleton for the Company.

Cleveland Ballet officially debuts in 1976. Ernie is Artistic Director and Dennis is Associate Director. Cleveland Dance Center becomes School of Cleveland Ballet, and the Horvath family still reigns supreme. I join forces with all of them in 1980, first as a guest instructor in the School.

I become Ballet Mistress of Cleveland Ballet in 1981. I'm now teaching the daily Company ballet class, as well as rehearsing the repertoire. After several years, I'm given the title and responsibility of Régisseur. A "keeper of the flame," so to speak. The nurturer of traditions.

When Ernie leaves Cleveland Ballet in 1983, that's when the "pinkie swear" happens. My indelible promise to dear friend Dennis Nahat: "I'm here as long as you're here. After that, I'm gone."

And so it begins. Dennis becomes sole Artistic Director, and I am his loyal Artistic Associate. The "right hand" who temporarily takes the helm, if the Artistic Director has to be off campus for a while.

Back to that pinkie promise. It doesn't just mean working together administratively. Dennis and I also get to perform together. His Friar Laurence to my Juliet's Nurse, in *Romeo and Juliet*. His Uncle Drosselmeyer to my Helga the Housekeeper, in *The Nutcracker*. His Dr. Coppélius to my Swanilda's Mom, in *Coppélia*. That pinkie lock? As tight as ever.

Taking Dennis Nahat's notes during a tech rehearsal of *The Nutcracker* at the State Theatre, in Cleveland, Ohio in the '90s.

This might be the best moment to mention that Dennis is an absolute master of pantomime and physical comedy. Anyone who's seen his Dr. Coppélius can back me up on that. "Genius" is not an exaggeration. So, I'm not only performing with him. I'm being coached by him. Over 31 years of artistic partnership, you learn a lot. No matter the role. The Stepmother in Agnes de Mille's *Fall River Legend*. The Countess in Donald McKayle's *District Storyville*. The list goes on.

ABT, Revisited

After leaving ABT in 1971, I find it really hard to go back to see the Company dance. The two times I tried in 1972 were excruciating. Not only because of watching what was going on, onstage. But, also, because of what I had to live through during intermissions. "Oh, Roni. We miss you so." "Oh, Roni. When are you coming back?"

I've already told you a gazillion reasons why I eventually move to Manhattan, Kansas. Just add those intermissions to the list. The passage of time definitely makes things easier. But it was acquiring a great new label, in the Fall of 1974, that really did the trick. How does "Assistant Professor of Dance at Kansas State University" strike you?

Then, in 1980, Erik and I move to Cleveland, Ohio. Shaker Heights, to be exact. So, flying to New York would now cost a lot less. Plus, it's a new decade at ABT. Lots of different dancers. And memories have a way of fading.

By 1984, I'm feeling like making a return visit. Cynthia is, of course, still performing like crazy. Erik is 16 and complaining that he's never seen his Aunt Cynthia dance. Obviously, her full-length *Swan Lake* is the indisputable choice.

It's the long Memorial Day weekend. Straight from LaGuardia, we stop at Shea Stadium (nowadays, Citi Field) to catch a Dodgers–Mets Saturday afternoon game. That night, before the curtain goes up at The Met, Erik is peppering me with questions.

ERIK (worried): "When does she come onstage? Will I be able to find her?"
ME (not worried): "You will."

Erik understands that Aunt Cynthia won't be in Act I, at the Palace. He knows he has to wait for Act II, at the Lake. But, on purpose, I don't tell him that the stage will be absolutely bare when she makes her entrance. Does his jaw ever drop! Total awe, from that moment on. "Wow, Mom. I knew she was important but…"

* * *

About two or three years later, I make my first solo trip back. To hang out with Cynthia at rehearsals and see every performance she's in. Heaven. Naturally, this trip also includes a Gregory *Swan Lake*. You can never see too many of those. The orchestra has stopped tuning. The performance has begun. I'm all atingle. It sounds so trite, but Cynthia is one of those ballerinas who is simply "born to dance" the White and Black Swans, Odette and Odile. But, it's her Odette that really defies description.

You're watching this breathtakingly beautiful creature. Half swan. Half woman. That's what makes her portrayal so poignant. And what tears so hard at your heartstrings. You're not just watching an amazing evocation of a bird. You're feeling for the Princess trapped inside. And Cynthia never stops reminding you.

That, my friends, is the essence of a Cynthia Gregory *Swan Lake*. So much that's impossible to describe. Such as her *bourrée* (sewing machine toes) departure in Act II, when the sheer force of evil Von Rothbart's spell tears her away from her pleading Prince. It's utter agony, watching this Swan/Woman being gradually separated from the man she's fallen in love with.

As Odette struggles to stay closer to Prince Siegfried, Von Rothbart's powers compel her further and further away, toward *him*. She fights this invisibly evil strength, inching closer and closer to Siegfried. Your heart is feeling the tug of hers. The Evil One's powers finally prevail. Ultimately, the overwhelmed Swan succumbs to her fate, gliding offstage in a coma of submission. It breaks your heart.

Next, her evilly seductive Odile. Finally, breaking your heart again in Act IV… and thunderous applause. In her dressing room afterwards, I hang back. I see Cynthia all the time. Better to let all those friends have their moments with her. While her dresser is helping her out of costume, I take yet another picture with my mental camera. This figure in eerily-pale makeup, wearing a mid-thigh, forest-green theater robe with black trim and belt. Pointe shoes, off. Feathers, off. Her short, dark-brown hair, still in its hairnet, held in place by the necessary black headband. The headpiece feathers had been covering all this. Clever. The illusion of longer hair, which

There it is. That heartbroken princess trapped inside a beautiful Swan. Cynthia Gregory with partner Ted Kivitt in *Swan Lake* at ABT (Photo by Martha Swope © New York Public Library for the Performing Arts).

Cynthia and I, two peas in a pod.

always has to be tucked away in a bun. It's now been deftly replaced by the comfort of a modern-day bob cut. That's Cynthia.

The friends are recalling moments that resonated. More often than not, her Act II departure. Suddenly I hear, "Can I touch your arm? To make sure it's not feathers?" Cynthia explains that she uses white body makeup.

"I love that body makeup. It makes my arms feel less like arms, and more like wings." (Honey, it ain't the body makeup.)

Later, we're talking about it. Just the two of us. Cynthia confesses, "I never remember my second act exit. And I *never* rehearse it. It just happens. Before every *Swan Lake*, I worry. What if *it's* not there anymore? The 'thing' everyone says I've got? What if it's gone? I make myself stop thinking and leave it up to God."

Don't worry, dear friend. During every *Swan Lake* I get to watch, while you're leaving it up to God, tears are welling in my eyes. Chills are swimming all over me. When the curtain comes down, I'm a limp rag doll. Emotions, completely spent.

At that moment, an odd question can creep into my head. Was that ever really me up there, so many years ago? Feels like a dream.

What a cliché. (Some clichés say it best?)

* * *

Cynthia isn't the only dear friend I'm visiting on this trip. There is, of course, also Gladys.

Pianist Gladys Celeste joined American Ballet Theatre in 1960. Ask any ABT dancer over the years. They'll most likely tell you that Gladys is the linchpin of the Company. She connects all of us. Every ABT dancer has his or her "Gladys Story." (Usually, more than one.) Cynthia Gregory, Christine ("Chrissy") Sarry, Marie Johansson, Elizabeth Carr. Sure. We might be from different decades. But we all know Gladys, so we all know each other.

Gladys, during her more than forty years with ABT, rises to Principal Pianist. Playing countless rehearsals, but also a featured soloist with the ABT Orchestra in the pit, during performances.

One day at The Met, Cynthia and I are grabbing a bite in the basement cafeteria. Gladys walks by, on her way to play a rehearsal she thinks I'd like to watch. A female soloist is working on the *Waltz* in *Les Sylphides*. That used to be my solo, and Gladys used to play my rehearsals. See ya' later, Cyn.

The *Waltz* is one of three female solos. The others are the *Mazurka* and the *Prelude*. One of the three ballerinas dancing these solos also performs the *Pas de Deux*. And the ballerina dancing the *Pas de Deux* gets to pick which of those three solos she wants to do. No historian, me. But it seems that many *Pas de Deux* ballerinas choose the slow and quiet *Prelude*. You dance it right before the *Pas de Deux*. Excellent warm-up? On the other hand, ballerinas who love to jump often pick the *Mazurka*.

Did any ballerina ever choose *The Waltz*? You bet. None other than Anna Pavlova. Since I know this gem of Fokine choreography so well, I'd like to think Pavlova chooses it because of its diverse "personalities." And, let's face it, "La Pavlova's" solos are full of different personalities.

In this *Waltz*, for instance, I feel like I go from cheerful, to playful, to gliding with smooth *bourrées* like a wisp among the trees, to quietly meditative, to bursting into an exuberant *cabriole derrière* (beating the legs together once in the back, then landing *arabesque*). It all feels like different parts of me that I can share with the audience.

The opening *grands jetés* (large leaps) are cheerfully lilting, emphasizing the gentle arc of the jump, like a rainbow. Like a delicious version of my power leaps as Queen of the Wilis. The second sequence has you landing a gentle *grand jeté en tournant* in an *allongé attitude*. After running three steps in place on pointe, you end with a tiny leap off your pointe shoe into a *demi-plié* in a low *arabesque*. Like a feather, wafting to the ground. Magical.

Why magical? Because, at the same time I'm running those three feather-like steps on pointe, I get to perform one of the most enchanting gestures in all ballet. The "calling" gesture. First, I float my hands and wrists collar-bone height, with elbows aside. Allowing both arms to gently breathe upward, with fingers downward. Then, gently lifting my fingers, let's say, to the height of a microphone, I waft my right hand forward and my left out to the side.

It sounds simple, but practicing this gesture in *The Waltz* always feels a bit like meditation. So gentle. So focused. So exacting. All without appearing to be so.

Can you tell that I adore this *Les Sylphides Waltz*? And rehearsing it was equally wonderful. Because my rehearsals were with ABT Régisseur, Dimitri Romanoff. In the world of ballet, the Régisseur is kind of like the "keeper of the flame" of all the traditions. And Dimitri has obviously been minding those traditional ballet flames for a long, long time.

As a youth in Los Angeles, Dimitri studied with Michel Fokine.[12] Yes, the choreographer of *Les Sylphides*. Could he have been a fly on the wall when Master Fokine was coaching ballerina Nathalie Krassovska, back in the late '30s? For the Ballet Russe de Monte Carlo's premiere in 1938?

Judging from the way Dimitri eventually coached me in the *Les Sylphides Waltz*, he was committed to every detail as much as Fokine was. We spent fifteen minutes on just that one "calling gesture." He had me watching my two pinkie fingers tracing invisible parallel lines, as they glided through the air in front of me. Again and again. Turns out, the details are the magic.

Back to today's rehearsal. It's about to start. There are four of us in the room. The dancer. The Ballet Master, who's been "running the rehearsal" and teaching the choreography. Gladys. And one guest. Me.

But, no. There's one more "presence" in the studio. The ubiquitous videocassette machine, attached to its small TV monitor. That's how a Ballet Master teaches a dancer a role that he himself has never danced.

Problem is, TV is such a two-dimensional medium. There's nothing organic about the *ports de bras* you're seeing on it. Nothing showing the "heart" that goes along with the arm movements. *That* you can't get from a TV monitor. On that screen, you can only see someone dancing from the outside, in. You can't see where the movement is originating. From the inside, out.

But, I digress. Gladys is forging ahead, playing the ever-helpful "learning tempo." A lot slower than the eventual "performance" tempo. Perfect for when the steps are still a little unfamiliar. This lovely soloist has been taught well. The steps are all there, but Dimitri's magic is not. Only Gladys and I know the touches that are missing, remembering them from all those rehearsals years ago. I mumble to Gladys, "We sure could use Dimitri."

All of a sudden, Gladys's fingers stop playing. She stands up.

GLADYS: "You know, Roni was coached by Dimitri. Would you like to hear what she remembers?"
DANCER: "Yes. P-l-e-a-s-e."

I spend what's left of the rehearsal hour demonstrating every detail I still so vividly recall. I even remember two more phrases of Fokine wisdom, passed on by Dimitri: The *Mazurka grand jeté* is *pushed* forward, from behind. The *Waltz grand jeté* is *pulled* forward, from in front.

And that, folks, is how tradition continues. Down to the pinkies, and all. Just like the cliché says. Passed on from generation to generation. With generous helpings from the rehearsal pianist, and the keeper of the flame.

Remember, at the beginning of all this, hearing about the diverse "personalities" I find in my beloved *Waltz*? Cheerful? Playful? Smoothly gliding? Meditative? Exuberant? Well, let's hear it for Gladys's depth of artistry. Her playing has been reflecting Chopin's personality changes throughout this extraordinary music. Which has been helping the dancer reflect those same personality changes in Fokine's extraordinary choreography.

When the dancer is about to try the whole thing from the top, Gladys whispers to me, "I'm going to push her. It's time." And, just like that, she ups the tempo from a "learning" one, to a "nearly performance" one. Don't look now, but I think it's Gladys who's been "running" one heckuva rehearsal.

The Cleveland Browns

In 1984, I'm happily ensconced at the Cleveland Ballet when I get an amazing phone call. It's Dr. John Bergfeld, orthopedic surgeon to both Cleveland Ballet and the Cleveland Browns. Dr. Bergfeld heard about my "Ballet Movement for the Athlete" presentation in Kansas City seven years ago. Now he wants to hook me up with the Cleveland Browns' Strength Trainer, Dave Redding. Dave wants me to work with the players in general, and cornerback Hanford Dixon in particular. To sell his guys on this idea, he invites me to teach a class for them.

Why a ballet class? After successfully adding muscle mass to the players, Dave wants an off-season, weight-bearing activity to help their legs acclimate and ward off injury. Case in point? Bob Golic's two inflamed Achilles tendons, after switching from New England Patriots linebacker to Cleveland Browns Nose Guard. The guy who has to be strong enough to take out the Center. All that extra muscle. Could *movement-based* cross-training help? Could ballet?

Dave tells me that if the players are "sold" on the class, he'll set up a 12-week program at their off-season training site, on the campus of Baldwin Wallace University. Wondering what kind of "studio space" I'll have? Only a regulation football field. All 100 yards of it.

Before we begin my "audition class," Dave takes me aside.

Dave: "I want you to kill 'em. I want them to think ballet is the hardest thing they've ever done."
Me: "No problem."

(Did I mention that Dave also takes the class? I recently texted him to say thanks for all his help back then. I received a one-sentence response: "My butt *still* hurts.")

How do I manage to make the players think ballet is the toughest thing in the world? For starters, by making them stretch with their legs up on the barre *my* way. With *straight knees.* And later, by having them jump off two feet, turn around once in the air, and stick the landing, on balance. Tough enough?

Okay. "Audition class," taught. Players, won over. Program, set up. Maybe the first in the NFL at the time? Teaching this class is going to be different. The sheer size of my "students" ensures that. One Offensive Line player is 6'8" and 275 lbs.[13]

I'm definitely going to be adjusting some of my "tried-and-trues." Take the day Mr. 275-pounder is stretching with his leg up on the barre at a right angle. Both arms overhead, throughout the entire sequence. I call it my "Look, Ma, no hands" approach.

First, he bends forward toward his leg on the barre, before coming back up. Then he tries bending back as far as possible. Usually, I make sure to guide each student for safety the first time they try it. My left hand on their upper back, with my left elbow bracing against my waist. My right hand, pulling them gently back towards me. "Don't worry. I've got you." My standard line.

Suddenly, "Don't worry. I've got you" is not accurate. This guy's massive weight is slowly bending my knees and arching me backwards, closer and closer to the floor. My instinct to scream wins out over my instinct to laugh, "H-E-L-P!" Bob Golic runs to my rescue.

A word about this barre the Browns have for me at Baldwin Wallace. After telling Dave we'll need one along a wall of his choice, he asks, how high? I touch the wall, to indicate the height.

Dave: "That's not high enough, Roni. These guys are big."
Me: "I know. But, when they put their legs up on that barre, I'm going to want their legs to be *straight*."

We end up compromising. The barre starts off at my suggested height. Then it continues at Dave's.

Mind you, this barre has to support a lot of muscle. It's made out of heavy-duty black iron, maybe 2½ inches thick. And it's riveted to the wall with heavy-duty bolts. What about that two-height compromise? In the end, the only one who can stretch on the high barre with straight legs … is me.

Some more adjustments. No way all the different shapes and sizes in this ballet class can move at the same rate. And once you ditch moving in unison, music isn't necessary. When I need to energize them, I simply scream and clap to eight, over and over again. The players are looking puzzled.

Me: "What's the matter?"
One Player: "Where's Nine? Where's Ten?"

Of course. They're used to reps. I explain that ballet class music is mostly written in eights.

ANOTHER PLAYER: "Well why don't we have music?"
ME: "We can, if you want."

Are they going to like solo piano? I try it. They go with the counts.

Another area where our paths differ? A football player measures his "vertical" jump. Translation: How high he can jump off two legs from a standing position, his fingertips stretched upward. He tries once. Measures the height. Tries again.

Ballet dancers do that move, but many times in succession, while alternating beating one leg in front of the other. Bending our knees on each landing. The height of our jump is determined by the tempo of the music. Quality over quantity?

There's another vertical jump we dancers do. We call it a single *tour en l'air*. It means jumping off both feet and revolving 360°. Then, landing in the same spot. The male ballet dancer must perfect the double *tour en l'air*. Some have been known to do a triple. I do a single. I ask the players to try this single *tour en l'air* to increase their body awareness in space. It might help them while turning to catch an over-the-shoulder pass.

These professional athletes can't do something I can do. It drives them crazy. In retaliation, they measure my vertical jump. Utterly dismal. I counter with who can jump higher in a forward leap, or *grand jeté*. (Heh! Heh! Heh!)

* * *

One early success: Mike Baab, the Center. Mike is recovering from arthroscopic knee surgery. He needs to build confidence in that knee, not just strength. I have Mike stand on a cushioned mat. First, holding the barre with both hands. Then, without. Keeping his heels together, he "comfortably" rotates his legs outward from his hips.

Now, he bends both knees (*demi-plié*), keeping them out over the little toe of each foot. Then, he pushes his toes down at the same moment he jumps off the floor with straight knees. He then lands again with knees bent in that properly-aligned 1st position *demi-plié* again. These mechanics feel totally foreign to the non-dancer. Totally "opposite." My student is puzzled.

MIKE: "Why do I have to straighten my knees in the air? Frogs are the best jumpers, and they keep their knees bent."
RONI: "Frogs knees are already strong, and they are not rehabbing from arthroscopic surgery."

The mechanics of correctly bending and straightening and bending and straightening and bending, while jumping, is going to strengthen that knee. Surprise, surprise. Because Mike now has confidence in his arthroscopic knee, he's able to master the basic mechanics of *chassé, grand jeté en tournant* (colloquially, *tour jeté*). He can repeat it in an unending string across all 100 yards. It's become his favorite exercise. Why? That ballet step has an unmistakable bouncing-ball rhythm to it. When *that* kicks in, it becomes downright fun. Not all the players do it as well. Mike is a star.

About six months later, Mike and his beautiful wife Lolis come to Cleveland

Ballet's Grand Opening performance at the completely refurbished State Theatre on Playhouse Square. During one of the intermissions, I introduce Mike and Lolis to Artistic Director Dennis Nahat. Dennis has brilliantly choreographed the evening's premiere. *Celebrations and Ode*, performed to Beethoven's Seventh and Ninth Symphonies.

> **DENNIS:** "Roni tells me she's been teaching you ballet."
> **MIKE:** "Yes. And she taught me how to bend my knees when I land from a jump."
> **DENNIS:** "Goooooood."

Dino Hall, eat your heart out!

My star student really knows his stuff.

When Mike and Lolis host a "company" Halloween party, all of Cuyahoga County can hear me cry out: "I have nothing to wear!"

Browns Equipment Manager to the rescue. I show up as, what else? A Cleveland Brown. Helmet, and all. (Minus, thankfully, the shoulder pads.) I'm sporting a bright orange "1" on my white regulation "away" jersey, and a "1" on my regulation helmet. Dino Hall's number, Special Teams. Regulation socks, pants, belt. I get to keep the belt.

Now, fast forward from Halloween to New Year's Eve. Cleveland Ballet is entertaining its audience with this year's rendition of *The Nutty Nutcracker*, the celebrity-sprinkled parody performance of their treasured Holiday Classic.

Picture the Battle Scene between the Mice and the Soldiers. Then picture Mike Baab, decked out in all his Cleveland Browns uniform-and-helmet glory, suddenly jumping out from the wings. To screams of recognition from the ecstatic audience, here's Mike chasing the Mouse King all around the stage. Trying to pull off that huge Mouse King's head.

Did somebody just close a loop here?

Another success story is Cornerback Hanford Dixon, the player Dave had hoped I'd be able to help in particular. Hanford's the one who names the bleachers the "Dawg Pound," because he shakes his fist and "woofs" at his fellow cornerback, Frank Minnifield. What does Dave Redding want me to help Hanford with? He puts it this way:

DAVE: "Hanford is fast enough to get to the ball. His problem is catching it."
ME: "I can work on that."

Now all I have to do is come up with something.

Okay. Refocusing, while turning. A catch is easier when the ball is in front of you. When looking back over your shoulder, the faster you can refocus, the sooner you can "soften" your hands for the catch.

Let's have Hanford jump four quarter turns to the right. Wall, wall, wall, front again. First, his legs must be rotated slightly outward from his hips, to protect and strengthen his knees. Then, he must land each jump in a modified ballet 5th position. First, with his left heel covering his right big toe then switching, switching, switching. Yes, changing feet when landing each jump. He also has to turn his head to the next wall *while he's in the air* ... and clap his hands once at the same time. Lots of coordination going on here. Lots of moving parts, emulating the complexities of catching a ball over your shoulder, while running as fast as you can.

I love this stuff. I even have something up my sleeve for errant field goal attempts. Also up my sleeve? Working on knees that can't seem to straighten. Too much musculature built up around a slightly bent knee can cause frequent hamstring injuries. Time to start stretching ... properly.

The Wednesday Ballet Class lasts for 12 weeks. Attendance is voluntary. Never less than six players. Never more than 18. Redding, naturally, is happier with the larger classes. I prefer the smaller ones. More individual instruction. (I must never own my own Ballet School. I'd be bankrupt in a week.)

Back home, Erik, now 16, has been pestering me to see a practice. The school year finally ends. He gets to tag along and watch The Wednesday Ballet Class.

I'm collecting my things after class, when I suddenly look up. Erik's about 30 feet away, chatting it up with the players. (Not shy.) Pretty soon, one of them saunters by.

He's asking another player, "Who *is* that kid? He not only told me where I played college ball. He named my entire starting lineup, and reminded me of plays I forgot I made." That's my boy. A tomboy's son, through and through.

(Erik may have gotten my sports gene, but the ballet one? Not so much. When Dennis Nahat sees a long-legged,14-year-old Erik at the School of Cleveland Ballet's studios, he asks when he'll see him [and his legs] in ballet class. Erik's reply? "Well, I guess that just means I'll be the tallest sportscaster in the business!" You can't win 'em all.)

After the '84 season, the coaches finish their final evaluation of the program. There seems to be a significant reduction in groin injuries. I'm not surprised.

Just for kicks, I also ask if any player wants to sum up how the ballet class helped. Bob Golic wins the prize: "If you can't get around 'em, jump over 'em."

Everything's pointing to a return engagement in Spring '85. But, Fate has something else in mind for me, just around the corner. No, I don't work with the Cleveland Browns again. But, several Browns stay in touch and still do my exercises.

* * *

It goes without saying that, during my 12 weeks of classes with the Browns, many cameras were clicking constantly. Turns out, Dr. John Bergfeld is my best cheerleader. About a year after that coach's evaluation, I receive a manila envelope. Dr. Bergfeld's slideshow, gleaned from all those pictures of the Wednesday Ballet Class. He's been lecturing around the country with these photos as his centerpiece. Touting, among other things, the reduction in groin injuries. Now, these slides are mine to keep. Apparently, one of them goes out over the Associated Press wire.

Meanwhile, my dad's in the hospital, recovering nicely after pancreatic surgery. He's reading the *Miami Herald* in his hospital bed one morning. His surgeon pops in to chat. Something catches the Doc's eye on the back of Dad's newspaper.

Doc: "Look at that. A football player doing a ballet leap."
Dad (flipping over the page): "Hey. That's my daughter in the air with him."

I like to think my friend Albert Einstein would be proud. Got an absurd idea, anyone?

Cue Stage Left: San Jose

"What's in a name?" Dear, dear Juliet. To answer that, I need to begin with the name "Cleveland Ballet." The name Dennis Nahat and Ernie Horvath gave to their nascent ballet company at its 1976 debut.

Poof. Now, it's 1984. "Enter stage left," from the West coast, Californians Karen Loewenstern and Anita Del Grande. Two enterprising women from San Jose. And, have they got a vision.

Training the Cleveland Browns in Spring of 1984 at their off-season training site on the campus of Baldwin Wallace University (©Paul Tople—USA TODAY NETWORK).

They want an "instant ballet company." Not ten years building one. And they want a co-venture with an existing professional company. The hunt is on.

March 1985. The only ballet company left on Karen's dance card is Cleveland Ballet. The program she attends? Artistic Director Dennis Nahat's storybook production of *Coppélia*. Could this be fate? You see, back in December of '71, Karen's husband-to-be, Walter Loewenstern, took her to see American Ballet Theatre at the Kennedy Center. Their very first date. Her very first ballet. And it's none other than *Coppélia*. Then-ABT soloist Dennis Nahat receives hearty applause for his hilarious turn as The Priest in Act III. By evening's end, Karen has fallen completely in love with *Coppélia*.

Now, in 1985, she's head-over-heels again. This time with Cleveland Ballet's production. Nobody tells a story better than Dennis Nahat. Dinner with Dennis after the show. Instant chemistry between the two. The rest is history.

Karen and Anita return to San Jose and agree that Cleveland Ballet is the one. The feeling is mutual. Believe it or not, Dennis has also been searching for a city to hook up with. He's been favoring San Jose. It's the one city that doesn't already have a ballet company he'd have to merge with.

On cue, Cleveland and San Jose give birth to *San Jose Cleveland Ballet*. Every program we present in Cleveland now travels cross-country to be performed in San Jose. At their Center for the Performing Arts, designed by the Frank Lloyd Wright Foundation.

Our Cleveland Ballet Orchestra musicians are *not* making the trip with us. Our

Music Director and Conductor, Dwight Oltman, is. And Maestro Oltman will be conducting the San Jose Symphony Orchestra for our performances. Different musicians. Same gifted baton.

Hark, sweet Juliet. Here's what's in a name. At home, we're still Cleveland Ballet, for our loyal audience. But, out West, we're now San Jose Cleveland Ballet. Two major cities. One lucky professional ballet company.[14]

Now, it's the Thanksgiving Holiday in 1985. But, before the Friday night San Jose premiere of Dennis Nahat's magical production of *The Nutcracker*, we're offering a free Children's Performance. And Karen Loewenstern needs to find funding for it. She hears that Apple co-founder and tech entrepreneur Steve Wozniak is all about helping kids. "Woz." The half-man, half-pixie, himself. Equal parts wonder, curiosity, enthusiasm.

This time, I'll call it kismet. Karen and Woz attend the same Mayor's Breakfast. Never one to snub kismet, Karen breaks the ice:

This co-venture is really working! Karen Loewenstern, Anita Del Grande, and me with principal dancers Raymond Rodriguez and Karen Gabay (center) in 1987, after our full-length *Swan Lake* in San Jose.

Karen: "Mr. Wozniak. My name is Karen Loewenstern, and I'm...."

Woz (interrupting): "I know who you are. Your husband's ROLM poster has been hanging on my garage wall for years."

Yes, Karen's husband, Walter Loewenstern, is the "L" in the tech company ROLM, founded by Gene Richeson, Ken Oshman, Walter Loewenstern, Robert Maxfield. (Just the year before, IBM acquired ROLM.)

Karen and Woz make a date to talk turkey. Karen's modest figure in mind? $25,000. But, Woz is getting so excited about that free Children's Performance that Karen takes a deep breath and adds a zero. Woz doesn't even blink. He writes the check. Signs it, "Woz." Is this the prankster in him? Turns out, that's the way he signs *all* his checks.

Not only is Woz's money good. He dives right in and joins the Board. The Free Children's Performance funding is in place. And then some. And the opening night of Dennis's production of *The Nutcracker* is a big hit.

A year later, in 1986, Dennis realizes the rest of his co-venture. The School of San Jose Cleveland Ballet hits the road, running. Dennis sends me westward to start things off for the first four months. A faculty of one. Twenty classes a week. Pre-Ballet, all the way up to the most advanced. Plus, adults.

In my Advanced Ballet class, I meet Elizabeth Farotte, Crystal Hernandez, Ariel Hoffman, Janine Kreft, and Kathryn Zuhr. Five teenage girls who are really strong dancers. I mean *en pointe*, strong. I dub them The Fab Five.

The wheels in my mind begin spinning like crazy. Time to talk about the time-honored "rite of passage" at Cleveland Ballet. Every year during *Nutcracker* season, the strongest female students in the most advanced class cover certain spots in "The Dance of the Snowflakes." Dubbed "Snow." Snow? Sounds light and flaky, right? Think again. "Snow" is Dennis's cardio-killer choreography that closes Act I.

Dennis uses 16 Snowflakes. But there are also at least two or three different casts of *The Nutcracker's* two female principal roles, Maria (Clara) and the Tsarina (Sugar Plum Fairy). That's four to six different "Snow" spots that need covering. Who fills all those vacant spots in each show? Yup. The strongest female dance students from the most advanced class.

What if, in three short months, I can teach "Snow" to the San Jose Fab Five? What if Dennis watches a run-through and gives the thumbs-up? Imagine the excitement if students from the fledgling School, in their first year, can perform with the Cleveland Snowflakes. Now *this* is a "co-venture."

The Fab Five *really* want to give this a shot. But, it's no walk in the park. Even Company dancers have to gradually build up the stamina to "get through" Snow. Muscle endurance. Cardio endurance. Blood, sweat, and tears isn't a cliché for nothing. On their day of reckoning, Dennis gives his long-awaited thumbs up. The Fab Five have pulled it off. (To this day, some of these women reminisce about "Snow in San Jose" on Facebook.)

But local "participation" doesn't end with the Fab Five. Every storybook production needs Supers. *Supernumeraries.* The "extra" men, women, girls and boys that appear onstage, mostly in non-dancing roles, who aren't contracted company members.

The Nutcracker has lots of Supers. Spanish Guards. Russian Guards. A Priest leading little Carolers in song. A Chestnut Vendor selling hot chestnuts to the adorable children. Even a Major Domo, in charge of the wondrous Ballroom scene.

This year, I'm teaching all the Supers' roles. And I love it. I run the auditions, too. Guess which impish, overgrown child ends up as the Chestnut Vendor? Doling out bags of hot chestnuts to Carolers that include his own two children? Hint: He's a generous half man, half pixie.

Woz is in heaven. And he doesn't stop there. *Swan Lake. Romeo and Juliet.* He's a Guard. A Page. A Spear-Carrier. A Banquet Server. In absolute awe of the dancers. Now, he's got the best seat in the house; onstage, with them.

Roasted chestnuts are not the only things Woz is giving away. Any Company member who wants one is the instant owner of an Apple II. Chiseled in my memory forever: the two hours he spends "customizing" mine. All those bells and whistles.

And the giving just keeps on coming. Cleveland is about to premiere Dennis's poignant, full-length *Romeo and Juliet.* When Woz flies in for Opening Night, he's mesmerized. He can't wait until San Jose sees this masterful production.

But then, Dennis delivers some troubling news. The stage at San Jose's Center for the Performing Arts is not "deep" enough. It has only five wings. "R & J" needs

Here I am posing with (from left to right) Anita Del Grande, Stella Beer, and Steve Wozniak, backstage at the San Jose Center for the Performing Arts, to celebrate another successful performance by the San Jose Cleveland Ballet.

seven. Dollars magically materialize for a complete stagehouse renovation. More dollars for the Patron Lounge. *And*, Dennis's dressing room/office. The Pixie strikes … again and again and again.

The Woz. He's actually half pixie, half *mensch*. Classic definition: A person of honor and integrity. My definition: A really fabulous human being.

This thriving, two-city arrangement sadly comes to a crashing halt in 2000, when the Cleveland Board closes down the Cleveland end of the co-venture. Fear not. Right on cue, San Jose steps in to save the day … *and* the ballet company. The entire operation moves westward. To what is now it's *only* home. Dancers, costumes. Sets. The whole shebang. And, the name? *Ballet San Jose*. Juliet. Over and out.

Everybody's Mother

I join Cleveland Ballet as Ballet Mistress in 1981. That same year, I make my debut as Helga The Housekeeper in the Party Scene of our annual production of *The Nutcracker*. And it never stops after that. A never-ending string of "old lady parts." Or so they're affectionately called.

These time-honored performing opportunities most often arise in the "story" ballets, multi-act productions telling a fairytale. Here, the chances to play somebody's mother, or a king or queen, are infinite. Even one-act offerings can include a stepmother. Or a red-light district "Madam."

Company dancers sometimes fill these roles. But, they're also a godsend for, let's say, a former dancer, now retired and a member of the Company rehearsal staff. Someone who still has performing in her soul. Older now. Still in very good shape. But nowhere near the *incredible* shape of someone who can still perform *en pointe*. Sound like anybody we know?

These old-lady parts are

"You *will* marry Paris," says Lady Capulet to her daughter Juliet, performed by Cynthia Gregory in 1988 (Photo by Susan Telecky).

referred to as "character roles," for the characters we portray in a story. Sometimes these story "characters" wear a flat shoe. Others, sporting a 1–2 inch heel, known as "character shoes."

Even a mid–1980s move up from Ballet Mistress to Artistic Associate can't keep me away from "the stage." (She says, dramatically.) Lucky, lucky me. Still learning from Dennis, while performing his choreography. Learning about pantomime. Learning about the stagecraft of transferring ballets from the studio to the stage.

In 1998, when promoting her upcoming film, *Stepmom*, Susan Sarandon gave an interview that became seared into my brain: "Now I play everybody's mother," she said. Well, she might as well have been talking about me. Thanks, Ms. Sarandon for that terrific line.

Exactly how many times do I portray Everybody's Mother? The list:

Swanilda's Mom
Siegfried's Mom
Juliet's Nurse
Juliet's Mom
Lizzie's Stepmom
Giselle's Mom

The Countess (polite for Madam… "mother" to her "girls?")
Flemming's Mom
Maria's Mom

For now, let's just stick with Dennis's charming production of *Coppélia* on our European tour in 1990, in which (you guessed it), I play the Mother.

* * *

When we perform *Coppélia*, Dennis often portrays Dr. Coppélius himself. But today, Rudolf Nureyev, now in his 50s, is preparing for his debut in the role. And the Cleveland San Jose Ballet is in Dublin. (Ireland, not Ohio.) It is 1990, and we're performing in an interesting venue. It used to be called "The Point Depot," because it was a train station. Now it's just called The Point. One of those multi-purpose concert-and-events spaces that transforms itself, as needed. For us, "Presto." It becomes a theater.

Roughly a month ago, Dennis met up with Rudolf in Europe. Over the span of a few days, he taught him the role of Dr. Coppélius. Now, Rudolf has met up with the Company at The Point and is scheduled to rehearse all his choreography in Act II.

Allow me to set the scene. Rudolf is up onstage. I'm in the wings, watching. Dennis is in the audience, on the "God Mic." So called, because he can tell everyone in the theater what to do. Without being seen.

Rudolf is having trouble remembering his choreography. It's very understandable. That's because there are no ballet steps. Just lots of pantomime and lots of props. Very effective. V-e-r-y complicated. After a few minutes of watching this, Dennis can no longer contain himself.

Dennis: "Rudolf. Just a minute. I'm on my way up."
Rudolf, to Me: *"Tell him one foot on stage, I leave."*
Me (blurting, in one breath): "Dennis. Rudolf says if you put one foot on the stage, he's gone."
Dennis: "Fine."
Rudolf, to Me: *"Come. You teach."*

A playful moment between Juliet (Karen Gabay) and her Nurse in 1986 (Photo by Susan Telecky).

Wait a minute. Sure, I've been watching Dennis do Dr. Coppélius for years. And I can imitate him pretty well. But teach every move? Exactly? With precise counts? Never. Dennis knows this. What follows is wonderful comedy.

I begin to show Rudolf something that's not quite right. I hear a throat clear, over the God Mic. I shoot a hasty glance out into the house. Dennis is frantically pantomiming the exact move. I teach it accurately to Rudolf. Fact: I'm shaking in my boots. Fact: Rudolf is enjoying this immensely. He can be quite the imp.

This imp is, by no means, finished. Before curtain for the Orchestra Dress Rehearsal, he approaches me.

RUDOLF: *"Where you be Act II?"*
ME: *"Watching, in the downstage left wing."*
RUDOLF: *"Too far. You be there."* (Pointing to the upstage right wing.)

Upstage right happens to be the location of Dr. Coppélius's Work Table. Multiple flasks, of assorted sizes and colored liquids. A winding tube with vapor spilling out. A bottle of a questionable brew. Two goblets. All the magic happens here.

Dr. Coppélius should run over to his Work Table only when he needs to make a brew or fetch a prop. But Rudolf just keeps running over to me in the wings, anytime he needs to find out what comes next.

So I'm ensconced in the wing nearest said Work Table. Doing my best to "cue" him through this humorously challenging scene, where Dr. Coppélius is determined to turn his beloved, life-sized doll Coppélia (who's actually Swanilda in disguise) into a living, breathing companion.

How? By draining the "life-force," one body part at a time, from a passed-out Franz (who made the mistake of drinking one of Coppélius's dubious concoctions). And seeming to "infuse" it into the wooden body of his life-size creation. Swanilda goes along with the gag. "Eyes." "Shoulders." "Arms." "Legs." Get the picture?

Rudolf runs wild-eyed towards the wing, as I'm frantically raising and lowering my shoulders. Or stroking an arm. Or a leg. In every rehearsal, he orders me to sit closer to the wing's edge. The better to see me. Then, the God Mic: "Roni, we can see you." So I obediently scoot back a little further into the wing. Until the next time.

Second Act shenanigans isn't the only choreography Rudolf has to master. But when it comes to actual steps and actual dancing, he's absolutely amazing. Let's talk about Act III. The dance has four village couples, including Swanilda's Mom and Dr. Coppélius. In a twist of irony, the music for this fun-filled romp is none other than that familiar "Dawn" variation in Act III. Yes, the exact same music I danced to for my very first "tutu" variation when I was 14 years old!

Because Dennis's choreography has so much built-in humor, many of the funniest moves require a high level of physical comedy. Well, to pull off this high level of comedy, you need a really strong partner. And a trustworthy one. Someone you're not afraid to take risks with.

Rudolf is just that partner. He's strong *and* trustworthy. In all those off-balance spinning moments. Even during my pratfall into a sideways split, when my tailbone's only protection is Dr. Coppélius's strong arms under my armpits, cushioning my fall.

I'm totally "protected." Every time. It's safe to say that the "prima donna" part

Yes, I actually danced with Rudolf Nureyev! (Photo by Dennis Nahat).

of Rudolf, offstage, is completely out of the picture when he sets foot onstage. Out there, he is consistently reliable. And blessed with fabulous partnering instincts. Some male dancers still worry about how *they* are looking when partnering the woman. Not Rudolf. His only concern? Making *her* look good. But, when the dancing is over, watch out. The mischievous imp is back in full force.

* * *

Guess what follows that comedic romp by us "characters?" "From the ridiculous to the sublime." It's none other than the poignantly serene *Pas de Deux* celebrating the wedding of Swanilda and Franz.

The introduction to that *adagio* is several slow-tempo phrases of tranquil melody. During that time, Swanilda and Franz enter from upstage right. They walk a slow, counter-clockwise circle around the stage, finishing more or less where they started. But, but, but, but, but… During the penultimate of those *adagio* phrases, they pass by the balcony of Dr. Coppélius's toy shop, looking up at Dr. C and Mama. At which point, I must be calmly in place to tearfully wave my handkerchief at my daughter and her soon-to-be husband.

But, remember. We're talkin' about The Imp here. Following our comedic romp, Rudolf precedes me through the toy shop front door and easily ascends those tricky off-stage spiral stairs, unencumbered. Once on the balcony, he stands ready to greet me.

I, on the other hand, am running through that same stage-level toy shop front door, with my full petticoats and costume skirt slung over my right elbow. My right hand is now free to grab the handles of two empty beer mugs from Prop Guy. This leaves my left hand free to hold the handrail of said tricky off-stage spiral stairs … all while wearing 2"-heeled character shoes. Needless to say, one of those mugs is upright, but the other is bound to be askew. This doesn't matter, because both mugs are empty.

Or are they? The Imp has instructed his dresser to fill *his* mug with hot tea and honey and lemon. So waiting Prop Guy has to loop the handle of the upright mug-with-beverage through my index finger. I must then grasp the empty and askew mug with my free right thumb. All, with my crinolines and skirt hanging off my elbow.

This left hand has three jobs. Hold handrail. Part the velvet curtains. Hand both mugs to the awaiting Dr. Coppélius. Finally, my right hand is free to grab the handkerchief tucked into my bosom. Then, I look as serene as the melody, and wave said handkerchief right on time. To my daughter, who's gazing at me lovingly from below. And I accomplish all this, while still out of breath from our dance. Perspiration still pouring down my face. Luckily, the audience thinks I'm crying, as I blot the sweat beads too close to my eyes.

Rudolf. The Imp.

* * *

"Swanilda's Mom" and Rudolf's coach aren't the only hats I wear in this Dublin production of *Coppélia*. The other, also behind the scenes, is teaching the five adorable "village children" their choreography. Three boys and two girls. This "mothering" never stops.

The older of the two girls is especially memorable. An 11-year-old who looks like she's eight. The story of *my* life. The pale blue eyes looking out beyond the very long, black eyelashes. The round face with such rosy cheeks. The obligatory freckles. The reddish-brown curls all over the place. Precious.

She confides in me that she has just started *en pointe*. Would I mind looking at her standing in her pointe shoes? Her stance is beautiful. She's a natural. As with most beginners, she can use a little help with tying her pointe shoe ribbons. Would she like to watch me tie mine?

As I sit to put on my pointe shoes, I grab some fresh lamb's wool from the box in my dance bag. Lamb's wool is used to cushion the toes from the hard and unforgiving floor. I'm showing her how I mold this lamb's wool to my toes, when she interrupts me.

> **IRISH LASS:** "Your lamb's wool comes from a box?"
> **ME:** "Yes. Where does yours come from?"
> **IRISH LASS:** "Oh. We have a barbed wire fence around our farm. If I need more lamb's wool, I just go out and pick it off the fence. When the sheep jump over, the little babies can't go as high. Their tummies graze the top and leave some wool on the wire. My father wants to make the fence higher. My mother says I need the lamb's wool."

There are no words.

Once a Mahler...

Have I mentioned that my sisters and I are legendary composer Gustav Mahler's closest living relatives? Technically, we are first cousins, three times removed.

My great-grandfather, Rudolf, and Gustav were first cousins, because their fathers (David and Bernhard) were brothers. That makes my grandfather, Wilheim, a first cousin, *once* removed. My father, Paul, a first cousin, *twice* removed, and Stephanie, Ronnie, and Lyn first cousins, *three times* removed. Pretty special, huh?

In the summer of 1969, it finally happens. I get to perform the Fourth Song in Antony Tudor's *Dark Elegies*. Choreographed to Gustav Mahler's *Kindertotenlieder*. Gustav and Roni, on stage together with American Ballet Theatre. At The Met, no less. I'm not going to say it, but.... Okay, it doesn't get any better than this.

Before dancing any role for the first time, friends often give you a little token gift called a "happy." Before my first *Elegies*, an orchestra pal presents me with what looks like a campaign button at first glance. It's not. The button says "Mahler Grooves." Columbia Records is apparently commemorating their reissuing of all the Mahler symphonies.

The top half of the button is orange, background to the "Mahler." The bottom half is red, background to the "Grooves." I

Grandpa Wilheim, Gustav's first cousin, once removed. Here, far left, with (continuing from left to right) his brothers Paul and John (Hans), and sister Hilda in Vienna (circa 1900).

immediately pin this fabulous "happy" to my winter coat. It goes everywhere I go. After a while, I forget it's there.

Once, when getting off a crowded elevator, I hear, "So long, Mahler." How does he know my name? Oh. The button.

Even better is when I'm getting off the Long Island Rail Road at the Flushing Avenue station to go to the unemployment office. As the train pulls away, the conductor leans out and waves. "I'll vote for 'em, lady."

It takes me a minute to get it. Last June, in the New York City democratic primary, brazen novelist Norman Mailer really shook things up as a candidate for Mayor. His running mate was NYC newspaper columnist Jimmy Breslin, going for City Council President.[15] I guess my politically-minded conductor thinks Mr. Grooves is Mr. *Mailer's* running mate?

Once, when performing in San Jose in the '90s, a terrible cold leads me to the nearest CVS. I'm assisted by a shy, good-looking young man whose name tag reads, "R. Mahler." I squeal, "I'm R. Mahler. Roni." He squeals, "I'm R. Mahler. Robert." He tells his mom and dad.

Within days, I receive an invitation to the annual Mahler Festival, "Mahler-Fest," held on the University of Colorado Campus. Within weeks, I'm off to Boulder.

Soon after walking into the lobby of the Festival's main exhibition hall, I hear a gasp right next to me. A woman I do not know grabs my wrist and practically drags me over to one of the murals. An etching of Gustav Mahler and his family, riding in a horse-drawn buggy.

"Look straight ahead," she commands. "Look straight ahead," ensuring that I'm in profile. Then, to her friends, "She's Justine. You see it? The image of Justine!"

Justine was Gustav's favorite sister, born when he was eight years old. Maybe because her next three siblings all die in infancy, little Justine has recurring fantasies of death. She lies down, lights candles around the edge of her bed, and remains motionless for hours at a time.[16]

They say all the Mahlers are complicated. Hmmmm….

Epilogue: Performing Career

Former athletes and dancers fall into two buckets. *Bucket #1*: The type who can easily walk away.

The more things change…

Never looking back. Happy as a clam. *Bucket #2*: Those for whom playing/performing has always been like oxygen. They must find another way to keep breathing. I'm definitely a "2nd bucket-er." ("2nd bucketeer?")

When athletes can no longer play? Not everyone can, or wants to, coach. But there's always TV commentary, doing play-by-plays. Fantasy camp appearances?

What about Roni? What happens when the chance to play "everybody's mother" is unceremoniously lurched out from under her feet?

In 2011, an all-too-common monster rears its ugly head. The founding director of a ballet company is forced out by the powers-that-be. Dennis Nahat is forced out of Ballet San Jose. Our pinkie promise, that I would stay with the company only as long as he did, is cast in stone. I leave the company, too.

Do I miss performing? My career was so enriched and expanded by George Balanchine, Valerie Bettis, Agnes de Mille, Flemming Flindt, Frederic Franklin, Una Kai, Nora Kaye, José Limón, Beppe Menegatti, Dennis Nahat, Jerome Robbins, Herbert Ross, and Antony Tudor. How do you *not* miss that?

Do I miss being onstage? *And how.* Remember oxygen? Remember how, for me, there's nothing like moving to music and captivating your audience. The lights? The costumes? Most of all, having the chance to "disturb" all those molecules in the air, so the audience can feel their gentle vibration? Trying to make all those folks feel the same joy and freedom, when they're watching me, as I feel when I'm dancing for them?

As I'm leaving Ballet San Jose, how many times do I hear, "But, Roni. You're 69. You can't have gone on much longer anyway." Just a darn minute. Frederic Franklin performed Friar Laurence into his mid–90s, in ABT's *Romeo and Juliet* at The Met.[17]

Apparently, in rehearsals, he might falter once or twice. Walking to the wrong side of the stage. Omitting some important pantomime. But when it's "curtain up," my dear Uncle Fred is spot on and brilliant. Every cue, every gesture. Far beyond anything he's done in rehearsal.

It's as if, when onstage, this little switch inside him flips on. All he needs is a costume, some lights, and that audience. Then, he's instantly everything he's always been. And more. At 95.

…The more they stay the same! (Photo by Susan Telecky).

Lucky for me, my teaching career has always been chugging right alongside my performing one. Starting with those long-ago Saturday mornings in Wilmington, Delaware, when I was 19. Yes, I've fallen completely in love with the art of sculpting and molding ballet students. Teaching is now my oxygen.

And that's why this Epilogue is aimed so narrowly at performing. Because I'm going to teach forever. You have to breathe, right?

Finale
Curtain Calls

Kansas State Legacy

In 1996, the Kansas State Dance Program establishes the Roni Mahler Award, honoring the person who has done the most to promote dance in the community that year. To my surprise and delight, I am its first recipient.

Back in 1968, a fire had destroyed Kansas State's Nichols Gymnasium. It was a burnt-out shell when I arrived in the fall of 1974, to teach ballet in the HPER Department. For six years, every ballet class I taught was in Room 304 of Ahearn Field House. When I left what was now the HPER*D* Department, in the spring of 1980, Nichols Gymnasium was still a burnt-out shell.

An initial renovation is completed in 1985. Fast forward another 14 years. The aptly-renamed Nichols Hall now houses the Department of Communication Studies, Theatre, and Dance. In 1999, it's the proud host of four new studios, the largest of which is Room 008.

That's the Roni Mahler Studio. As you descend the ramp, you're accompanied by eight or so framed photos on the wall to your right. Highlighting my years at K-State. I still can't get over it. Now, every guest ballet class I come back to teach at KSU has my name on the door. And not posthumously.

International Ballet Competition

In 2014, I lead the two-week Teacher Training program for the International Ballet Competition (IBC) in Jackson, Mississippi. Edward Villella is serving as Jury Chair. After many stellar years of performing with George Balanchine's New York City Ballet, he's recently left his post as Artistic Director of Miami City Ballet, a job he held through 2012. What a welcoming personality he has. It's a pleasure to interact with him, and to mine his brain about Mr. B.

But that's the performing side of this multifaceted, quadrennial event. My responsibilities are entirely pedagogical. The Teacher Training Program gives me the chance to share my classroom techniques and philosophies with the attending ballet teachers. All those hours in Madame Swoboda's classroom, the years on the road learning how to use my own body as an instrument, the wisdom gleaned from

At the 1999 dedication of the Roni Mahler Studio in Nichols Hall, at Kansas State University.

all the legends I worked with at the National Ballet and ABT, too numerous to list. Every experience, a part of my personal ballet DNA, now refracted through "the lens of me" to my students. A lifetime of important lessons, hard-earned.

Many of these same teachers have students simultaneously taking daily classes in the IBC two-week Ballet School Intensive. What the teachers work on with me, they try out on their own students, back at the dorms. Instant gratification for them. Positive feedback for me.

128 Ballet Class Albums & 6 DVDs

Over the years, I teach for many "dance conventions." Dance Masters of America (DMA), Dance Educators of America (DEA), and Professional Dance Teachers Association (PDTA) ... to name a few. What a wonderful chance to share my love and knowledge of ballet with dance studio owners and their students, all over the country.

But it all starts back in 1965 (at the ripe old age of 23). I land my first-ever job teaching ballet at a dance convention. I'm hired for the Summer Dance Caravan Tour. And rehired, and rehired ... for the next 10 out of 11 years.

I immediately learn that all the ballet technique and variations I present have to be choreographed to music from albums created by either Statler Records or Dance

What a joy performing for all those Dance Caravan teachers, over all those years!

Records, Inc. And so begins the adventure of codifying my ballet teaching knowledge and recording it for use in dance studios all over the country.

Over the years, I record 128 albums in all, if you count as "two" the "music only" and "vocal overlay" versions of the same album. These ballet class albums address all ages, and all levels and aspects of technique. Most dance studios don't have live accompaniment for classes. Ballet class albums are their lifeline.[1]

In 1966, I begin collaborating with the incomparable Harriet Cavalli as my pianist. Selecting the music is her bailiwick. She comes to each preparatory session with armfuls of what can sometimes only be described as "sheet music scraps." I swear. One is a clef in height and only about five inches long. "This is a really jolly 2/4. Perfect for the little ones."

Then Harriet begins taking beginner-level classes, to better understand the nuances. Why some allegro music helps you jump and soar, and others don't.

The recording process is an adventure in itself. Scene: RCA Studios in New York City, in the late '60s. Harriet is the only one in the "live" studio. I am safely ensconced in the glass-enclosed engineer's booth. Where I can do no harm.

I suddenly realize that this time-honored approach of playing the music in isolation isn't working. The hardest thing for a pianist is to keep a steady tempo when there's no one dancing.

"Wait, Harriet. I'll come to you." My engineer argues, "Your sound will be picked up. These mics are very sensitive." Insisting I'll be a mouse, I prevail. In the live studio for the rest of the session, I pantomime the steps. That's all Harriet needs.

For instance, I've choreographed to the gorgeous "Kingdom of the Shades" entrance from *La Bayadère*, for my first Statler Records Advanced Class *adagio*. That famous and seemingly endless line of penché arabesques. Tilting toward the floor, as the leg behind gets higher and higher. (On a ramp, no less.)

ME: "Harriet. Do you want to run it once together, to be sure?"
HARRIET: "Nah. I'll just practice on tape."

Her rendition is flawless. Perfectly syncing with my pantomimed gestures to that haunting melody. I remain motionless at the end, waiting until she lifts her foot off the pianissimo (soft) pedal. We are both close to tears. It's so moving. Such a bond. A-a-a-n-d … cut.

Once all the tracks are "in the can," it's time to record the vocal overlays. My "Music Only" version of the album will allow teachers to vary the exercises, while the "Vocal Overlay" version allows for more repetition. Now, Harriet and I switch places. She's with the engineer in the glass-enclosed sound booth and I'm set up in the studio on a high stool, with a music stand for my copious notes. On a slightly lower stool to my right sits a cup of water and a container of coffee. I'm wearing headphones. Just add the ubiquitous dangling cigarette and I could be a weary Frank Sinatra in the wee hours. Plowing through, to "make it a wrap."

Harriet is such a trouper. Because she's been taking ballet class, she can tell if I get my words mixed up when I don't notice. The engineer, of course, knows *bupkis* about ballet. Once, Harriet catches me saying "close to pointe on fifth," instead of the correct "close to fifth on pointe."

In every ballet class, each exercise at the barre is immediately repeated, facing the other way, to use the other leg. The engineer just "repeats" the music. Can a sound engineer at the famous RCA recording studios not have a sense of tempo? Those "repeated" versions are definitely running faster than Harriet's originals.

The only thing missing is the dangling cigarette and the coffee container.

And the engineer can't hear the difference. So, Harriet and I have to keep telling him.

Frustrated up to his tin ears, he suddenly yells, "Look. I'm no *Mozz*-art." He actually pronounces "Mozart" like comic-book snoring "Zs." If we break out laughing, he'll never fix things. Can't speak for Harriet, but I'm peeing my pants. And, *Mozzz*art finally fixes the problem.

Every album comes with its own set of class exercise descriptions. I've often been described as "detail-oriented, to a fault." Hence, my notes are extensive, if not annoyingly copious. At K-State, I argue that these are my "published" works.

My albums, with their accompanying notes tucked inside the cover, sell really well. For a while there, my voice becomes pretty recognizable. At D.C.'s National Airport, while requesting a boarding pass, I hear a man's voice behind me.

"Are you Roni Mahler?" I answer, "Why?" He explains, "My wife teaches to your records at The Y. I'd know that voice anywhere." For years, dancers in professional companies of every genre tell me they "grew up" with my records.

It takes me until 2014 to arrive, kicking and screaming, into the 21st Century. That's when dance educator Rhee Gold invites me to author a set of six teacher-training DVDs, "The Complete Guide to Teaching Ballet." One teacher buys it and calls me up to exclaim: "I've just had Miss Roni in my living room for more than 5½ hours!"

I feel like I've scraped my brain for everything I know about teaching ballet. A daunting but fulfilling task. Thanks, Rhee Gold.

Thank You, Z-O-O-M

On February 28, 2020, I move from Henderson, Nevada, to San Francisco. My sister Stephanie has been living there for eight years, because that's where her daughter, Kristyn; son-in-law, Cole; and granddaughters, Piper and Mara, live.

Twelve days after I arrive, Covid shuts down the city. What's a ballet teacher to do? Especially one for whom teaching is oxygen? Hello, Zoom. A lifesaver for so many dancers during the pandemic. A lifesaver for me. All made possible by the untiring efforts of Belinda McGuire. Former Juilliard student and now professional contemporary dancer extraordinaire.

In my case, teaching on Zoom involves a pretty steep learning curve. Like finding ways to effectively correct your students without the now-unavailable "hands-on" technique. Or finally figuring out how to create a "foot-cam" for lower-body specifics, and a "torso-cam" for port de bras and épaulement (use of the head, arms, and shoulders). Most alien of all: sitting and watching your students on a computer screen for so much of the class.

With a lot of "electronics" help from these same students, I slowly become more tech-savvy. And less prone to disconnecting myself from the class and having to sign back in again. Or inadvertently reversing the order of the CD tracks. Their patience is beyond commendable. We spend a lot of time laughing.

Over the next 2–3 years, many students naturally return to the ballet studio. But a lot of them stick with me and, together, we have carved out a double success story. They have made exciting progress. And I have been able to keep on breathing.

Watching the Green Grass Disappear...

Maybe this would be a good time for me to remember that this book's title is *Tomboy Ballerina*. *Ballerina* is part of the story. *Tomboy* is the other. I've already said goodbye to the ballet stage. Now might be as good a time as any to accept the inevitable and say goodbye to that other "stage." *My* Yankee Stadium. The old one. The *real* one.

I'm talking about saying goodbye to my beloved *former* Yankee Stadium. The original one, built in 1923.

It's 2008 and I'm now back in my native New York City, teaching ballet all over the city. (The Ailey School, Ballet Tech, The Juilliard School, Joffrey Ballet School, to name a few.)

It's 4:00 in the afternoon on Friday, September 19. I've just learned that my last ballet class has been canceled. It suddenly dawns on me. Tonight, the Yanks begin a three-game series with the Baltimore Orioles. Their last, before they tear everything down. If there's a snowball's-chance-in-Hades to sit in *my* Yankee Stadium … the *real* one … one last time, this is it.

While riding the "4" train to 161st and River Avenue, I'm calculating that my best chance to score a seat will be in the bleachers. I've never sat in the bleachers before, but how bad could it be?

When I phone my son Erik (now in Kansas, working in sportscasting) and tell him my plan, he strongly disagrees. "Mom, the Bleacher Creatures can be a pretty rowdy bunch. Don't do it! There's got to be a single reserved seat *somewhere* in the third deck."

Erik is spot-on. I end up buying a single reserved seat in the third deck, just like he said, a little past third base, in left field. For my first game in July of '51, we also had third-deck seats, but a little past first base, in right field.

It turns out, tonight's game against the Orioles is vintage Yankees. Closer Mariano Rivera "saves" a 3–2 Yankee victory. Brett Gardner makes a warning-track catch after banging into the centerfield wall.[2] Classic.

And then it's over. Frank Sinatra's "New York, New York" is filling the Stadium. Just about everyone in the crowd of 54,136 is standing. They always announce the attendance, and not one of us is going anywhere.

Twenty minutes later, the cleaning crew is collecting half-eaten popcorn boxes around my immovable feet. It really seems as if no one, including me, wants to leave. Name the clichés. Moistening eyes. A lump in the throat. Goosebumps. All of the above.

It's getting late. I muster just enough self-discipline to make my way to the aisle on my right. With no one behind me, I leave the Stadium the only way I can bear to. I walk *slowly backwards* down that same incline I first scaled in 1951. I watch that vast sea of green expanse. First, a bold stripe. Then, a thin stripe. Then, a sliver. Then it disappears.

Fifteen years later, my son is still teasing me about that. Here, celebrating that KRSL's Erik Stone has been awarded first place by the Kansas Association of Broadcasters, for small market sports play-by-play.

I stand there for a few more seconds, staring at "no more magic green ocean." Then I turn to my left and go home.

I keep promising myself I'll get to the gleaming new Yankee Stadium. Hasn't happened yet.

Once a Tomboy...

Was I destined to be a tomboy? Before I was born, my dad was certain I was going to be a boy. Ronnie *is* a boy's name. Even as a small child, my voice *is* very low. My curly hair *is* always cut very short.

And the evidence keeps piling up. At seven, racing a boy across a frozen pond. Losing, *only be*cause I plunge through the cracked ice. At ten, falling out of a tree into a pile of November leaves. *Only* because I forget to take off my woolen gloves. And in 5th grade, this Roosevelt Elementary Field Day Champ is already tuning up for Queen of the Wilis. I win the Hop-Skip-Jump!

Posing in a bathing suit on the beach at 12. Feet apart. Ribs expanding. Shoulders, definitely wider than hips. Peter Pan, meet Superman ... about to take flight? Is it any wonder that, when I grow up to be a ballerina, my athleticism is front and center?

Maybe once a tomboy, always a tomboy? In 1964, Evan Jenkins of the *Washington Star Sunday Magazine* writes, "Roni Mahler is a beautiful young ballet dancer who, pound for pound, is probably stronger than the average professional football player."[3]

And the *Washington Evening Star*'s Harry MacArthur describes, "...a lovely, lithe dancer with what football broadcasters call great moves and she is as much fun to watch as any shifty halfback."[4]

So dear, dear Valerie Bettis. When the National Ballet debuts in 1963 ... and you choreograph that Tomboy role for me, in your *Early Voyagers* premiere... Do you get it? Do you get that you're asking me to dance the story of my life?

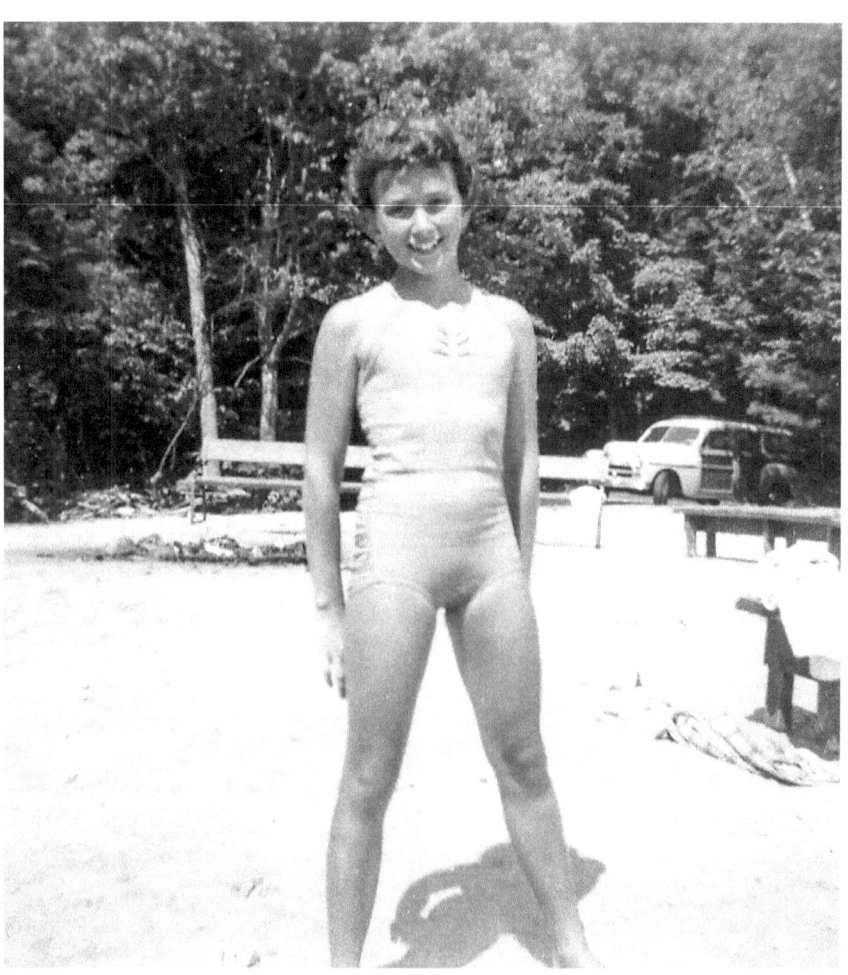

Team Gratitude

Okay, fans, today's lineup...
Leading off, **Family**:
To my mother, Ethel Butwenig Mahler, who meticulously choreographed every opportunity for me to succeed, including the chance to be a butterfly before I ever met a first position.

To my father, Paul Mahler, for not playing God after all.

To my older sister, Stephanie Mahler Fredericks, for her quick wit and childhood memories.

To my younger sister, Lynbarbra Mahler, for paving my way to Kansas State University.

To my son, Erik Mahler Stone, who knows more about baseball than I do.

To my niece, Kristyn Fredericks Medeiros, and "nephew-in-law" Cole Medeiros, for their smiles and invaluable and knowledgeable support.

To my great-nieces, Piper Hart Medeiros and Mara Mahler Medeiros, for graciously giving up their "time," so Mommy and Daddy could answer my questions.

Batting 2nd, **Guidance**:
At the top of this list is my pandemic-inspired diligent ballet student and tireless Virtual Assistant, Anna Wolfe Climenhaga. Heartfelt gratitude goes out to you, Anna. You never wavered as you held my hand through 2½ years of three manuscript drafts of endless corrections and endless word processing. And to your son, Toby Merlin Taylor, for navigating the shark-filled waters of computer-world for us.

There are also so many others without whose early encouragement this book would never have kept chugging along. First, Janet Sunderland, an author. Thanks, Janet, for reading my earliest attempt at writing this memoir.

My thanks also goes out to former *New York Times* dance critic Anna Kisselgoff. You helped me get my feet wet in the mystifying waters of authorship. And dance critic Renée Renouf Hall. Your consistent support and connections have been invaluable.

Robert (Bobby) Barnett and Cynthia Crain. Without you two, I would probably never have found the perfect home for my story. Your insights and über-useful information formed the foundation upon which I could continue to build. Dr. Doris Bersing, your wisdom and clarity were always spot on. And Elizabeth Foxwell, your guidance and support ... immeasurable.

A special shoutout to my friend since Junior High School, Sheena Macpherson.

Your reading and editing skills helped fan the flames, when this book was but an embryo. And to Nancy Fuerst Hexter. Emblazoned in my memory is not only your generosity, but your example of undying determination, as you mastered the Mandarin alphabet. What a model for the fortitude to never give up on this book. And Alicia Washburn and Michelle Harris, for keeping the dream alive. And Mel Norcutt, for the same.

Here's to Mike Mitchell, whose iconic 1964 photograph of George Balanchine coaching me endows me with a truly indelible gift. To DanceLife's Rhee Gold, and Nancy and Arthur Stone, for your immeasurable support. Of course, to Nina Deacon, Meg Fensholt-Anderson, Cynthia Gregory, Stephanie Schiro Ronco and Nancy Whyte. Courageous early beta readers, all. And to Larkin Yaeger, whose marketing ideas rise to the level of consultant.

Batting 3rd, **Memory Helpers**:

I've been blessed with a bunch of them. Starting with my older sister, Stephanie Mahler Fredericks, for those valuable childhood details and giving me, "Not so fast, Chickie!" Moving on to my son, Erik Mahler Stone. Your computer mind provided myriad baseball gems. Not to mention infallible fact-checking skills.

There are no words for my life-long friend, Cynthia Gregory. Archiver of my photos. Keeper of the flame for all things ABT. Sixty-one years of seeing each other through thick and thin. Thanks for riding the Seesaw of Life with me, Cyn, and never jumping off.

Dennis Nahat, for our shared and cherished life, both onstage and off, and for being the brother I never had. I've run out of adjectives. Pantomime, anyone? And Karen and Walter Loewenstern, for your beautiful story that gave birth to Ballet San Jose … and so much more.

To Phyllis Rosenberg Constan, my brave Camp Wicosuta buddy. With me, as I scaled Mt. Washington. And still with me, tackling chapter after chapter after chapter of this book.

Karen and Edward Seaton. For your 49 years of friendship, without which the phone call with Mickey Mantle would never have happened. Ned Seaton. Without you, no photographs from *The Manhattan Mercury*. Bill Felber, for nudging me onto the path that ultimately led to That Amazing Phone Call.

Lolis and Mike Baab. For a friendship that began when Mike signed up for ballet class as a Cleveland Brown. And for Dave Redding, whose sore butt gave me the best quote in the book.

Special shoutouts to Paula Tracy, for your knack with ABT dates. To Shirley Weishaar Brink and Linda Phillips Rogers, for your Ballet Russe tidbits with a Hoosier twist. And to a stunning mother/daughter duo: Carolyn Martin Santonicola's Mother, for never throwing out a Ballet Russe itinerary or program. And to Carolyn, the best tour bus seatmate ever, complete with a delicious Southern accent.

To Judy Mack Saffer, for your Greenwich Village recollections and so many unforgettable meals. And Lucy Maybury King and Patricia Mideke Bloom. For your National Ballet nuggets, recalled with such warmth and laughter.

Now Batting Clean-Up (who else?), **My Collaborator**:

Stepping up to the plate, the multi-talented Caroline O'Connor. Her ability to clarify while condensing. Her sleuthing skills. All eclipsed only by her uncanny knack for dragging out of me that which I would've preferred to keep inside. And for Rory, Emmet, Susan, and Kitty … for sharing her with me.

Coaching in the Dugout: **My Zoom Class Enablers**

The Juilliard Guinea Pig Gang, who persevered through my very first attempt at electronic teaching: Laura Careless, Julia Mayo, Belinda McGuire, Laura Mead, Navarra Novy-Williams, and Annika Sheaff.

And subsequently, all my Zoom Students, steadfast in their pursuit of ballet excellence, no matter how many miles and time zones separate us. Not to mention the studio owners, spouses, parents … and pets … who tirelessly support their endeavors.

And Warming Up in the Bullpen: **Every future ballet dancer**

Mme. Swoboda patiently instilled in me so many precious nuggets of knowledge. I will lovingly continue to channel them into newly eager hearts and minds. With my own twist, of course.

To you all … my ever-evolving gratitude.

Chapter Notes

Prologue

1. Two years later, my ballet classes with Mme. Swoboda begin. I find out that I actually saw one of Madame's former students perform that day. Norma Vance danced the role of "The Bird" (flute) in *Peter and the Wolf*.
2. Anna Kisselgoff, "Irma Duncan Dead; Disciple of Isadora." *The New York Times* (1977), 28.
3. Nineteen years later, Chujoy would distinguish himself as co-author, with P.W. Manchester, of *The Dance Encyclopedia*.
4. "Maria Swoboda Dies; Noted Ballet Teacher." *The New York Times* (1987), 8.
5. Swoboda, Maria. 1976. Interview by Joan Kramer. *Interview with Maria Swoboda*. NYPL Performing Arts Dance Division (1976).
6. Murray Schumach, "Babe Ruth, Baseball Idol, Dies At 53 After Lingering Illness." *The New York Times* (1948), 1.
7. "The Billboard Music Popularity Charts." *The Billboard* (1954).
8. "Hebron Police Report: 2010 Annual Report." *Annual Report For The Town of Hebron New Hampshire For the Fiscal Year Ending December 31, 2010* (2011).
9. The Associated Press. "Ike Gellis, Sports Editor, 80." *The New York Times* (1988).
10. Robert Creamer, "When Brooklyn Won." *Sports Illustrated* (1955), 57–58.
11. Lynn Garafola, *Diaghilev's Ballets Russes*. (New York: Oxford University Press, 1989), 175–176.
12. Jack Anderson, *The One and Only: The Ballet Russe de Monte Carlo*. (New York: Dance Books Limited, 2010), 10.
13. Jack Anderson, *The One and Only: The Ballet Russe de Monte Carlo*. (New York: Dance Books Limited, 2010), 154.
14. That worn-out, shankless pointe shoe? Dance merchants actually *sell* it now, complete with ribbons. It's called a "Pre-Pointe" shoe. Marketing, have you no end?
15. Jack Anderson, "Frederic Franklin, Inventive and Charismatic Ballet Star, Is Dead at 98." *The New York Times* (2013), 10.
16. Jack Anderson, "Leon Danielian, 75, Ballet Star Known for His Wide Repertory." *The New York Times* (1997b), 22.
17. Jack Anderson, "Alexandra Danilova, Ballerina and Teacher, Dies at 93." *The New York Times* (1997a), 20.
18. Program for "Jacob's Pillow Dance Festival, 11th Season—1952—First Week." (1952), 27–28.
19. Jack Anderson, "Nathalie Krassovska, 86, Dancer Particularly Known for 'Giselle,' Dies." *The New York Times* (2005), 14.
20. Mary Clark, "Mia Slavenska." *The Guardian* (2002).
21. Jennifer Dunning, "James Starbuck, 85, TV Dance Innovator." *The New York Times* (1997), 20.
22. Jack Anderson, "Igor Youskevitch, Master of Classical Ballet Style, Dies at 82." *The New York Times* (1994), 21.
23. "Lee Remick," *IMDb*.
24. Jack Anderson, *The One and Only: The Ballet Russe de Monte Carlo*. (New York: Dance Books Limited, 2010), 222.
25. How "perfect" to be hearing that news from Mr. Katz. Before taking some shrapnel in his right eye during World War II, he'd been a promising pitching prospect in the Yankees farm system. So, I end up with one of the best high school teachers ever, all because he had to let go of his baseball dreams.
26. Tyler Kepner, "Don Larsen Became an Unlikely Legend in 9 Perfect Innings." *The New York Times* (2020), 6.
27. History of Model United Nations (NMUN)." *National Model United Nations*.
28. "What Sol Wrought." *Time Magazine* (1959).
29. "Music: Ballet on Film." *Time Magazine* (1956).
30. "New York Yankees vs. Pittsburgh Pirates October 13, 1960 Box Score." *Baseball Almanac*.

Act One

1. Homer Bigart, "17-Inch Snow Cripples City Area; Schools Shut, Suburbs Isolated as Blizzard Hits Eastern States." *The New York Times* (1960), 1.
2. George Balanchine and Francis Mason, *101 Stories of the Great Ballets*. (New York: Anchor Books, 1989), 473–474.

3. Jack Anderson, *The One and Only: The Ballet Russe de Monte Carlo*. (New York: Dance Books Limited, 2010).

4. Walter Terry, *Walter Terry's Ballet Guide* (New York: Popular Library, 1977), 286.

5. Jack Anderson, *The One and Only: The Ballet Russe de Monte Carlo*. (New York: Dance Books Limited, 2010), 16-17.

6. Ten years later, Karinska shares the first-ever Oscar awarded for costumes in a *color* film, with co-designer Dorothy Jeakins. The film: *Joan of Arc*.

7. "War Memorial Opera House," *San Francisco Opera*.

8. Walter Terry, *Walter Terry's Ballet Guide* (New York: Popular Library, 1977), 48-49.

9. Jack Anderson, *The One and Only: The Ballet Russe de Monte Carlo*. (New York: Dance Books Limited, 2010), 179.

10. Walter Terry, *Walter Terry's Ballet Guide* (New York: Popular Library, 1977), 123.

11. Jack Anderson, *The One and Only: The Ballet Russe de Monte Carlo*. (New York: Dance Books Limited, 2010), 160.

12. In 2000, all three versions of the storied "Ballet Russes" have a reunion weekend. When a teaching obligation is postponed to the very same weekend because of a Florida hurricane, my hopes of attending are dashed, like waves against shoreline rocks.

13. Jack Anderson, *The One and Only: The Ballet Russe de Monte Carlo*. (New York: Dance Books Limited, 2010), 110-111.

14. Ultimately, Suzanne is one "favorite" who keeps her private life separate. Other "favorites" end up marrying Mr. Balanchine, including Maria Tallchief and Tanaquil Le Clercq.

15. Leslie Norton. Frederic Franklin: A Biography of the Ballet Star. (Jefferson, North Carolina: McFarland, 2007), 143.

16. "Ballet: Time to Start Pushing." *Time Magazine* (1963).

17. Walter Terry, *Walter Terry's Ballet Guide* (New York: Popular Library, 1977), 179.

18. Walter Terry, *Walter Terry's Ballet Guide* (New York: Popular Library, 1977), 313-314.

19. "The Philadelphia Academy of Music." *The New York Times* (1857).

20. Later, Kai becomes Artistic Director of the New Zealand, now Royal New Zealand Ballet, and Ballet Mistress for both the Royal Danish Ballet and the Kansas City Ballet.

21. Walter Terry, *Walter Terry's Ballet Guide* (New York: Popular Library, 1977), 268.

22. The Czárdas is the national folk dance of Hungary. *Raymonda*, the name of the full-length ballet, is also the name of the Hungarian Princess at the heart of the story. So, all the *Pas de Dix* choreography is well-seasoned with Czárdas sprinklings.

23. George Balanchine and Francis Mason, *101 Stories of the Great Ballets*. (New York: Anchor Books, 1989), 139.

24. Anna Kisselgoff, "Tanaquil Le Clercq, 71, Ballerina Who Dazzled Dance World." *The New York Times* (2001).

25. George Balanchine and Francis Mason, *101 Stories of the Great Ballets*. (New York: Anchor Books, 1989), 388.

26. Lisa Rinehart, "Secrets of *Serenade*." *Dance Magazine* (2010).

27. Evan Jenkins, "That Something Extra." *The Sunday Star* (1954).

28. There's no way I can ever anticipate receiving the note that Mike Mitchell sends along with the photo. What's quoted next is a small snippet of the whole.

29. Anita Gates, "Bob McGrath, Longtime 'Sesame Street' Star, Dies at 90." *The New York Times* (2022), 25.

30. In the mid-'60s, Bob becomes a well-known recording artist in Japan. His specialty: Irish and other folk songs, sung in Japanese. If you're not sure what he does from 1969 on, just ask Bert and Ernie.

31. Dunning, Jennifer. "James Starbuck, 85, TV Dance Innovator." *The New York Times* (1997), 20.

32. "'Comedians' on Stage At the California." *The San Bernadino County Sun* (1962).

33. Adam Hetrick, "Revisit Leslie Uggams in the Tony-Winning *Hallelujah, Baby!*" *Playbill* (2019).

34. Adam Bernstein, "Jean M. Riddell, 100, dies; patron of the arts." *The Washington Post* (2010).

35. Anna Kisselgoff, "Ivan Nagy, Star of American Ballet Theater, Is Dead at 70." *The New York Times* (2014), 16.

36. John Martin, "Notable Ballets by City Company." *The New York Times* (1950).

37. Walter Terry, *Walter Terry's Ballet Guide* (New York: Popular Library, 1977), 94-98.

38. Thank you, Lisa Telthorst.

39. Years later, while conducting for New York City Ballet, de Rosa is tapped as Music Director of Miami City Ballet by the Founding Director, Edward Villella. He later serves as same for Pittsburgh Ballet Theatre and Boston Ballet. Maestro de Rosa: nuanced, sensitive, a real dancer's conductor.

Second Intermission

1. Anthony Mason, "Kennedy condolence letters—some of the 800,000 sent to Jackie Kennedy—published online." *CBS News* (2014).

Act Two

1. Walter Terry, *Walter Terry's Ballet Guide* (New York: Popular Library, 1977), 318-323.

2. Walter Terry, *Walter Terry's Ballet Guide* (New York: Popular Library, 1977), 316.

3. Years later, after Joe Montana has won the Super Bowl with yet another of his storied two-minute drills, I am reading all about it in the paper the next day. A reporter (hoping for some dramatic insight?) asks him what is going through

his mind right before the clock restarts after the two-minute warning. "I throw to the open guy, then throw to the open guy, then throw to the open g..." Of course, that's the only way.
  4. Walter Terry, *Walter Terry's Ballet Guide* (New York: Popular Library, 1977), 155–157.
  5. "Giselle." *The Marius Petipa Society*.
  6. Sarah Kaufman, "Ballerina Natalia Makarova: 'Being spontaneous, it's what saved me.'" *The Washington Post* (2012).
  7. Michael Barson, "Herbert Ross." *Encyclopedia Britannica* (2014).
  8. Burt A. Folkart, "Nora Kaye, Renowned U.S. Ballerina, Is Dead at 67." *Los Angeles Times* (1987).
  9. Clive Barnes, "Dance: 'Moor's Pavane.'" *The New York Times* (1970b), 47.
  10. "Les Noces." *New York City Ballet*.
  11. "The Moor's Pavane." *American Ballet Theatre*.

Third Intermission

  1. Don McDonagh, "Ballet Theater Stars New Teams in Two Works." *The New York Times* (1970), 38.
  2. Clive Barnes, "Dance: Debuts in 'Giselle.'" *The New York Times* (1970b), 43.
  3. "Pas de Quatre." *American Ballet Theatre*.
  4. Janice Berman, "Ballet San Jose breathes new life into 'Giselle.'" *San Francisco Chronicle* (2006).
  5. Jack Anderson, " Lucia Chase of Ballet Theater Is Dead." *The New York Times* (1986), 15.
  6. Anna Kisselgoff, "Dance View: Lucia Chase Helped Create The Ballet World We Know." *The New York Times* (1986), 17.
  7. "Pillar of Fire." *American Ballet Theatre*.

Act Three

  1. Alessandra Stanley, "Maples in Spotlight on Opening Night." *The New York Times* (1992), 3.
  2. Ray Blount, Jr., "Ballet Dancer On a Ball Field." *The New York Times* (1978).
  3. "2003 | Gary Spani | Linebacker." *Chiefs Hall of Honor*.
  4. "Packers Hall of Fame Inductees." *Packers Hall of Fame and Studio Tours*.
  5. "Anatomy of the Foot." *Arthritis Foundation*.
  6. George Balanchine and Francis Mason, *101 Stories of the Great Ballets*. (New York: Anchor Books, 1989), 137.
  7. Craig Muder, "MANTLE JOINS 50-HOME RUN CLUB." *National Baseball Hall of Fame*.
  8. Nick Anapolis, "MANTLE HITS 565-FOOT HOME RUN." *National Baseball Hall of Fame*.
  9. Steve Jacobsen, "Death Hits Painfully Close to Home Again for Mickey Mantle." *Los Angeles Times* (1994).
  10. William Longgood, "Mantle Sees Murder From Wheelchair." *New York World-Telegram and Sun* (1951).
  11. Mickey Mantle, "Time in a Bottle." *Sports Illustrated* (1994).
  12. "Dimitri Romanoff, Dancer and Teacher Of Ballet, Dies at 86." *The New York Times* (1994), 26.
  13. Back in 1984, you could land that job at that size. Not today.
  14. When performances eventually take us to *other* cities, we dance as Cleveland San Jose Ballet.
  15. Richard Reeves, "Mailer and Breslin Enter Race; Promise a 'Serious' Drive—Laurino Quits Contest." *The New York Times* (1969), 24.
  16. Kurt Blaukopf, *Gustav Mahler*. (London: Allen Lane, 1973), 19–20.
  17. Claudia La Rocco, "Such Sweet Sorrow (and Such Dramatic Death)." *The New York Times* (2010), 3.

Finale

  1. Two generations of dance teachers have begged me to write a book containing all my helpful teaching methods and insights. I heard you then. I haven't forgotten you now. The next book is coming.
  2. Associated Press. "Yanks CF Gardner sparkles as stadium's final series begins." *ESPN* (2008).
  3. Evan Jenkins, "That Something Extra." *The Sunday Star* (1964), 104.
  4. Harry MacArthur, "Our National Ballet Comes Home Dancing." *The Evening Star* (1965).

Bibliography

Anapolis, Nick. "Mantle Hits 565-Foot Home Run." *National Baseball Hall of Fame.* Accessed October 5, 2023. https://baseballhall.org/discover/inside-pitch/mantle-hits-565-foot-home-run.

"Anatomy of the Foot." *Arthritis Foundation.* Accessed November 14, 2023. https://www.arthritis.org/health-wellness/about-arthritis/where-it-hurts/anatomy-of-the-foot.

Anderson, Jack. 1986. "Lucia Chase Of Ballet Theater Is Dead." *The New York Times.* January 10. https://www.nytimes.com/1986/01/10/obituaries/lucia-chase-of-ballet-theater-is-dead.html.

Anderson, Jack. 1994. "Igor Youskevitch, Master of Classical Ballet Style, Dies at 82." *The New York Times.* June 14. https://www.nytimes.com/1994/06/14/obituaries/igor-youskevitch-master-of-classical-ballet-style-dies-at-82.html.

Anderson, Jack. 1997a. "Alexandra Danilova, Ballerina and Teacher, Dies at 93." *The New York Times.* July 15. https://www.nytimes.com/1997/07/15/arts/alexandra-danilova-ballerina-and-teacher-dies-at-93.html.

Anderson, Jack. 1997b. "Leon Danielian, 75, Ballet Star Known for His Wide Repertory." *The New York Times.* March 12. https://www.nytimes.com/1997/03/12/arts/leon-danielian-75-ballet-star-known-for-his-wide-repertory.html.

Anderson, Jack. 2005. "Nathalie Krassovska, 86, Dancer Particularly Known for 'Giselle,' Dies." *The New York Times.* February 11. https://www.nytimes.com/2005/02/11/arts/dance/nathalie-krassovska-86-dancer-particularly-known-for-giselle.html.

Anderson, Jack. 2013. "Frederic Franklin, Inventive and Charismatic Ballet Star, Is Dead at 98." *The New York Times.* May 5. https://www.nytimes.com/2013/05/06/arts/dance/frederic-franklin-inventive-ballet-star-dies-at-98.html.

Anderson, Jack. *The One and Only: The Ballet Russe de Monte Carlo.* Alton: Dance Books Limited, 2010.

The Associated Press. 1988. "Ike Gellis, Sports Editor, 80." *The New York Times.* April 29. https://www.nytimes.com/1988/04/29/obituaries/ike-gellis-sports-editor-80.html.

Associated Press. 2008. "Yanks CF Gardner sparkles as stadium's final series begins." *ESPN.* September 20. https://www.espn.com/mlb/recap/_/gameId/280919110.

Balanchine, George, and Francis Mason. *101 Stories of the Great Ballets.* New York: Anchor Books, 1989.

"Ballet: Time to Start Pushing." *Time Magazine.* January 11, 1963. https://content.time.com/time/subscriber/article/0,33009,873034,00.html.

Barnes, Clive. 1970a. "Dance: Debuts in 'Giselle.'" *The New York Times.* July 7. https://www.nytimes.com/1970/07/07/archives/dance-debuts-in-giselle-radius-and-kivitt-seen-with-ballet-theater.html?searchResultPosition=2.

Barnes, Clive. 1970b. "Dance: 'Moor's Pavane.'" *The New York Times.* June 29. https://www.nytimes.com/1970/06/29/archives/dance-moors-pavane-limon-work-performed-by-ballet-theater.html.

Barson, Michael. 2014. "Herbert Ross." *Encyclopedia Britannica.* March 19. https://www.britannica.com/biography/Herbert-Ross.

Berman, Janice. 2006. "Ballet San Jose breathes new life into 'Giselle.'" *San Francisco Chronicle.* November 18.

Bernstein, Adam. 2010. "Jean M. Riddell, 100, dies; patron of the arts." *The Washington Post.* September 24. https://www.washingtonpost.com/wp-dyn/content/article/2010/09/23/AR2010092307596.html.

Bigart, Homer. 1960. "17-Inch Snow Cripples City Area; Schools Shut, Suburbs Isolated as Blizzard Hits Eastern States." *The New York Times.* December 13. https://timesmachine.nytimes.com/timesmachine/1960/12/13/issue.html.

"The Billboard Music Popularity Charts." *The Billboard.* December 18, 1954.

Blaukopf, Kurt. *Gustav Mahler.* London: Allen Lane, 1973.

Blount Jr., Ray. 1978. "Ballet Dancer On a Ball Field." *The New York Times.* November 27. https://timesmachine.nytimes.com/timesmachine/1978/11/27/110973876.html?pageNumber=46.

Clark, Mary. 2002. "Mia Slavenska." *The Guardian.* December 11. https://www.theguardian.com/news/2002/dec/12/guardianobituaries.artsobituaries1.

"'Comedians' on Stage at the California." *The San Bernadino County Sun.* February 18, 1962.

Creamer, Robert. 1955. "When Brooklyn Won." *Sports Illustrated*. October 17. https://vault.si.com/vault/1955/10/17/42384#&gid=ci0258bfe6d01426ef&pid=42384---060---image.

"Dark Elegies." *American Ballet Theatre*. Accessed January 12, 2024. https://www.abt.org/ballet/dark-elegies/.

"Dimitri Romanoff, Dancer and Teacher of Ballet, Dies at 86." 1994. *The New York Times*. May 19. https://www.nytimes.com/1994/05/19/obituaries/dimitri-romanoff-dancer-and-teacher-of-ballet-dies-at-86.html.

Dunning, Jennifer. 1997. "James Starbuck, 85, TV Dance Innovator." *The New York Times*. August 19. https://www.nytimes.com/1997/08/19/arts/james-starbuck-85-tv-dance-innovator.html.

Folkart, Burt A. 1987. "Nora Kaye, Renowned U.S. Ballerina, Is Dead at 67." *Los Angeles Times*. March 1. https://www.latimes.com/archives/la-xpm-1987-03-01-mn-7059-story.html.

Garafola, Lynn. *Diaghilev's Ballets Russes*. New York: Oxford University Press, 1989.

Gates, Anita. 2022. "Bob McGrath, Longtime 'Sesame Street' Star, Dies at 90." *The New York Times*. December 4. https://www.nytimes.com/2022/12/04/arts/television/bob-mcgrath-dead.html.

"Giselle," *The Marius Petipa Society*. Accessed November 14, 2023. https://petipasociety.com/giselle/.

"Hebron Police Report: 2010 Annual Report." *Annual Report for the Town of Hebron, New Hampshire, For the Fiscal Year Ending December 31, 2010*. February 3, 2011.

Hetrick, Adam. 2019. "Revisit Leslie Uggams in the Tony-Winning Hallelujah, Baby!" *Playbill*. April 26. https://playbill.com/article/revisit-leslie-uggams-in-the-tony-winning-hallelujah-baby.

"History of Model United Nations (NMUN)." *National Model United Nations*. Accessed February 17, 2024. https://www.nmun.org/assets/documents/about-nmun/mission-and-history/nmun-history.pdf.

Jacobsen, Steve. 1994. "Death Hits Painfully Close to Home Again for Mickey Mantle." *Los Angeles Times*. March 20. https://www.latimes.com/archives/la-xpm-1994-03-20-sp-36363-story.html.

Jenkins, Evan. 1964. "That Something Extra." *The Sunday Star*. May 31.

Kaufman, Sarah. 2012. "Ballerina Natalia Makarova: 'Being Spontaneous, It's What Saved Me.'" *The Washington Post*. November 30. https://www.washingtonpost.com/entertainment/theater_dance/ballerina-natalia-makarova-being-spontaneous-its-what-saved-me/2012/11/29/68f72692-32da-11e2-9cfa-e41bac906cc9_story.html.

Kepner, Tyler. 2020. "Don Larsen Became an Unlikely Legend in 9 Perfect Innings." *The New York Times*. January 2. https://www.nytimes.com/2020/01/02/sports/baseball/don-larsen.html.

Kisselgoff, Anna. 1977. "Irma Duncan Dead; Disciple of Isadora." *The New York Times*. September 22. www.nytimes.com/1977/09/22/archives/irma-duncan-dead-disciple-of-isadora-foster-daughter-of-dancer-was.html.

Kisselgoff, Anna. 1986. "Dance View; Lucia Chase Helped Create The Ballet World We Know." *The New York Times*. January 19. https://www.nytimes.com/1986/01/19/arts/dance-view-lucia-chase-helped-create-the-ballet-world-we-know.html?pagewanted=all.

Kisselgoff, Anna. 2001. "Tanaquil Le Clercq, 71, Ballerina Who Dazzled Dance World." *The New York Times*. January 1. https://www.nytimes.com/2001/01/01/nyregion/tanaquil-le-clercq-71-ballerina-who-dazzled-dance-world.html.

Kisselgoff, Anna. 2014. "Ivan Nagy, Star of American Ballet Theater, Is Dead at 70." *The New York Times*. February 25. https://www.nytimes.com/2014/02/26/arts/dance/ivan-nagy-star-of-american-ballet-theater-is-dead-at-70.html.

La Rocco, Claudia. 2010. "Such Sweet Sorrow (and Such Dramatic Death)." *The New York Times*. July 6. https://www.nytimes.com/2010/07/07/arts/dance/07romeo.html.

"Lee Remick." *IMDb*. Accessed September 12, 2023. https://www.imdb.com/name/nm0001665/.

"Les Noces." *New York City Ballet*. Accessed. February 11, 2024. https://www.nycballet.com/discover/ballet-repertory/les-noces/.

Longgood, William. 1951. "Mantle Sees Murder From Wheelchair." *New York World-Telegram and Sun*. October 10.

MacArthur, Harry. 1965. "Our National Ballet Comes Home Dancing." *The Evening Star*. February 6.

Mantle, Mickey. 1994. "Time in a Bottle." *Sports Illustrated*. April 18. https://vault.si.com/vault/1994/04/18/time-in-a-bottle-after-42-years-of-alcohol-abuse-a-legendary-ballplayer-describes-his-life-of-self-destructive-behavior-and-hopes-his-recovery-will-finally-make-him-a-true-role-model.

"Maria Swoboda Dies; Noted Ballet Teacher." *The New York Times*. August 13, 1987. www.nytimes.com/1987/08/13/obituaries/maria-swoboda-dies-noted-ballet-teacher.html.

Martin, John. 1950. "Notable Ballets by City Company." *The New York Times*. November 30. https://timesmachine.nytimes.com/timesmachine/1950/11/30/94277245.html?pageNumber=41.

Mason, Anthony. 2014. "Kennedy condolence letters—some of the 800,000 sent to Jackie Kennedy—published online." *CBS News*. January 14. https://www.cbsnews.com/news/kennedy-condolence-letters-published-online/.

McDonagh, Don. 1970. "Ballet Theater Stars New Teams in Two Works" *The New York Times*. July 6. https://www.nytimes.com/1970/07/06/archives/ballet-theater-start-new-teams-in-two-works-serrano-and-fernandez.html?searchResultPosition=1.

"The Moor's Pavane." *American Ballet Theatre*. Accessed February 11, 2024. https://www.abt.org/ballet/the-moors-pavane/.

Muder, Craig. 2023. "Mantle Joins 50-Home Run Club." *National Baseball Hall of Fame*. Accessed October 5. https://baseballhall.org/discover/inside-pitch/mantle-joins-50-home-run-club.

"Music: Ballet on Film." 1956. *Time Magazine*. April 9 https://content.time.com/time/subscriber/article/0,33009,866880,00.html.

"New York Yankees vs. Pittsburgh Pirates October 13, 1960, Box Score." *Baseball Almanac*. Accessed November 23, 2023. https://www.baseball-almanac.com/box-scores/boxscore.php?boxid=196010130PIT.

Norton, Leslie. 2007. *Frederic Franklin: A Biography of the Ballet Star*. Jefferson, North Carolina: McFarland.

"Packers Hall of Fame Inductees." *Packers Hall of Fame and Studio Tours*. Accessed November 1, 2023. https://www.packershofandtours.com/explore/hall-of-fame/hall-of-fame-inductees.

"Pas de Quatre." *American Ballet Theatre*. Accessed February 11, 2024. https://www.abt.org/ballet/pas-de-quatre/.

"The Philadelphia Academy of Music." 1857. *The New York Times*. February 26. https://timesmachine.nytimes.com/timesmachine/1857/02/26/77071283.html?pageNumber=1.

"Pillar of Fire." *American Ballet Theatre*. Accessed January 12, 2024. https://www.abt.org/ballet/pillar-of-fire/.

Program for "Jacob's Pillow Dance Festival, 11th Season - 1952 - First Week." 27–28 June 1952. Accessed September 24, 2023. https://archives.jacobspillow.org/Detail/objects/4790.

Reeves, Richard. 1969. "Mailer and Breslin Enter Race; Promise a 'Serious' Drive—Laurino Quits Contest." *The New York Times*. May 2. https://www.nytimes.com/1969/05/02/archives/mailer-and-breslin-enter-race-promise-a-serious-drive-laurino-quits.html.

Rinehart, Lisa. 2010. "Secrets of *Serenade*." *Dance Magazine*. August 25. https://www.dancemagazine.com/secrets_of_iserenadei.

Schumach, Murray. 1948. "Babe Ruth, Baseball Idol, Dies At 53 After Lingering Illness." *The New York Times*. August 17. https://www.nytimes.com/1948/08/17/archives/famous-diamond-star-fought-losing-battle-against-cancer-for-2-years.html.

"Serenade." *The George Balanchine Trust*. Accessed September 23, 2023. https://www.balanchine.com/Ballet/serenade.

Stanley, Alessandra. 1992. "Maples in Spotlight on Opening Night." *The New York Times*. August 4. https://www.nytimes.com/1992/08/04/nyregion/maples-in-spotlight-on-opening-night.html.

Swoboda, Maria. 1976. Interview by Joan Kramer. *Interview with Maria Swoboda*, NYPL Performing Arts Dance Division. June 22–29.

Terry, Walter. *Walter Terry's Ballet Guide*. New York: Popular Library, 1977.

"2003" | Gary Spani | "Linebacker" *Chiefs Hall of Honor*. Accessed November 1, 2023. https://www.chiefs.com/hallofhonor/players/garyspani.

"War Memorial Opera House." *San Francisco Opera*. Accessed December 10, 2023. https://www.sfopera.com/about/venue/war-memorial-opera-house/.

"What Sol Wrought." 1959. *Time Magazine*. April 27. https://content.time.com/time/subscriber/article/0,33009,811062,00.html.

Index

Numbers in **_bold italics_** indicate pages with illustrations.

The Ailey School 212
Al & Dick's Steakhouse 24
Albert Leonard Junior High School 18–19
Alice's Unbirthday Party 28–29
Alonso, Alicia 31, 58
Alston, Walter 23
Alvin Ailey (company) 44
American Alliance for Health, Physical Education, Recreation and Dance (AAHPERD) 169
American Ballet Theatre 51, 66, 73, 126–153, 154–157, 169–170, 172, 181–187, 193, 203, 205
Anatomy of a Murder (film) 32
Anderson, Jack 62
Arlington National Cemetery 124
Arova, Sonia **_100_**
Auditorium Theatre (Chicago) 136
Aurora's Wedding (from *The Sleeping Beauty*) 5

Baab, Lolis 189–191
Baab, Mike 189–191
Bailey, Pearl 111
Bakst, Léon 7, 63
Balanchine, George 3, 30–31, 68, 70–72, 81, 89–90, 94–**_105_**, 106, 124, 134, 138, 175–176, 181, 205, 207
Ballet Academy East 128
Ballet Imperial (ballet) 70–73, 81
Ballet Movement for the Athlete (presentation) 169, 187
Ballet Russe de Monte Carlo 17, 24, 28–32, 37–38, 42–44, 48–50, 54–55, 59–89, 91, 110, 186
Ballet Russe de Monte Carlo School of Ballet 24–50, 53–58, 91
Ballet San Jose 105, 155, 197, 205; *see also* San Jose Cleveland Ballet

Ballet Tech 212
Ballets Russes 24, 147
Baltimore Orioles 212
Barnard College 44
Barnes, Clive 146
Bathilde (role, *Giselle*) 73
Battersea, London 175
Battey, Jean 92, 155
Bauer, Hank 23
La Bayadère 210
Baylis, Meredith 10, 66
Le Beau Danube (ballet) 30
Beer, Stella **_196_**
Bergfeld, Dr. John 187, 192
Berman, Janice 155
Berra, Yogi 23, 67, 89
Berson (Hauser), Roberta **_9_**, **_11_**, 73
Bettis, Valerie 30, 90–94, 145, 205, 214
Bewley, Lois 28
Big/Lead Swans (role, *Swan Lake*) 32, 79–83, 88, 90–92, 128–130
Bill Bailey, Won't You Please Come Home (song) 111
"The Black Duchess" (painting) 143
"Bleacher Creatures" 212
The Blue Danube (waltz, Strauss) 26
Blum, René 24
Bolger, Ray 33
Bolshoi Ballet 7, 46–48, 122–123
Boston, Massachusetts 84
Bournonville, August 155
Bradlee, Ben 125
Brahms Quintet (ballet) **_136_**
Breslin, Jimmy 204
Bristol, New Hampshire 20–21
Brooklyn Academy of Music 79, 82, 88–89, 108–109, **_136_**, 154
Brooklyn Dodgers 22–24, 40–41, 183
Bruhn, Erik 3, 126, 140–143

Brunson, Perry 38
Bryant, Theopilis 168–169
Buchwald, Art 125
Bunton, Dr. Norma 165
Burr, Marilyn 117, 159–160
Butler University 73
Button, Dick 28
Byrne, Tommy 23

Caesar, Sid 31, 110
Calegari, Maria 99
Camp Wicosuta 20–21
Campanella, Roy 23
Caplan, Max 22–23
Capp, James ("Jimmy") 71, 75, 84–90
Caprichos (ballet) 143–146
Carnaval (ballet) 30
The Carnival of the Animals (suite) 174
Carr, Elizabeth 185
Carroll, Lewis 28
Caton, Edward 35–36
Cavalli, Harriet 209–211
Celebrations and Ode (ballet) 190
Celeste, Gladys 185–187
Cerrito, Fanny 155
Chapman, Marina 79
Chapman, Rachel 80–81
Charles River 84
Chicago Civic Opera 7, 83
Children's Professional Class (Swoboda School of Ballet) 7–11
Chopin, Frédéric 37, 62, 187
The Chordettes 18
Christensen, Lew 116
Chujoy, Anatole 7
Citi Field 183
Clark Hotel 62, 69
Cleveland 78–81, 181–182, 187–197
Cleveland Ballet 131, 181–182, 187–203; *see also* San Jose Cleveland Ballet
Cleveland Browns 187–192

227

Index

Cleveland Dance Center 181
Clorinda (role, *Le Combat*) 116–118
Coca, Imogene 31, 110
Coca-Cola 85, 108
Coffman, Paul 167
Cole, Nat King 111
Coll, David **144**
Collins, Eugene 89
Columbia Records 203
Le Combat (or *The Duel*) (ballet) 116–118
The Comedians (ballet) 110
The Complete Guide to Teaching Ballet (videos, Roni Mahler) 211
Con Amore (ballet) 116
Concerto (ballet) 128, 133
Convention Hall (Philadelphia) 53–54
Coppélia 32–34, 38, 83, 112, 116, 118–121, 159–160, 182, 193, 198–202
Corelli, Juan 115
Le Corsaire (ballet) 169, 172–174
The Countess (role, *District Storyville*) 182, 198
The Court Jester (film) 31
COVID 211
Cronkite, Walter 124

d'Addario, Edith 89
Dance, Ballerina, Dance (song, Nat King Cole) 111
Dance Caravan 208–209
Dance Educators of America 208
Dance Magazine 1, 105
Dance Masters of America 208
Dance News 7, 94
Dance of the Snowflakes (divertissement, *The Nutcracker*) 195
Dance Records, Inc. 208–209
Danielian, Leon 17, 24, 29–30, 62
Daniels, Dorothy 37
Danilova, Alexandra 17, 24, 29–31, 62, 89
Danses Concertantes (ballet) 30
D'Antuono, Eleanor 32, 129, **134**, **136**
Dark Elegies (ballet) 157, 203
Dawn (*L'Aurore*) (variation, *Coppélia*) 32, 34, 112, 118, 200
Days of Wine and Roses (film) 32
de Beaumont, Étienne 65
de Brauw, Cornelie ("Corrie") 72, 86
dégagé 36
Delarova, Eugenia 144

Del Grande, Anita 192–**194**, 195–**196**, 197
de Mille, Agnes 3, 30, 127, 144, 146–149, 181–182, 205
Denham, Sergei J. 24, 33, 50, 60, 83
Denton, Texas 107–108
Department of HPER/HPERD 165–166, 181, 207
de Rosa, Maestro Ottavio 119–120
Des Moines, Iowa 79
Dewey, John 42
Diaghilev, Serge 24, 147
Die Fledermaus (opera) 171–172
DiMaggio, Joe 13, 180
Dirty Dancing (film) 162–163
Disney, Walt 113
District Storyville (ballet) 182
Divertissement D'Auber (ballet) 154
Dixon, Hanford 187, 191
Dobrynin, Anatoly 123
Dr. Coppélius (role, *Coppélia*) 118–121, 182, 198–202
Dolin, Anton 155
Don Quixote (ballet) 38, 87, 159–160
Dorothy Chandler Pavilion 151–152
Dragomanovic, Sonja 91
Drew, Roderick 116, 122–123
Dublin, Ireland 198–203
Dubno, Julia 128
Duncan, Irma 6
Duncan, Isadora 6, 57
Dyche, Anita 89
The Dying Swan (ballet) 174–175

Ebel, Evelyn 90
Einstein, Albert 113–121, 166–167, 192
Les Elfes (ballet) 86–87
Everett, Ellen 127
Ewing, Tom 155

Fall River Legend (ballet) 144, 147, 182
Farotte, Elizabeth 195
Felber, Bill 177
Female Matchmaker (role, *Les Noches*) 147–148
Fernandez, Royes 149
Fine Arts Quartet 136
Firebird (ballet) 175
Fitzgerald, Hester 37
Flemming's Mother (role, *The Red Shoes: Legs of Fire*) 198
Flower Girl (role, *Gaîté Parisienne*) 144
Fokine, Michel 30–31, 37, 62–64, 86–87, 93, 174, 185–187
fondu & adagio 36

Forbes Field 49
Fordham University 44
The Four Georges Restaurant 123
The Four Temperaments (ballet) 94, 97–99, 105–106
Fracci, Carla 3, 140–141
Francine's Luncheonette 150
Franck, César 83–85
Franck, Daniel 116
Frank Lloyd Wright Foundation 193
Franklin, Frederic 3, 29–30, 50, 83–86, 89–94, 97, 103–104, 114, 116–121, 124, 126, 154, 158, 205
Franz (role, *Coppélia*) 116, 118–121, 200–202
frappé 26, 36
Fredericks, Stephanie (Mahler) 5, 7–8, **12**–14, **16**–17, 34, **165**, 174, 203, 211
Friar Laurence (role, *Romeo and Juliet*) 30, 182, 205

Gabay, Karen **194**, **199**
Gaîté Parisienne (ballet) 18, 30, 65–68, 144
Gala Performance (ballet) 133–134
Gardner, Brett 212
Gehrig, Lou 12–13
Gellis, Isaac ("Ike") 22
Gibson, Vince 167
Gill, William J. 161
Gilliam, Jim 23
Giselle (ballet) 7, 30–31, 46–48, 58, 73, 78, 137–143, 146, 155, 198
Giselle's Mother (role, *Giselle*) 155, 198
Gladstein, Robert 128, **144**
Glazunov, Alexander 94–95
Gluck, Christoph 57
Gold, Rhee 211
Golden Earrings (song) 113
Golic, Bob 187–188, 192
Googie's 69
Grahn, Lucile 155
grand battement 26, 36
Grand Central 24, 39
Grand Pas Classique d'Auber (ballet) 169, 172
Grand Pas Glazunov (ballet) 134
grand plié 36
Grantzeva, Tatiana 29–30
Grebel, Stevan 99–**100**
Gregory, Cynthia 1–3, 129–**136**, 137, 141, 146, 149–151, 154, 170, 183–**184**, 185
Grimm, Bob 23
Grisi, Carlotta 155
Guggenheim Logan, Polly 123

Index

H. Upmann No. 12 78
Hall, Dino 190–191
Hallelujah, Baby (musical) 111
Hamilton, Dr. William 114
Harkness Ballet School 162
Hathaway, Robert 172
Heineman, Helen 107
Heiss, Carol 28
Heiss, Nancy 28
Helga the Housekeeper (role, *The Nutcracker*) 182, 197
Hellman (Covan), Judith 90
Henderson, Skitch 112
Hennessy, Christine 10
Hernandez, Crystal 195
Hill, Martha **136**
Hodges, Gil 23, 40
Hoffman, Ariel 195
Horvath, Debby 181
Horvath, Ernest 181
Horvath, Helen 181
Horvath, Ian ("Ernie") 181–182, 192
Houston Jazz Ballet Company 162
Hurok, Sol 46
Hwang, Grace 103

International Ballet Competition 116, 207–208
Ishimoto, May 92, 112
Israel, Gail 84–85, 87, 89
Italian Ballerina (role, *Gala Performance*) 133–134

Jeffers, Josephine 37
Jenkins, Evan 214
Jennings, Sandra 101–103
The Joffrey Ballet 89, 181
Joffrey Ballet School 89, 212
Johansson, Marie 185
Johnson, Lucy Baines 103
Juliet's Mother (role, *Romeo and Juliet*) 198
Juliet's Nurse (role, *Romeo and Juliet*) 182, 198–199
The Juilliard School 212

Kabalevsky, Dmitry 110
Kai, Una 94–95, 103, 205
Kansas City, Missouri 169, 180, 187
Kansas State University 103, 165–176, 181, 207–208
Kaye, Nora 3, 144–145, 205
Kelder, Michael Linda 176
Kennedy, Jackie 103–104, 123–125
Kennedy, John F. 3, 49, 103, 122–125
Khrushchev, Nikita 123
Khrushcheva, Nina 123
Kindertotenlieder (composition, Gustav Mahler) 203

Kipling, Rudyard 95
Kirov Ballet 70, 140–141
Kivitt, Ted 133–135, 154, **184**
Klein, Virginia **9, 11**
Kokich, Kazimir 28, 38
KOMA (radio station) 178
Kotchoubey, Irene 24–25
Krassovska, Nathalie 29–31, 186
Kreft, Janine 195
KSAC (radio station) 178

Lakewood, New Jersey 36–38
Lambert, Margery 61
Lander, Toni 51, 127, 129–130, 133–134, 149
Laramie, Wyoming 77–78
Larkin, Moscelyne 84
Larsen, Don 40
Lawrence, Pauline 152–153
Le Clercq, Tanaquil 97
The Legend of the Pearl (ballet) 116
Lenox Hill Hospital 176–180
Lewis, C.L. 15
Lewis, Daniel 150
Limón, José 3, 149–153, 205
Lincoln Center 1, 137, 154, 172
Lipow, Dr. Eugene 114
The Little Mermaid (statue) 75
Little Swans (*Cygnets*) (role, *Swan Lake*) 31, 79, 82, 92, 128
Lizzie's Stepmom (role, *Fall River Legend*) 198
Loew's Capitol Theatre 122–123
Loewenstern, Karen 192–**194**, 195–**196**
Loewenstern, Walter 193, 195
Long Island Rail Road 204
Los Angeles Philharmonic 152
Los Caprichos (etchings) 143
Louis Falco Dance Company 149

MacArthur, Harry 214
Mack (Saffer), Judith ("Judy") 32, 49
MacMillan, Deborah 161
MacMillan, Kenneth 128, 133, 159–161
Macy's 28
Maglie, Sal 180
Mahler, Ethel 5–20, 44–45, 59, 80, 82, 106, 108–109, 119–120
Mahler, Gustav 152, 203–204
Mahler, Justine 204
Mahler, Dr. Lyn (Shelton) 6–8, **12**–13, 15, **165**, 172, 203
Mahler, Paul 5, 8–15, 22–23, 29, 35, 40–41, 44–45, 80, 82, 108–109, 192, 203
Mahler, Robert 204
Mahler, Wilheim **203**
MahlerFest 204

Mailer, Norman 204
"La maja desnuda" (painting) 143
Makarova, Natalia 3, 140–143
Malek, Peter 160–161
Manchester, P.W. 94, 154
Manhattan, Kansas 165–181
Mantle, Elvin "Mutt" 176, 179
Mantle, Mickey 1, 3, 13–15, 23, 35, 40–41, 49, 135, 176–181
Margolis, Craig 105
Maria's Mother (role, *The Nutcracker*) 198
Marks, Bruce 133–134, 149–151
Martin, Billy 23, 180
Martin (Santonicola), Carolyn 70–71, 76, 78
Martinez, Enrique 129
Martinelli (Menchaca), Carmela 73–74
Massine, Leon ("Lorca") 36
Massine, Léonide 18, 24, 30, 36, 65–66, 144
Mattingly, Don 180
Maxfield, Robert 195
May, Susan 37
Maybury (King), Lucy 90, 92, 96
Mazeroski, Bill 50
McCain, Dr. James 171
McCain Auditorium 171
McDonagh, Don 154
McDougald, Gil 23
McGrath, Bob 109–113
McGuire, Belinda 211
McKayle, Donald 182
McWilliams, Ralph 147
Melbourne, Florida 106–107
Mendelssohn, Felix 86–87
Menegatti, Beppe 140, 205
Merriweather Post, Marjorie 122
Metropolitan Opera House (Lincoln Center) 137, 140, 145, 147, 149, 152, 170, 183–185, 203, 205
Metropolitan Opera House (39th Street) 46–48, 58
Miami Herald 192
Mickey Mantle Day 135, 179
Mideke (Bloom), Patricia 90
Midsummer Night's Dream (composition, Mendelssohn) 86
Miller, Mitch 109–113
Minkus, Léon 87
Minkus Pas de Trois 87–89
Minsk, Russia 8
Mr. Sandman (song) 18–19
Mitchell, Mike 103–106
Model United Nations 41
Momentum (ballet, Nahat) 129
Moore, James ("Jimmy") 148
The Moor's Pavane (ballet) 149–153

Index

Mordkin, Mikhail 7, 155–156
Mother of the Groom (role, *Les Noches*) 147–148
Mount Moosilauke 20
Mount Sugarloaf 20
Mount Washington 20–21
Mount Washington Cog Railway 20
Muller, Jennifer 149–150
Munson, Thurman 179

Nagy, Ivan 116–118, 135–137, 140–141, 150–153, 159–160
Nahat, Dennis 129–131, **136**, 155, 181–**182**, 190–201, 205
National Airport 211
National Ballet of Washington, D.C. 30, 36, 89–121, 122–126, 145, 154–155, 208, 214
National Merit Scholarship 44
Neiman Marcus 31
Nelidova, Lydia 7
New Haven Railroad 39
New Orleans, Louisiana 108
New Rochelle High School 38–44, 56, 126
The New School 45–46
New York City Ballet 44, 68, 70, 81, 90, 94, 101, 114, 207
New York City Center 97, 140, 149
New York Herald Tribune 15
New York Post 22
The New York Times 15, 62, 146, 154
New York World-Telegram and Sun 176, 178
New York Yankees 1, 12–14, 22–23, 40–42, 49–50, 82, 135, 176–181, 212
Newman, Paul 33
Nichols, Kyra 99
Nichols Gymnasium/Hall 207–208
Nicoll, Charles 181
Niemi, Lisa 162–163
Nijinska, Bronislava 31, 147
Nijinsky, Vaslav 24, 63
1951 World Series 176
1955 World Series 22–24
1956 World Series 40
1958 World Series 41
1960 World Series 50, 82
Les Noces (ballet) 147–148
Nordlinger, Gerson, Jr. 122–123
Novak, Nina, 31–32, 43–45, 61, 79–80, 87
Nureyev, Rudolf 173, 198–**201**, 202
The Nutcracker (ballet) 68, 116, 182, 194–197
The Nutty Nutcracker (ballet) 191

Offenbach, Jacques 65
Oh Captain! (musical) 31
Oklahoma Lung Association 177–178
Oltman, Dwight 194
The Omen (film, 1976) 32
101 Strings (orchestra) 113
Orfeo ed Euridice (opera) 57
Orr, Terry **136**
Oshman, Ken 195
Oswald, Lee Harvey 124
Othello (ballet, Corelli) 115
Othello (play) 149

Paquita (ballet) 159–160
Paredes, Marcos 128
Parkinson, Georgina 159–161, 175
Pas de Dix (ballet, Balanchine) 94–96, 124, 134–135
Pas de Quatre (ballet, Dolin) 155
Pasadena, California 87–88
Pavlova, Anna 24, 174, 185
The Perils of Pauline (film) 38
Peter and the Wolf (ballet) 5
Petipa, Marius 70, 95, 118
Philadelphia Academy of Music 57, 93–94
The Philadelphia Orchestra 57
Phillips (Rogers), Linda 73
Piano Concerto No. 2 (concerto, Tchaikovsky) 70
Pittsburgh Pirates 49, 82
Pleasant, Richard 145, 156
Plisetskaya, Maya 123
Pocatello, Idaho 85–86
Podres, Johnny 23
The Point Depot/The Point 198
Pourmel, Sophie 81, 87
Prayer (*La Prière*) (variation, *Coppélia*) 32
prima ballerina 2, 8
Professional Dance Teachers Association 208
Prokofiev, Sergei 46, 133
Puccini, Giacomo 170
Pulcinella Variations (ballet, Smuin) 129

Rachmaninoff, Sergei 7
Radio City Music Hall 46, 78
Rainbow Room 111
RCA Studios 209–211
Red Rock, Wyoming 77–78
Red Wing Camp for Girls 21
Redding, Dave 187–191
Reese, Pee Wee 23
Régisseur 181, 186
Remick, Lee 32
Richardson, Naomi 46–48
Richeson, Gene 195
Riddell, Jean 114, 124
Rigler, Julie 90

Rivera, Mariano 212
Riverdale, New York 41, 45, 59–60
Robbins, Jerome 3, 74, 146–148, 205
Robinson, Jackie 23
Rodeo (ballet) 30
"Rodina" 36–38
Rodriguez, Raymond **194**
ROLM 195
Romanoff, Dimitri 186–187
Romanov, Boris 10
Romeo and Juliet (ballet) 3, 46, 159–161, 182, 205
rond de jambe en l'air 32, 36, 58
rond de jambe par terre 26, 36
Roni Mahler Studio 207–208
A Rose for Miss Emily (ballet) 149
Rosenberg, Lillian 6
Rosenberg (Constan), Phyllis 20–21, 32
Ross, Herbert 3, 143, 205
Round, Roy 175
Round, Tobias 175
Ruby, Jack 124
Russell, Paul 108, 162, 169, 172–**173**, 174
Russian Ballerina (role, *Gala Performance*) 133–134
Ruth, Babe 12

St. Petersburg 7, 95, 118, 129
Saint-Saëns, Camille 174
Salerno, Libby 37
San Francisco Chronicle 155
San Jose Cleveland Ballet/ Cleveland San Jose Ballet 192–203; *see also* Cleveland Ballet; Ballet San Jose
Der Sandmann (short story) 118
Sandy Amorós 23, 41
Sarah Lawrence College 44–46, 149
Sarandon, Susan 198
Sarry, Christine 185
Scanlon, Jennifer 151–152
Schéhérazade (ballet) 63–64
School of American Ballet 6, 89–90, 97, 99
School of Cleveland Ballet 181, 192
School of San Jose Cleveland Ballet 195
Schrafft's 7
Seaton, Edward 177
Seaton, Karen 177
Seravalli, Rosanna 128
Serenade (ballet) 94, 99–103, 115
Serrano, Lupe 145–146
serré & battu 36

Index

Sesame Street (TV show) 109–110, 113
Seven Arts Center 33
Seventh Symphony (ballet, Massine) 30
Shaker Heights 182
Shea Stadium 183
Shelton, Dr. Lewis 165
Shirley (Aristedes), Suanne 73–74
Siegfried's Mother (role, *Swan Lake*) 198
Sing Along with Mitch (TV show) 110–113
Slavenska, Mia 28–31, 91
Slavin, Eugene 38, 84, 89
The Sleeping Beauty 26–27, 30, 38, 41, 57
The Sleeping Beauty, Act III (from *The Sleeping Beauty*) 38, 41
Smith, Valerie 28, 70
Smith, William 57
Smuin, Michael 129
Snider, Duke 23
Sorkin, Leonard 136–137
Spani, Gary 167
Sports Illustrated, "Time in a Bottle" (article) 180
Starbuck, James 29, 31, 110–113, 116
Starr, Dr. Mortimer P. 169
State Theatre (Cleveland) 182, 190
Statler Records 208–210
Steinbrenner, George 179
Stengel, Casey 180
Stepmom (film) 198
Stone, Arthur ("Art") 126
Stone, Erik Mahler 1, 117, 126–*127*, 134–*135*, 155, 158–*159*, 164–166, 175, 182–183, 192, 212–*213*
Strauss II, Johann 26, 53
A Streetcar Named Desire (ballet) 30–31, 91
Streltzov, Catherine 83
Stretton, Ross 160–161
Subotin, Michael 74
Suites for Two Pianos (composition, Arensky) 110
Supernumeraries 195–196, 202–203
Swan Lake (ballet) 30–31, 61, 73, 79–83, 90–92, 103–104, 122–123, 127–133, 159, 183–185, 194, 196
Swan Lake, Act II (from *Swan Lake*) 31, 61, 73, 79–83, 90–92, 103–104, 127–133, 159
Swann, Lynn 167

Swanilda's Mother (role, *Coppélia*) 182, 198
Swayze, Patrick 162–*163*, 164
Swayze, Patsy 162–163
Sweet Bird of Youth (play) 33
Swoboda, Maria (Yurieva) 3, 7–11, 14–20, 24–38, 41, 43–44, 52–58, 73–75, 83, 126, 140, 174, *175*
Swoboda, Vescheslav 7
Swoboda School of Ballet 7–11, 15–17, 24
Swoboda-Yurieva School of Ballet 7
Sydney, Australia 159–162
Sydney Festival Ballet 159–162
Les Sylphides (ballet, Fokine) 5, 36–37, 62–64, 68, 86, 88, 93, 107–109, 155–156, 185–187
Les Sylphides, Pas de Deux 37, 62, 185
Symphonic Variations (composition, Franck) 83

Taglioni, Marie 155
Tancred (role, *Le Combat*) 116–118
Tarczynski, Richard ("Dick") 60–61
tendu 17, 26, 36
Tennyson, Paula 72
Théâtre du Châtelet 24
Le Théâtre Impérial de l'Opéra 118
Thème Slave Varié (from *Coppélia*) 83
Three Virgins and a Devil (ballet) 181
Thurston, James 107–108
Tippet, Clark 169–*172*
Titus, Mary Ellen 178
Titus, Ralph 178
Tomb of the Unknown Soldier 124
The Tonight Show 112
Tosca (opera) 70
Tribute (ballet) 83–86, 88–89, 109
True, Roy 177
Tudor, Antony 3, 133–*136*, 144, 156–157, 203, 205
TV Guide 113
Tyven, Gertrude 10, 63

Udall, Stewart 123
Uggams, Leslie 111–113
Ulanova, Galina 46–48
Uncle Drosselmeyer (role, *The Nutcracker*) 182
University for Man 176
University of Colorado 204

Vance, Norma 10, 63
Varna, Bulgaria 116
Verdak, George 73
Verdy, Violette 114–116
Vienna, Austria 8, 203
Villella, Edward 207
Violin Concerto in E Minor, Op. 64 (concerto, Mendelssohn) 86
Vodehnal, Andrea 37, 60, 79–82, 84–86, 89, 104, 118
Voice of America (radio broadcast) 116
Voices of Spring (waltz, Strauss II) 53
von Aroldingen, Karin 99

Wallace, Jim 162–164
War Memorial Opera House 70–73
Warburg, Felix M. 99
Washington Evening Star 214
Washington Post 93, 155
Washington Redskins 114
Washington Star Sunday Magazine 214
Waterbury, Connecticut 145, 155–156
Waterbury Clock Company 156
Weishaar (Brink), Shirley 32–33, 48–49, 73
Where's Charley? (film) 33
The White House 103–104, 123–125
Wilkinson, Raven 32
The Will Rogers Follies (musical) 162
Wilmington, Delaware 83, 206
Wilson, June 37
Wilson, Sallie *134*, 149
Wozniak, Steve ("Woz") 194–*196*, 197

Yankee Stadium 2, 13, 22, 48–49, 177, 180–181, 212–213
Yezer, Franklin 84, 89
Yom Kippur 58
Young, Gayle 130–133, *136*
Your Show of Shows (TV show) 31, 110
Youskevitch, Igor 29, 31, 36, 58, 78
Youskevitch, Maria 36, 66

Zagreb Opera House 91
Zawatzki, Mary Kay 167
Zide, Rochelle "Chellie" 32
Zimmer, Don 23
Zoom 211
Zuhr, Kathryn 195
Zynda, James *144*

www.ingramcontent.com/pod-product-compliance
Lightning Source LLC
Chambersburg PA
CBHW060341010526
44117CB00017B/2918